The Nightmare

Other Books by Ernest Hartmann

The Biology of Dreaming

Adolescents in a Mental Hospital
(WITH BETTY A. GLASSER, MILTON GREENBLATT,
MAIDA H. SOLOMON, AND DANIEL LEVINSON)

Sleep and Dreaming

The Functions of Sleep

The Sleeping Pill

THE

NIGHTMARE

The Psychology and Biology of Terrifying Dreams

ERNEST HARTMANN

Basic Books, Inc., Publishers   New York

Library of Congress Cataloging in Publication Data

Hartmann, Ernest.
  The nightmare.

  Includes bibliographical references and index.
  1. Nightmares—Psychological aspects. 2. Nightmares—
Physiological aspects. I. Title. [DNLM: 1. Dreams.
2. Sleep Disorders. WM 188 H333n]
BF1099.N53H37 1984   154.6'32   83-46070
ISBN 0-465-05109-X

CONTENTS

v

CONTENTS

ACKNOWLEDGMENTS

I AM keeping this page of acknowledgments short, though the list of my debts is long, and I hope my gratitude will be long-lasting. I could write a paragraph or a page about each individual who is mentioned below.

First, I would like to thank my collaborators in the research projects summarized in this book covering the period of 1975 to the present. These include Susan Adelman, George Brennan, Roberta Falke, J. Gila Lindsley, Walter Mitchell, Molly Oldfield, Diane Russ, Ilana Sivan, Barry Skoff, and George Zwilling, all of whom worked in my laboratory. Also, Sally Adinolfi, Robert Blitz, Wynne Burr, and Bessel van der Kolk, my collaborators at the Veterans Administration; Steven Cooper at the Massachusetts Health Center; James Butcher, Grant Dahlstrom, and Martin Zelin, whose help was essential in the psychological studies involving the Minnesota Multiphasic Personality Inventory; and Philip Holzman, Deborah L. Leavy, and Margie Solovay, who helped with the pendulum tracking studies.

I am grateful to my colleagues, friends, and coworkers who were kind enough to read the manuscript or parts of it and make any number of useful suggestions. These include Myron Sharaf on several occasions, Patricia Brune, Eva Hartmann, Larry Hartmann, Anton Kris,

Acknowledgments

Walter Mitchell, Kimberly Sloan, and Bessel van der Kolk. My colleagues Paul Myerson and Milton Kramer made helpful suggestions on hearing the work presented, though they did not have a chance to read this manuscript. I am indebted to my friend and colleague, Roger Broughton, and my friend and teacher, Charles Fisher, for their earlier work on nightmares as well as for personal discussions, which made my work possible. And I owe special thanks to Charles Fisher for making available to me a great deal of unpublished interview material from his own studies. And I thank Richard LaBrie and Roland Branconnier for help with methodological, statistical, and computer problems over the years.

Research in psychiatry and related fields, especially clinical research in the real world of hospitals, patients, and human volunteers, lives a precarious existence. I see it as a frail but valuable creature—a canary or a bird of paradise living on crumbs, on bits and pieces of time, space, and money left by the larger voracious creatures called teaching, clinical care, and administration. For the fact that the research work did get done, and this book written, I therefore acknowledge the direct and indirect help of a number of important chairmen, directors, and bosses: Harold Goldberg, Clinical Director, West-Ros-Park Mental Health Center, Gus DeBaggis, Area Director, West-Ros-Park Mental Health Center, Gerard O'Connor of Boston State Hospital and the Department of Mental Health, Paul Myerson and Richard Shader, past and present chairmen of the Department of Psychiatry, Tufts University School of Medicine, and Joseph Cohen, Chief of Medicine, Lemuel Shattuck Hospital.

PART I

The Nightmare
and the
Nightmare Sufferer

"Oh, to dream once more the untroubled dreams of childhood!"

Drawing by Whitney Darrow, Jr.; © 1973 The New Yorker Magazine, Inc.

CHAPTER 1

Introduction: A New View of Nightmares

NIGHTMARES have fascinated us for centuries because they are so frightening, so primitive, so unlike waking experience. They are often alien to us, yet obviously ours, too, as though we have given birth to a monster. Just because they are so intense and "different," understanding them and when and why they occur can teach us much about the human mind. Nightmares are like a split in the earth, a canyon allowing us to examine the strata or layers they expose.

What is a nightmare? Who has them? How and why do they occur? In this book I shall attempt to answer some old questions, using new information. By so doing I shall offer ideas about vulnerability to schizophrenia, the creative personality, and genius and madness. Along the way, I shall also examine the origins of our fantasies of half-humans or androids and our conception of hell. I shall discuss the relationship between nightmares and dreaming, and I hope that a better understanding of nightmares will also increase our understanding of dreaming in general. And finally I shall propose a new theory on the development of nightmares in terms of boundaries in the mind: I shall discuss how a psychological predisposition to thin boundaries may bear a pervasive influence on nightmares, sensitivity, and mental illness.

We do not like to think much about nightmares for two good and related reasons—we do not like being frightened, and we do not like being helpless or out of control. The nightmare is an extreme version of these two unpleasant states. Yet I believe nightmares are of great interest for those very reasons. We all felt helpless, out of control, and frightened as little children. For some of us these feelings persisted into adult life. There is a strong tendency to deny these states of mind rather than to face them and attempt to understand them. Understanding nightmares and examining when they occur will help us to understand ourselves. Examining the workings and the structure of the mind under extreme situations such as in a nightmare will help us better to understand its normal functioning.

Over the past years, my colleagues and I studied in depth nearly one hundred persons who suffered frequent nightmares as a lifelong condition. We compared them with those who suffered traumatic nightmares, others who had nightmares only under certain conditions, and with still others who suffered night terrors. Using information from these studies, we are now able to answer the basic questions of the determinants of nightmares; that is, under what conditions and in what persons they occur.

In chapter 2, I review knowledge acquired from the sleep laboratory. Observing nightmares as they take place in the laboratory gives us a chance to examine such factors as the stage of sleep from which they arise and the physiology of the sleeper. The most important result of the laboratory investigations—one that has critical implications for the study of nightmares—is that we now realize that two, or perhaps three, very different phenomena have in the past all been lumped together as "nightmares." One of these is the night terror, sometimes called incubus attack, or terror attack. After experiencing a night terror, the sleeper does not remember a dream; he either remembers nothing at all or simply recalls waking in fright. True nightmares, sometimes called dream anxiety attacks, are long, vivid, frightening dreams, which awaken the sleeper and are usually clearly recalled. The two are biologically as well as psychologically different and, as we shall see, are experienced by dissimilar persons. Any attempt at understanding must keep them distinct.

In chapter 3, I consider nightmare data from many past studies—their frequency, when they occur, the conditions that make them more or less severe. I also examine various theories that have been proposed to account for why nightmares happen. The theories, of course, have varied with the orientation of the theorist and the nature of his or her time. Thus nightmares have, over time, been ascribed to demons, to altered blood flow in the brain, to powerful sexual wishes. Some of these theories appear to be hammering square pegs into round holes—nightmares just do not fit neatly, especially since the authors try to make a single explanation fit both nightmares and night terrors.

In chapter 4, I attempt to answer the question of who has nightmares. As a psychiatrist and psychoanalyst, I see patients who report nightmares to me in the course of treatment. But rather than relying only on this clinical experience, I also attempt to examine nightmares in "pure culture." Over the last five years, I have studied a large number of adults who have nightmares at least once per week as a lifetime or longterm condition and fifty of them took part in two formal research studies. These admittedly form an extreme group, but my hope is that here, as so often happens in science, a study of extremes can shed a clearer light on the normal range. And in addition to the formal studies of the fifty extreme nightmare sufferers, I have also studied more than forty persons with less extreme nightmare conditions; these studies have helped me to re-examine hypotheses derived from the extreme group. I have been able to study in detail the kinds of nightmares that occur most frequently; under what conditions nightmares become more frequent or more severe; the extent to which there is a family history of nightmares and of mental illness; the effect of trauma on these nightmares; and—perhaps most important—the personality characteristics, development, pathology, lifestyles, and relationships of people who suffer nightmares.

I then go on in chapter 5 to examine other groups that have or might be expected to have nightmares. It is well

Introduction: A New View of Nightmares

known that war veterans frequently experience nightmares, and I explore whether such veterans are similar
to the persons described in chapter 4. I examine several
other groups, including schizophrenic patients, in order
to test the hypothesis that people with frequent nightmares are vulnerable to mental illness, and that we could
thus expect to find a similar relationship starting from
the other side—that is, we would find that schizophrenics
do indeed suffer frequent nightmares. Also, since our
studies reveal that people with frequent nightmares often
turn out to be very open to their own unconscious
processes—and often are artistic persons—I also try to
determine whether people chosen on the basis of artistic
achievement or occupation might turn out to be people
with nightmares. Using the findings from these investigations I am then able to explore in some depth the oft-
postulated link between genius and madness.

In chapter 6, I use all the information gathered in the
previous studies to formulate a general theory of who
has nightmares. I consider various possibilities such as
that longterm nightmares result from early childhood
trauma. I am led to characterize persons with frequent
nightmares in terms of unusual openness, defenselessness, vulnerability, and difficulty with certain ego functions. The term I come up with that describes them best
is "thin boundaries," thin in many realms, including
sleep-wake boundaries, ego boundaries, and interpersonal
boundaries. I examine twenty different ways in which
we use the term boundaries and find that in all senses
persons with frequent nightmares have thinner or more
permeable boundaries than most people. It appears that
having thin boundaries, as opposed to heavy rigid

boundaries, may be related to being more artistic, more aware of one's own inner feelings and those of others, and it may also make one more vulnerable to some types of mental illness.

In Part II, I consider clinical aspects of nightmares. First, nightmares are dreams and presumably can be interpreted as dreams (chapter 7). In the case of post-traumatic nightmares with repetitive content involving trauma, an attempt to free associate is seldom "free." The dreamer is led straight back to the traumatic event or experience with no or very few other associations. In other cases—for instance with persons who have frequent nightmares of being chased, hurt, or killed—free association often leads quickly to childhood fears of a very primitive kind.

In chapter 8 I discuss the complex problem of post-traumatic nightmares. They are very common in children and quite common in adults after operations, serious accidents, and various violent or traumatic events. Although they resemble ordinary nightmares in some ways, there are enough differences so that I believe the chronic post-traumatic nightmare, forming part of the post-traumatic stress disorder, must be considered as a psychological and physiological process different from ordinary nightmares and from night terrors.

Nightmares, night terrors, and post-traumatic nightmares can be intensely painful and disturbing to those who suffer from them. In chapter 9, nightmares, night terrors, and post-traumatic nightmares are taken up as clinical problems. I discuss the natural history, the diagnosis and the prognosis of these conditions, and the treatments in cases where specific treatment is required.

Introduction: A New View of Nightmares

Most often true nightmares do not require treatment in themselves, though they may indicate the presence of other conditions requiring treatment. However, acute post-traumatic nightmares can benefit from treatment, and severe night terrors can be greatly helped by treatment.

In chapter 10, I return to our main discussion in trying to understand the basic nature of the nightmare—here, by examining its chemical and biological substrata. Since nightmares are especially intense emotional and frightening dreams, it is possible that their biology is simply an exaggeration of the biology of dreaming, of which we are beginning to gain fuller understanding. But there may be an additional more specific biology of the nightmare: I discuss a large but scattered literature on the pharmacology of nightmares; a number of drugs with relatively specific actions appear to induce nightmares while others appear to block or reduce the incidence of nightmares. This gives us some hint of the underlying biology of the nightmare as being somewhat different from that of dreaming. And I suggest that the biology of the nightmare may also lead us to an understanding of the underlying biology of boundaries in the mind.

CHAPTER 2

What Is a Nightmare?

A GENERALLY accepted definition of nightmare is *waking up from sleep terrified* (without an external cause) or *something from inside that awakens a person with a scared feeling.* We can accept this as a broad definition of all nightmarelike phenomena, but we will see that it includes several very different conditions.

A nightmare is a very well-defined psychological and biological phenomenon. In order to discuss it clearly, we must first distinguish it from other closely related phenomena with which it is often confused. Specifically, it is necessary to make a distinction between two quite different biopsychological phenomenon—the night terror and the nightmare. The sleep laboratory has helped us make this conceptual distinction. Here is an example of a classical night terror, as described in the laboratory studies of Charles Fisher, who has done much of the original work on this condition:

What Is a Nightmare?

Fifty minutes after sleep onset during stage 4 sleep, a body movement occurs, HS [the subject] rolls over screaming repeatedly, "Help, help." He mutters about swallowing something and choking. His pulse rate has increased from 60 to 90 per minute during the 15 seconds it takes him to awaken. He quickly falls asleep again, and later has no recall for the event (Fisher et al. 1974).

The most common vocalization is simply a scream. The sleeper does not remember a dream but sometimes remembers feeling crushed or suffocated. A mother will typically report, "My five-year-old screams and screams a half hour or so after falling asleep. I go in and he's sort of half awake, standing up. It takes five minutes for him to come out of it. Then he just falls back asleep peacefully." The child says, "I don't remember anything. I sleep okay, but Mommy says I scream a lot in my sleep."

Here, on the other hand, is a nightmare from my laboratory. Ellen, a twenty-four-year-old woman, sleeping in the lab as part of a study, awoke at 7:50 A.M. after a nineteen–minute REM-period (see table 2–1 for definition of this and other terms).

TECHNICIAN: Anything going on?
ELLEN: I know I dreamt something. Oh, yeah. I was at this man's house. . . . I can't remember who it was. And um, the first part of the dream there was a trial in his house. And the last part of the dream there was a big storm . . . an awful rainstorm. It poured like I've never seen it pour before and there was all these frogs all over the street outside. . . . I don't know if it was this dream or the dream before. . . . I had a really

11

TABLE 2-1
Table of Terms

Term	Definition or Explanation
Daymare	A daydream which becomes increasingly frightening and "nightmarish" so that it frightens and arouses the daydreamer much as a nightmare awakens the dreamer at night. A rare phenomenon, but described by many of the persons with frequent nightmares (chapter 4).
D-nightmare	Same as Nightmare. Refers to the fact that the nightmare arises from D-sleep.
D-sleep	Dreaming or desynchronized sleep, also known as REM-sleep.
Dream anxiety attack	Same as Nightmare.
Hypnagogic jerk	A sudden involuntary muscular movement or jerk occurring during sleep onset. A very common phenomenon, only rarely accompanied by frightening imagery.
Hypnagogic "nightmare"	A type of nightmare experienced immediately upon falling asleep or before one is quite asleep. These are unusual; subjectively they resemble nightmares more than night terrors; they are often found in patients with narcolepsy.
Incubus attack	An older term, referring usually to what we now call night terror. The incubus is a frightening creature imagined as sitting on the sleeper.
Nightmare	A long, frightening dream awakening the sleeper out of D-sleep, usually in the second half of the night or sleep period.
Night terror	A sudden arousal from slow-wave sleep (stage 3 or 4 sleep), usually early in the night; includes marked fear, frequently screaming, autonomic arousal, and often body movement with little or no dream recall or recollection of the experience.
NREM-sleep	Same as S-sleep.
REM-nightmare	Same as Nightmare. Refers to the fact that the nightmare arises from rapid eye movement (REM) sleep, also known as D-sleep.

TABLE 2–1 *(continued)*

Term	Definition or Explanation
REM-anxiety dream	Same as Nightmare.
REM-sleep	Same as D-sleep.
Sleepwalking–terror episode	Refers to a prolonged episode of night terror which involves body movement, getting out of bed, walking about.
Somnambulism (sleepwalking)	Episodes of body movement, getting up and sometimes getting out of bed and walking without full awakening. These arise from stage 3–4 sleep, early in the night. Related to night terror, but can occur separately.
S-sleep	Synchronized sleep, also referred to as NREM (nonrapid eye movement) sleep.
Stage 4 nightmare	Same as Night terror. (The term is unfortunate, since it suggests a connection with the nightmare, which is quite different; see text.)
Stage 2 nightmare	Refers to the more unusual phenomenon—which has been seen in the laboratory occasionally—of arousal from stage 2 sleep with anxiety. These arousals are unusual and are not completely understood; however, the best evidence is that they are similar to night terrors, but in milder form.
Traumatic nightmare	A long, frightening dream usually consisting of an exact or almost exact memory of a traumatic event (see chapter 8). Traumatic nightmares appear, in many senses, to be dreams. However, in some cases these dream- or memorylike nightmares arise from stage 2 sleep, rather than or as well as from REM-sleep; they may represent an exception to the nightmare vs. night terror dichotomy, not fitting clearly into either group.

awful dream. . . . I was at my parents' house and they had gone out to some party . . . or something like that and I was home alone. Suddenly, this guy from next door came over and he just kind of walked through the house. And I asked him what he needed and he told me he was having trouble moving his house. And it turned out that he was having some kind of legal trouble so that he had to move his house a certain number of feet. And in the dream I went out into the yard and he had moved his whole house and it crashed into my parents' house. . . . All this stuff just started happening. His house slipped and it started crashing and then there was these two trucks that just kind of came flying down towards me. It was just like a disaster. Everything that possibly could have gone wrong did. . . . Then something else happened. . . . I don't remember . . . and I really got scared and I started to run. And this other guy ran after me and caught me . . . and I kept struggling. I remember struggling. While we were struggling, I thought how much stronger he was than me, but I knew that I could hurt him . . . but I didn't want to hurt him. I don't remember what happened after that. I woke up.

TECHNICIAN: Would you call this a nightmare?

ELLEN: Yeah.

More commonly, someone will report a long dream ending something like, "Then this huge man, or maybe some kind of monster, started after me; I tried to run but I couldn't get away. He caught up to me and just then I woke up terrified."

Some differences between night terrors and nightmares

14

are obvious from these accounts. We can learn more about the distinctions—and about dreaming in general— if we review the characteristics of a typical night of sleep, as we have learned about it in the last thirty years of sleep laboratory research.

As a person falls asleep, his brain waves go through certain characteristic changes, classified as stages 1, 2, 3, and 4. The waking EEG is characterized by alpha waves (brain waves of eight to twelve cycles per second) and low-voltage activity of mixed frequency. As the person falls asleep, he enters stage 1, considered the lightest stage of sleep, and begins to show a reduction of alpha-activity. This stage is characterized by low-voltage de-synchronized activity and sometimes by low-voltage, regular activity at four to six cycles per second. After a few seconds or minutes, this stage gives way to stage 2, a pattern showing frequent spindle-shaped tracings at thirteen to fifteen cycles per second (sleep spindles) and certain high-voltage spikes known as K-complexes. Soon thereafter, in stage 3, delta waves—high-voltage activity at 0.5 to 2.5 cycles per second—make their appearance. Eventually, in stage 4, the delta waves occupy the major part of the record.

The division of sleep into stages 1 through 4 is an arbitrary demarcation of a continuous process. In fact, sleep is a cyclical process, with four or five periods of emergence from stages 2, 3, and 4 to a stage similar to stage 1 (figure 2–1). The periods of emergence are characterized not only by stage 1 EEG patterns and by rapid conjugate eye movements (REM's) but by a host of other distinguishing factors, including irregularity in pulse rate, respiratory rate, and blood pressure; the

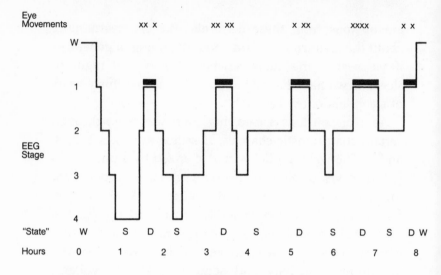

FIGURE 2–1

A Typical Night's Sleep in a Young Adult

NOTE: The four EEG "stages of sleep" are described in the text. The "states" are W—Waking; S—Synchronized sleep, also referred to as NREM (nonrapid eye movement) sleep; D—Desynchronized or Dreaming sleep, also referred to as REM (rapid eye movement) sleep.

presence of full or partial penile erections; and generalized muscular atony (absent muscle tone) interrupted by sporadic movements in small muscle groups. These periods differ from typical stage 1 sleep (although they exhibit the same EEG pattern) as well as from the other three stages. Persons awakened during periods of emergence frequently—60 to 90 percent of the time—report that they have been dreaming, while persons awakened from stages 2, 3, or 4 sleep very seldom report dreams. Because of their distinctive traits and specific neurophysiological and chemical character, these periods are now almost universally seen as constituting a separate state of sleep, referred to as D-sleep (desynchronized or dreaming sleep). This view is reinforced by the fact that similar periods of sleep are experienced by nearly all mammals and birds studied. The remainder of the sleep period is referred to as S-sleep (synchronized sleep). These two states of sleep are also known as REM-sleep (rapid eye movement sleep) and NREM-sleep (nonrapid eye movement sleep), as paradoxical sleep and orthodox sleep, and as active sleep and quiet sleep.

There are several other important characteristics of the typical night's sleep. First, there are four or five D-periods (REM or dreaming sleep) during the night, and the total time taken up by them is about one and a half hours, a little more than 20 percent of the total sleep time. There is some variation, of course, but all the many hundreds of people studied have such D-periods, and in young adults these periods almost always take up 20 to 25 percent of the total night's sleep. The first D-period occurs about seventy to one hundred twenty minutes after the onset of sleep; the interval may be longer in some normal persons, but it is significantly shorter only in a few unusual clinical conditions including the disease known as narcolepsy. Narcolepsy is a condition characterized by sudden irresistible attacks of sleep in the daytime as well as other related symptoms.

The cyclical nature of sleep is quite regular and reliable; a D-period occurs about every ninety to one hundred minutes during the night. The first D-period tends to be the shortest, usually lasting less than ten minutes; the later D-periods may last fifteen to forty minutes each. Most D-time occurs in the last third of the night, whereas most stage 4 sleep occurs in the first third of the night (see figure 2–1). S-sleep (synchronized or non-REM sleep) can be neatly organized according to depth; stage 1 is the lightest stage, and stage 4 is the deepest stage, as measured by arousal threshold and by the appearance of the EEG. D-sleep (desynchronized, dreaming, or REM-sleep), however, does not fit into that continuum. Human EEG data alone might indicate that D-sleep is a light sleep. But the arousal threshold (difficulty of arousal) in animals is higher in D-sleep than in S-sleep, and resting muscle potential is lowest during D-sleep. Thus, D-sleep is neither truly light sleep nor deep sleep but a qualitatively different kind of sleep.

Now that we have examined the general characteristics of sleep, we can look more closely at the chief differences between nightmares and night terrors: the night terror occurs early during the sleep period, usually within two hours of sleep onset. It consists of a simple awakening in terror, most often accompanied by a scream, by sweating, by body movements, and sometimes by sleep-walking. Studies in a sleep laboratory show that the night terror occurs usually in sleep stage 3 or 4 (see figure 2–2)—deep or slow-wave sleep—most commonly during the first hours of sleep. During the fifteen to sixty seconds of awakening, tremendous autonomic nervous system changes can be recorded: pulse and respiratory rates sometimes double. Sleepers do not remember the night terror as they might a dream. Either they recall nothing at all and are only aware of the episode because they are told of it, or they are aware of a single frightening image—"something is sitting on me," "I am choking," "something is closing in on me" (Fisher et al. 1973b, 1974; Broughton 1968).

The typical nightmare is a very different experience. It

What Is a Nightmare?

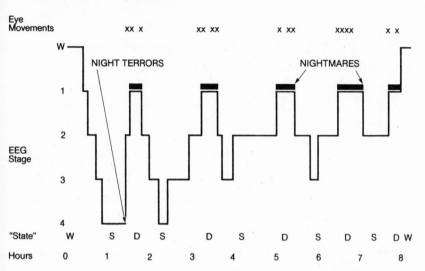

FIGURE 2–2

Night Terrors and Nightmares in the Sleep Laboratory

NOTE: Night terrors occur early (often within an hour of falling asleep), during stage 3 or 4 sleep. Nightmares occur toward morning, during REM or dreaming sleep (see text).

usually occurs later during the night, or the second half of the sleep period. Sleep laboratory studies show it arises during a period of D-sleep (figure 2–2). There may be some increase in autonomic measures—pulse, respiration, and so on—but not to the extent found during a night terror. Finally, the nightmare is definitely a dream— a long, frightening dream which awakens the sleeper. It is clearly remembered as a very detailed, vivid, and intense dream experience (Fisher, Byrne, and Edwards 1968).

Another way to emphasize the difference is to be aware that a nightmare is a dream, and like other dreams, occurs over a period of five to thirty minutes; one awakes from it, perhaps quickly, and may recall a long, detailed, frightening dream; the awakening itself is not remarkable. A night terror is not a dream, but the unusual awakening itself; it has been called a "disorder of arousal" (Broughton 1968). Something internal or external (it can even be an experimenter) arouses the sleeper, and the arousal itself is unusual, characterized by rapid changes in the nervous system. The arousal may include motor activity and sleep walking. This arousal itself *is* the night terror. One study showed that a night terror episode could be induced, in a child prone to night terrors, by pulling the child upright, producing a partial arousal (Kales and Jacobson 1968). This indicates that night terror is not a long, ongoing process from which the sleeper awakens, but rather is something involved in the arousal itself.

A sleep laboratory can confirm the diagnosis of nightmare or night terror, but this is usually not necessary. Even without the use of sleep laboratory data, I can almost always find out clinically whether a patient has nightmares or night terrors (although he or she may refer to either one as a "nightmare") by asking, "Are your nightmares dreams?" The question seems simplistic both to people who suffer from nightmares and to those who experience night terrors. Those with nightmares answer, "Of course." They have no doubt that their nightmares are very frightening dreams. They cannot imagine a nightmare that is not a dream, and after waking from one, they nearly always remember having had a long dream that they can recount in vivid detail. Usually the dream is complicated, with elements that become more and more frightening as the dream lengthens: ". . . and then the monster was chasing me and I couldn't get away"; "the people I had been talking with now had evil looks on their faces; after a while they pulled out knives; somebody slashed my arm." Night terror victims find my question equally absurd. Asked if their nightmares are dreams, they reply, "No, of course not." They sometimes remember dreams, like anyone else, but they know that their episodes of terror are quite different from their dreams.

I have emphasized these differences at length to help us make sense of past and present work on nightmares. I hope it is clear that the person in the classical descriptions of "nightmares" who sits upright in bed, or gets out of bed, screaming, with a glazed expression on his face, is a person having a night terror, not a nightmare. Nightmares and night terrors are indeed quite different phenomena psychologically, physiologically, and occur in quite different persons, as we shall see.

However, life is never quite this simple. Unfortunately, there are cases in which the type of experience is not entirely clear, even when one asks all the right questions. This can be due to poor memory, or poor descriptive abilities on the part of the patient or subject. Or it can be the fact that the person actually has both nightmares and night terrors concurrently—I have seen six or seven such cases—that makes description of and delineation between them difficult. But there are also cases that cannot be explained in these ways. There may be other rarer phenomena falling within the general term nightmare. For instance, Fisher in his original laboratory studies found what he called a "stage 2 nightmare." These were much more like night terrors than nightmares, as we have described them. They seemed to represent mild or less prominent forms of night terrors and, indeed, stage 2 sleep is in most ways a milder, less prominent form of stage 4 sleep. Some cases of post-traumatic nightmares in soldiers sound quite similar. They were described as starting out with feelings of terror and a great deal of movement, vocalization, and so on, and they were indeed found in laboratory studies to occur during stage 2 sleep (Schlosberg and Benjamin 1978). These could be considered a subgroup of the night terror phenomenon. However, we have seen a case in which the same "dream"—an almost exact replay of the wartime trauma—occurred at very different times of night and from different stages of sleep, including D-sleep as well as stage 2.* We shall discuss such post-traumatic nightmares further in Part II. I believe they represent something different from either classical nightmares or night terrors.

Just to complicate matters further, nightmarelike phenomena have also occasionally been described as occurring at sleep onset (Gastaut and Broughton 1964). These seem to occur out of stage 1 sleep—a time often characterized by somewhat dreamlike "hypnagogic" imagery, hypnagogic referring to a state between wakefulness and sleep (see table 2–1). These sleep onset "nightmares" consist of frightening hypnagogic imagery leading to an awakening, or rather a pulling back from a not-quite-asleep state. These may be considered an intense form of an experience most of us have at times, called the "hypnagogic jerk" in which we are suddenly jerked back awake while falling asleep. "Nightmares" of sleep onset can also be episodes of sleep paralysis—inability to move

---

* Similar cases have been reported to me by other sleep researchers, including Peretz Lavie and Milton Kramer.

What Is a Nightmare?

while apparently awake—and of hypnagogic hallucina-tions, both of which are common in narcoleptic patients and occasionally occur in others. These episodes are not usually experienced as nightmares but as an especially intense hypnagogic hallucination, or a hallucination combined with the experience of paralysis, sometimes assuming a nightmarelike quality. All these phenomena of falling asleep can also occur, though more rarely, while waking up at the end of sleep.

Despite these exceptions, we will not go far astray by concentrating primarily on two basic forms of "night-mares"—the nightmare proper and the often misidenti-fied night terror. Current evidence strongly suggests that psychological or personality characteristics of persons who experience nightmares are different from those who suffer night terrors. For instance, I recently analyzed information from thirty adults with severe night terrors, but no nightmares (Hartmann, Greenwald, and Brune 1982). These persons turned out not to resemble in the least the nightmare sufferers we studied in detail who will be described in chapter 4. The nightmare sufferers had some features of schizophrenia or a vulnerability to schizophrenia; they had artistic tendencies and a kind of openness and sensitivity.

The night terror sufferers could not be characterized in this way. They included all kinds of people with no specific psychopathology and no particular artistic ten-dencies; their psychological tests did not show the unusual characteristics found in the tests of the nightmare suffer-ers. Many were psychologically quite average; some had psychopathology, but not of any single type; a subgroup seemed unusually tightly controlled, but the relationship of this characteristic to night terrors (were they "holding in" or "holding down" angry impulses excessively?) was not clear.*

The basic subject of this book is the nightmare—the long, frightening dream arising from D- or REM-sleep. However, I shall discuss night terrors again in chapter 9 under clinical approaches and treatment. In the next chapter, we shall review our knowledge of nightmares and past attempts at understanding them.

---

* Material collected by other authors is consistent with this distinction. Dr. Charles Fisher, who performed some of the first laboratory studies of nightmares and night terrors fifteen years ago, made available to me detailed notes on nightmare content and his interviews with his subjects who had frequent nightmares as well as those who had frequent night terrors. I carefully reviewed his notes, and indeed his group with frequent nightmares had many schizophrenic and borderline features. This was not the case with the subjects who had night terrors, even though these were especially severe cases who experienced night terrors repeatedly in the laboratory. These results are entirely compatible with my data.

CHAPTER 3

What Do We Know
about Nightmares?

Frequency of Nightmares Among Adults

How frequently do nightmares occur in various adult populations?* In sleep laboratory studies of normal sub-

* The following pages summarize what we know about nightmares from previous surveys and research studies. The data must be taken with several grains of salt: There are two sources of difficulty in obtaining answers even to simple questions such as, "What is the frequency of nightmares?" One is the problem discussed in the previous chapter—the lack of differentiation between nightmares and night terrors; in other words, the fact that there are at least two distinct phenomena that have traditionally been called nightmares. A group of people simply asked how often they have nightmares will probably not distinguish between the different phenomena. Secondly, there is the further question of the demarcation between nightmares, bad dreams, and dreams in general. A nightmare is a particular kind of dream and the best I

jects, reports of nightmares are extremely rare. We have reported that out of 3000, only one nightmare was recorded (Hartmann 1970a). Others, too, have reported that nightmares are less frequent in the laboratory than at home so that our number must be taken as an estimate of nightmares in the sleep laboratory and not of nightmares in general.

Psychologists Marvin Feldman and Michael Hersen (1967) reported on the frequency of nightmares in a college freshmen population whose age was approximately eighteen. In this group, 5 percent reported nightmares "frequent" (one per week or more), 24 percent reported nightmares "sometimes" (one per month), 47 percent reported nightmares "seldom" (one per year or more), and 24 percent reported nightmares "never" (less than one a year). The subjects with nightmares were not asked for how long they had had this pattern. These figures are somewhat higher than those reported by most others, possibly because the subjects were students in a psychology class and were especially interested in reporting their dreams and nightmares.

In a separate study, Hersen (1972) also examined nightmare frequency in a population of psychiatric inpatients and found that 7 percent reported "frequent nightmares," again, approximately one per week or

---

can do in terms of a simple definition is that it is "a long, frightening dream that wakes one during REM-sleep (D-sleep)." This simple definition at least makes it clear that I cannot do what I am sometimes asked to do: differentiate between a nightmare and a dream. A nightmare *is* a dream. Dreams with no anxiety, dreams with anxiety, and nightmares all arise from REM-sleep, and naturally there are borderline cases. The problem is that surveys, questionnaires, and other such data-gathering instruments will inevitably include (without making distinctions) varying amounts of these different dream phenomena.

more. Interestingly, 43 percent of this psychiatric patient group reported never having nightmares. In both of the above studies, there were no significant differences between the sexes.

Bixler and associates (1979a) reported a wide prevalence of nightmares "as a current problem" in 5 percent of a sample of 1000 persons in a metropolitan area. Bixler and associates (1979b) also found, in a national survey of over 4000 physicians, that 4 percent of the patients had reported nightmares as one of their complaints; the severity and frequency of nightmares is not mentioned; nightmares were usually not the chief complaint (the reason for seeing the physician), but were mentioned in the course of the interviews. Dennis and Kathryn Belicky (1982) in a survey of 314 college students found that overall 26 percent reported less than one nightmare per year, 64 percent reported between one per month and one per year, and 10 percent more than one per month.

These results, as well as more informal surveys, give us a general picture of nightmare frequencies, but we do not have very exact figures: about 30 to 50 percent of adults remember at least an occasional nightmare, perhaps one per year. Thus, my estimate of the average incidence of nightmares in the adult population would be one or two per year.

My studies suggest that elderly persons (in their sixties and seventies) who have previously had nightmares may continue having them; and elderly persons who do not have a history of frequent nightmares, like anyone else, if subjected to stress, trauma, and other factors discussed below, will sometimes have them. However, my impression is that overall the incidence of nightmares decreases somewhat with age and is relatively low in healthy older persons. But there are at least two situations frequent in old age that increase the incidence of nightmares. One is greater need for medication; several different kinds of drugs can increase the incidence of nightmares (see chapter 10). Second is the onset of periods of mental illness; periods of depression are quite frequent and are sometimes associated with nightmares in the elderly.

Frequency of Nightmares Among Children

The Berkeley study of 252 children studied from age seven through fourteen made available data to show frequency of nightmares of these children at different ages (1954) (figure 3–1). Among the children, 5 to 10 percent had "disturbing dreams" (presumably nightmares) at least once per week at ages seven and eight; the incidence then decreased at ages nine and ten; disturbing dreams occurred very rarely in the eleven- to fourteen-year olds. In a large scale survey of 4,213 high school juniors and seniors in 1943–44, Jack Hertzman (1948) reported that 5.3 percent answered "yes" to the question "Are you bothered by nightmares, intense fears, by walking or talking in your sleep?" However, we do not know how many of them had nightmares as such or their frequency. R. H. Woodward and A. R. Mangus (1949) studied eight nervous traits in a group of 543 first graders (age about six). They report that 26 percent had the trait of "bad dreams," but the frequency is not given.

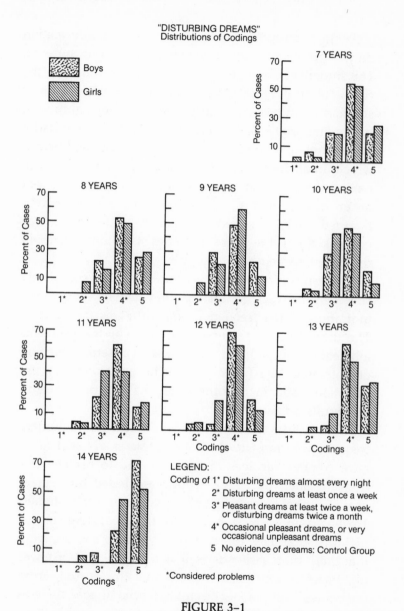

"DISTURBING DREAMS"
Distributions of Codings

LEGEND:

Coding of 1* Disturbing dreams almost every night

2* Disturbing dreams at least once a week

3* Pleasant dreams at least twice a week, or disturbing dreams twice a month

4* Occasional pleasant dreams, or very occasional unpleasant dreams

5 No evidence of dreams: Control Group

*Considered problems

FIGURE 3–1

Berkeley Study

NOTE: Reprinted with permission from J. MacFarlane, L. Allen, and M. Honzik, "A Developmental Study of the Behavior Problems of Normal Children Between Twenty-one Months and Fourteen Years." (Berkeley: University of California Press, 1954.)

Another study (Peterson 1981) obtained information on two groups of sixth graders (ages eleven to thirteen), 168 students in one group and 128 in the other. In the course of an interview, each student was asked if he or she had nightmares or had previously had nightmares. In the first group, 58 percent said they had never had a nightmare; 13 percent remembered past nightmares which had since stopped, and 29 percent were still having them. In the second group, 76 percent reported never having had nightmares while only 5 percent reported still having them. (Frequency of nightmares was not asked.) There were no consistent differences in response between boys and girls.

The results of these various studies are not completely consistent between groups, but they give us some rough indication of the frequency of nightmares in children. The differences in frequency warn us of the problems inherent to data gathering. Factors such as setting, method of obtaining data (interview versus questionnaire), expectations, and many others can make a difference in the results obtained.

There is little question that age influences nightmare frequency. In most textbooks nightmares are said to be most common at ages three to six and to become less frequent later, but these reports are based on a great deal of clinical experience rather than on research studies. Textbooks and clinicians speak of the great frequency of nightmares at ages three to six or four to six, implying that there is an earlier as well as a later period of fewer nightmares. I am not convinced that this is true. From interviews with parents of children who at ages three to five have definite nightmares, it appears to me that there

What Do We Know about Nightmares?

were often similar frightening arousals much earlier—as early as age one—that may well have involved nightmares. A number of psychiatrists and pediatricians have the same impression—Mack (1970) makes the point that nightmares or something very much like a nightmare may occur as early as age one. In fact, I would not be surprised if a considerable part of the non-specific "waking up crying" of younger children were actually pre-verbal nightmares—or possibly pre-verbal night terrors.

It is quite likely that nightmares can occur as early as dreams can occur; that is, probably late in the first year of life. What develops during the next few years may simply be the ability to report—the ability to define, conceptualize, and verbalize an experience to make it sound to the listener like a nightmare. In this sense, nightmares resemble dreams in general or waking perceptual experience, for that matter. A child does not relate a waking fantasy or give a detailed description of what he sees in the daytime until his verbal skills are sufficiently advanced. This takes place roughly around age three, but we do not doubt that perceptual experiences occur earlier, and indirect (behavioral) methods can be used to study them.

It is often argued that a child's ego must develop to a certain extent before anxiety can develop. The child must be able to structure his perceptions and give them some meaning before they can be felt to be frightening. However, such cognitive development has presumably progressed far enough by eight to twelve months to produce stranger anxiety—the first well-recognized childhood anxiety, which develops when the child realizes that the adult up there is *not* mother—that the large looming face above him is the "wrong face." Early nightmare experiences may well begin at this time, too. We cannot ask the nine-month-old dreamers, but I have been impressed with the frequency of stranger-anxiety themes in remembered early childhood nightmares and in the nightmares of adults as well:

> "Her face changed and she looked horrible, like a monster."
> "The face became larger and larger. I didn't know who it was; I screamed."
> "It wasn't my friend at the door, but this monster with a knife."
> "It wasn't my real husband I was with but an android creature who had taken his place."

This last theme, of course, has also invaded science fiction and horror literature, but its seed required no galactic winds to reach us; it was planted in the cracks of our developing minds when we were nine months old.

In any case, there is obviously a high incidence of nightmares before the age of five. Many of our subjects who have very frequent nightmares have reported a second peak in adolescence at the age of fourteen or fifteen, but such a peak did not show up in the Berkeley study data.

We may conclude that occasionally having nightmares is quite common for children as well as adults, especially children before the age of five or six.

What Do We Know about Nightmares?

Gender and Nightmare Frequency

Age clearly has a great deal to do with nightmare frequency; the influence of gender is not quite as clear. One gets the impression clinically that more women complain of nightmares than do men. In a study by Anthony Kales and associates (1980) of thirty volunteers with nightmares who answered a newspaper advertisement, only three were men. My own figures are not quite so extreme. Out of about sixty applicants for a nightmare study thirty-eight fulfilled our criteria of frequent nightmares with no night terrors or other problems; of these, twenty-seven were women and eleven were men (Hartmann et al. 1981b). In the Berkeley study, among the older children there was a slightly higher proportion of girls than boys reporting frightening dreams. The other studies cited, however, showed no difference between the sexes in nightmare frequency. Especially among young nightmare sufferers of two, three, and four years old—clinical experience suggests no difference in frequency between the two sexes, though I have found no published data on this point.

From these bits and pieces of information, my conclusion is that probably nightmares do not occur more frequently among women than among men, but that adult women are more willing to admit to having them than are adult men. This difference in attitude is not marked in children, but becomes more apparent with age. In our culture, having nightmares is thought of as being not especially manly, and is sometimes seen as

33

indicating fearfulness or childishness, an image that is hard for adult men to accept of themselves. This premise is not purely speculative: in interviews I conducted with about one hundred nightmare sufferers, I found a number of men who, although they admitted to having nightmares and talked about them, nonetheless found it difficult and embarrassing to do so; none of the women had this difficulty. The women either accepted the nightmares as being part of their personality makeup, or were terrified and disturbed, but they did not feel embarrassment in talking about them.

Overall, we can say that nightmares are found with equal frequency in boys and girls and probably also in men and women. Gender is not a determinant of nightmare frequency.

When Do Nightmares Occur? (What Produces or Prevents Nightmares?)

Now that we have a rough idea of the overall incidence of nightmares and its relationship to age and sex, we can ask what additional factors make nightmares more frequent or more intense. One factor that makes a difference is physical illness. It is a common clinical observation that children who do not otherwise have nightmares sometimes report having them during times of illness, especially febrile illness. Adults, too, frequently report more nightmares during times of illness (high fevers and operations, for example). There is some ques-

What Do We Know about Nightmares?

tion as to whether it is the actual illness itself or rather the stress that accompanies it that is important in this regard. Certain neurological diseases are sometimes associated with nightmares. Thus, there are epileptics who have nightmares as a kind of "aura" just preceding nocturnal seizures (Forster 1978, Boller et al. 1975). Encephalitis can be associated with nightmares. An extremely dramatic account of a nightmare during the rapid onset of post-encephalitic Parkinsonism is described by Oliver Sacks (1974). The patient had a vivid, incredibly frightening nightmare that he was caught in a sort of statue of himself and was unable to move or escape; by the next morning he was, in fact, caught by the onset of acute Parkinsonism and became a rigid almost immobile "statue" for many years until "released" by medication.

Mental illness is certainly associated in a general way with nightmares. It has frequently been noted (Detre and Jarecki 1971, Mack 1970) that nightmares occur at times of onset of psychosis, especially schizophrenic illness. Ernest Jones (1931, p. 15) notes that attacks of nightmares precede or accompany the development of hysteria and insanity and says this correlation has been reported also by many earlier writers. Depression often appears to be associated with an increase of nightmares, though there have been no solid studies of this observation. I have seen cases myself in which nightmares started or became more frequent during a depression—cases not treated with the almost ubiquitous antidepressant medication that makes interpretation more difficult—and then decreased or stopped as the depression was alleviated.

Stress of various kinds also makes a difference. Persons

who only occasionally or rarely have a nightmare are often unable to relate the experience to any particular stressful event or period. However, patients I have seen in psychotherapy and psychoanalysis who have many nightmares and also the research subjects I have studied (see chapter 4) report that periods of stress—almost any kind of stress—are associated with an increase in frequency and severity of nightmares. These periods of stress include times of examinations, job changes, or moves, and particularly, periods following the loss of important persons. Stress, unfortunately, is a very large and nonspecific concept. In my view, however, nightmares appear to be especially frequent in situations that involve helplessness or that remind a person of childhood feelings of helplessness.

Traumatic events, which can be considered an intense form of stress, clearly can produce nightmares—commonly for a period of days or weeks after the event and occasionally for longer periods. The trauma can be of many kinds—a simple witnessing of an accident or attack; waking up during a surgical operation; being the victim of a mugging or a rape; suffering serious injury; undergoing wartime traumas; and enduring years of concentration camp experiences. These traumatic nightmares, somewhat different from ordinary nightmares, will be discussed in detail in chapter 8.

Finally, it has become clear that certain medications make nightmares more frequent. This is especially true of l-DOPA used in the treatment of Parkinsonism; reserpine and related drugs used in the treatment of high blood pressure; and beta-adrenergic blockers used in the

What Do We Know about Nightmares?

treatment of high blood pressure and cardiac problems (see chapter 10).

It is worth asking whether there are factors that reduce the incidence of nightmares or are associated with fewer nightmares. Again, some medications have this effect (these are discussed in chapter 10). And on the psychological side, there is no question that in most persons a sense of safety or protection reduces nightmares. Parents regularly observe this in their children; and there is reason to believe it is true of adults as well. Interestingly, it is the sleep laboratory that leads me to this conclusion. Nightmares almost never occur spontaneously in the sleep laboratory in normal subjects, and even persons who report frequent nightmares at home have much fewer in the laboratory. This is surprising, since the laboratory situation is a strange experience in which a subject sleeps in an unfamiliar place with wires attached to his or her head and body, and with mysterious equipment in another room monitoring his or her sleep. Indeed, the sleep laboratory can be an annoying and disturbing place for some; a person often takes longer than usual to fall asleep on the first or second night in the laboratory. One would think that this would also be a frightening, stressful experience that might induce nightmares, but not so. A person who says he or she has a nightmare almost every night at home may have only an occasional nightmare in the laboratory. A person who occasionally has nightmares at home never seems to have them in the laboratory. Despite the superficial annoyance of sleeping in a laboratory, most people place a basic sense of trust in the doctors or the laboratory staff. They even have a sense of being protected or at least are convinced that they will not die or be attacked by monsters while they are attached to monitoring equipment. In fact, over the years, a number of subjects have told me that despite the wires and equipment, they enjoyed sleeping in the laboratory and felt safe because there was someone "watching over" them. One woman called the laboratory technician a guardian angel who watched over her while she slept. Along the same lines, some patients and research subjects have told me that they have nightmares mostly when sleeping alone; simply having someone else in the room reduces the frequency of nightmares considerably.

Theories about Nightmares

Now that we have discussed nightmares in terms of their frequency, and what influences them, we can begin to approach a related question, one that is central to this work: *Who has nightmares?* As we said, some are persons who have undergone trauma, some are persons taking certain medications, some are persons who go through stressful experiences, some are persons who go through frequent physical and mental illnesses. But this list is only a beginning. As we shall see, there are more revealing and richer ways of conceptualizing the nightmare sufferer. But before we can do that, let us begin by looking at what a number of authors have had to say about who has nightmares and under what conditions.

What Do We Know about Nightmares?

In a survey of psychiatric patients, Michael Hersen (1972) suggested that in general, more anxious patients have more nightmares. This is hardly very specific, but it supports the experience of many clinicians who base their conclusions on a few patients seen in psychoanalysis or psychotherapy. Marvin Feldman and Michael Hersen (1967) suggested that persons with thoughts about death or fears of death tend to have more nightmares than others. Ernest Jones (1931) suggested that persons who have nightmares are usually anxiety-neurotics (whom he sometimes calls neurasthenics). Kales and associates (1980), studying persons who reported at least twelve nightmares a year, found their subjects to be passive-dependent; to have feelings of insecurity or inferiority; and to be alienated, distrustful, or quick to withdraw emotionally. In my studies, I found that persons with a lifelong history of frequent nightmares were unusually open and undefended in their mental structure, with a tendency both to mental illness (schizophrenia) and to artistic expression (see chapter 4).

A great many authors have been interested in nightmares and have expressed thoughts about their nature and causes. Some of these developed out of research work on nightmares and have already been mentioned. Yet, there have not been many explicitly formulated theories about the nature of nightmares. In fact, for many authors including Sigmund Freud, nightmares were an annoyance, a stumbling block to developing a theory of dreams in general.

Early views were that nightmares involved visitations of devils or evil spirits (Roskoff 1869, Pinches 1906, Cox 1870). However, illustrations and descriptions suggest

FIGURE 3–2

The Nightmare by Henry Fusli. Used by permission of the Founders Society of the Detroit Institute of Arts. Gift of Mr. and Mrs. Bert L. Smokler and Mr. and Mrs. Lawrence A. Fleischman.

that the phenomena explained in this way may have been night terrors rather than nightmares (figure 3–2).

A number of nineteenth-century investigators have claimed that difficulty in breathing, partial suffocation, and reduced oxygen supply to the brain can produce

What Do We Know about Nightmares?

nightmares (Waller 1816, Radestock 1879). However, current evidence suggests that this is not the case. Several thousand patients have now been studied who have repeated episodes of apnea (cessation of respiratory airflow) during the night, often associated with marked reduction in blood oxygen saturation. Despite these serious problems, apneic patients almost never complain of nightmares (see chapter 10). On the other hand, we have seen in the last chapter that night terrors are sometimes produced when a subject with a history of night terrors is partially aroused from stage 4 sleep. Thus, if such a susceptible person also had an episode of suffocation or respiratory impairment, it could well produce a night terror. Possibly the earlier authors had seen such cases of pathologically induced night terrors.

Freud had surprisingly little to say about nightmares. Recognizing typical nightmares as dreams, he first tried to include them in his general view that dreams are fulfillments of wishes by suggesting that nightmares represent fulfillments of superego wishes (wishes for punishment) (Freud 1920). However, he was not satisfied with this view and suggested later that certain nightmares, especially traumatic nightmares, represent a repetition compulsion—a primitive tendency of the mind simply to repeat what has been experienced (Freud 1955). Most analysts do not find "repetition compulsion" an especially useful concept clinically or theoretically; it is not a term much used at present. And I suspect that Freud was not entirely happy with his explanation of nightmares since he never mentioned it in his voluminous later writings.

One theory, widely held but seldom stated explicitly,

41

suggests that guilt produces nightmares. John Mack (1970, pp. 46–47) gives a dramatic report of nightmares in a twelve-year-old boy, obviously related to guilt:

Nightmares following a murder that operated as a traumatic event were experienced by a twelve-year-old boy who stabbed to death a boy of six. Following the murder, he suffered from repeated punishment dreams and nightmares in which he relived the event, with various degrees of distortion. The killing occurred when the boy panicked after accidentally injuring the little child while playing mumblety-peg with a penknife. Not realizing how slight the injury was, he had suddenly become terrified that the screaming child would tell his mother, who would not believe the injury accidental. He had conjured up images in his mind of her "grabbing me and slapping me and taking me to the police. They'd beat me and handcuff me and take me to prison, and all the big guys would beat me up and smack me around." In a fit of irrational terror he stabbed the screaming child many times in the head to silence him. Although he was able "when I am conscious" to keep these struggles out of mind, in his dreams he relived many forms of assault and punishment, often awaking in terror or otherwise deeply upset. In one dream, a month after the killing, the dead boy's mother shot him in the head. So vivid was this dream that, after waking up in terror, his head hurt, and he felt that he was really dying from a head injury. In another dream a year later he went before the youth authorities and was discharged from the state correctional institution. Back in his home town, he went to school on the bus, and talked and joked happily with friends. He dreamed that when he got to school one of the boys began to tease him—"bugging" and "ranking," he called it. "We don't want a murderer in our school," the boy said. The patient struck him with his fist and killed him. He was sent back to the institution and entered the gate handcuffed, whereupon he awoke upset and in great

What Do We Know about Nightmares?

fear. In his dreams he repeated the expression of the violent impulses that had led him to kill the smaller child, while at the same time he always imposed upon himself a severe retaliatory punishment. Through the repeated dreams he sought to master this overwhelmingly disturbing traumatic experience, the memory of which afflicted him above all during sleep.

In literature, nightmares often visit a murderer or someone with a guilty conscience. For instance, Clarence, in Shakespeare's play *Richard III,* relates a long nightmare:

> O! then began the tempest to my soul.
> I pass'd, methought, the melancholy flood,
> With that grim ferryman which poets write of,
> Unto the kingdom of perpetual night.
> The first that there did greet my stranger soul,
> Was my great father-in-law, renowned Warwick;
> Who cried aloud, "What scourge for perjury
> Can this dark monarchy afford false Clarence?"
> And so he vanished; then came wandering by
> A shadow like an angel, with bright hair
> Dabbled in blood; and he shriek'd out aloud,
> "Clarence is come,—false, fleeting, perjur'd Clarence,
> That stabb'd me in the field by Tewksbury;—
> Seize on him! Furies, take him unto torment,"
> With that, methought, a legion of foul fiends
> Environ'd me, and howled in mine ears
> Such hideous cries, that with the very noise
> I trembled wak'd, and, for a season after,
> Could not believe but that I was in hell,
> Such terrible impression made my dream.

(lines 44–63)

Clarence obviously feels guilty about crimes he has committed, but this is not necessarily sufficient to produce a nightmare. Clarence is also in a position of helplessness—he is a prisoner in the tower of London suspecting (correctly) that he will soon be murdered by agents of Richard III.

This role of guilt seems reasonable and also, in a psychodynamic sense, it is consistent with Freud's notion of superego wishes or wishes for punishment portrayed in anxiety dreams. Indeed, among patients in analysis, one does hear anxiety dreams that clearly involve unexpressed guilt feelings. However, as I look over my records of severe nightmares, in patients and research subjects, I cannot find many such examples. Persons suffering from lifelong nightmares, whom I studied in detail, and also psychiatric patients suffering from the most severe nightmares, do not appear to be expressing feelings of guilt. Perhaps this is because the most serious childhood fears giving rise to these nightmares antedate the experience of guilt feelings, the capacity to develop and be aware of guilt for one's actions. Also, my impression is that guilt in an adult—in an undetected criminal, for instance—does not necessarily produce nightmares, unless the guilty person also finds himself in danger or helpless, as he was when a child (as is the case with Clarence). Guilt may certainly play a role but usually something more is required.

Ernest Jones (1931) formulated a hypothesis of what produces nightmares. He suggested, on the basis of his experience with patients in psychoanalysis, that nightmares represent a clash between an unusually powerful sexual wish—usually an incestuous wish—and unusually powerful repression, and he provided some dramatic examples. However, later authors have not substantiated this view, and I found no convincing evidence for it in my studies. Yet, there is always the possibility that the fears and the guilt about aggressive impulses also may hide wishes, including early sexual wishes.

Some psychoanalytic writers relate nightmares to the development of different forms of anxiety in children. For instance, John Benjamin (1961) emphasized that nightmares require first the perception of outside danger, which already occurs during the second half of the first year of life, and also require sufficient maturation to allow object-directed hostility and anger with a consequent increase in fear of object loss, which occurs in the second or third year. Presumably, nightmares occur when this conflict is especially strong. This is an attractive psychodynamic formulation of childhood nightmares. I am not certain, however, that only the fear of object loss, rather than other childhood fears, plays a role. John Mack (1970) provided some excellent examples of young children who developed nightmares in situations that can often be understood in terms of specific aggressive wishes and fears of punishment.

Harry, the oldest of four children, was three years and four months old when his third sibling and only brother was born. . . . At that time he became increasingly aggressive with his sisters and brother, demanded their toys and bit, kicked, tripped, and punched them, took putty off windows, or played in doorways to force people to step over him. Toward the end of her last pregnancy, Harry began to tell his mother that he hated her and intended to kill her and cut her stomach in order to remove the new baby and then cut it up. Sometimes he punched his mother in the abdomen so hard that it hurt her. The parents dealt with his behavior by scoldings and punishments, such as spankings and putting him in a chair in the corner, but also let him come into bed with them when he arose and walked around at night. After the baby's birth, the mother noticed that Harry seemed unhappy, smiled little, began again to suck his thumb, and cried easily; whereas his toilet training had been complete a year before, he now began to have frequent incidents of soiling and wet every night and frequently during the day.

About one month after the baby's birth Harry, who had not been known to have sleep disturbances, began to have nightmares. He awoke from these in terror, convinced that the events he described actually had occurred. Typically, he dreamt that a girl had come to hurt him or that a woman had killed him. It was very difficult for his parents to comfort him.

This boy is obviously fearful of punishment for his aggressive wishes toward his siblings, especially his newborn brother. The wishes and his fears become even more clear in subsequent therapy.

Both in children and in adults, nightmares have sometimes been seen as a sign of partial mental disintegration—perhaps a point part way from normality to psychosis. Thomas Detre (1971) mentioned nightmares as being prominent early signs of an oncoming psychosis, though he did not speak of the nature of the nightmares specifically. Mack (1970) spoke of the nightmare as part way towards a psychosis in the children and adolescents he studied. Michael Stone (1979) found that certain kinds of nightmares, especially dreams of body fragmentation and of the dreamer's death, are especially prominent in patients who are becoming psychotic. Harry Stack Sullivan (1962) stated "night terror and terror dreams of childhood are so closely related to schizophrenic panic states that it does violence to scientific method to separate the two. These eruptions of fear during sleep are important omens of future mental disorder."* I have also been struck clinically by the number of persons who have nightmares early in a psychotic episode or before they become psychotic.

I believe a relationship to psychosis may be important. However, since many adults and children continue to have nightmares for long periods without any progression towards psychosis, the concept of nightmares being part way from normality to psychosis must be considered simply one aspect or building block of a theory of nightmares. It does not explain much in itself, and it is compatible with the several possible psychodynamic explanations we have discussed.

One point on which there is agreement among many of the authors mentioned is that the nightmare involves some of the earliest, most profound anxieties, and the most profoundly terrifying fears to which we are all subject. Indeed, when we try to analyze nightmares (chapter 7), we are quickly led back to these early fears.

In reviewing these theories, it becomes clear that we have certain plausible pieces and building blocks of information. For instance, we can accept that nightmares are especially frequent in young children and that they increase during times of stress in older children and adults and especially in conditions involving helplessness.

* He appears to be referring to both night terrors and nightmares.

The relationship of nightmares and psychosis is a tantalizing possibility, but we do not yet know where it leads. Nightmares in children are certainly related to basic childhood fears, but there is considerable disagreement about the importance of early sexual impulses. A great deal more information about nightmares is needed, and in the next chapters I shall discuss data from my own studies and others as we look for answers especially to the questions, "Who has nightmares and under what conditions?"

CHAPTER 4

Who Has Nightmares? An Intensive Study of People with Frequent Nightmares

MANY OF US have experienced nightmares ourselves; we have had nightmares told to us at parties; and those of us who are clinicians have had nightmares related to us by patients. Some have drawn important conclusions from such material. In fact, Freud's work on nightmares, as well as Jones' and Mack's, is based entirely on nightmares recounted in treatment sessions. This approach has advantages—especially in that the patient is intimately known to the therapist or clinician, and (as Freud has pointed out) has every reason to be honest and forthright since describing his or her symptoms and problems is a way of obtaining help. However, there are disadvantages as well to gathering data only from patients. The patient, having serious problems, is in psychotherapy or other forms of treatment because of pain and suffering usually involving problems other than nightmares. With the exception of some veterans suffering from post-traumatic stress disorder, not many people see a therapist specifically for nightmares. Neither patient nor therapist is primarily interested in nightmares and often the information obtained about them is incidental. Also, the dynamics of the relationship with the therapist or analyst may influence the nightmares themselves as well as the way they are dealt with by patient and therapist.

Although I have learned much about nightmare sufferers by treating them clinically, a more fruitful approach to gaining a general understanding of nightmares is to study nightmare sufferers systematically. My collaborators and I were able to study in detail the characteristics of fifty subjects with a lifelong history of having frequent nightmares who were not patients but chosen purely on the basis of having nightmares. In a collaborative study, we also investigated forty war veterans with a history of nightmares in order to compare them with the civilian group.

The strategy I chose is based on the concepts of "pure culture" and "the extreme group." Sometimes it is useful in psychiatry and psychology—as it is in microbiology—to study something in a pure, uncontaminated form. For

Who Has Nightmares?

microbiologists, this means selecting one micro-organism and placing it in a sterile field with every precaution taken to ensure the organism will grow in isolation in the culture medium rather than with a profusion of other organisms. The same technique may sometimes be useful in research on human medical or psychological problems. One tries to find people who have whatever condition one is examining without having other related problems or confusing characteristics. Studying an "extreme group" simply means studying people who have a great deal of whatever one is examining. One hopes that if there are unusual characteristics to be found they will stand out sharply in such a group. For instance, I was interested for some years in people who required more sleep or less sleep than most of us—what were the characteristics of habitual long and short sleepers? My laboratory and others were unable to find anything interesting by simply taking a large normal population and trying to correlate aspects of life style, psychology, physiology with sleep duration. Nor did students who reported long or short sleep habits at a given time turn out to differ greatly from each other or from average sleepers (Webb and Friel 1971). But by studying extreme groups—regular long sleepers (persons who always slept over nine hours for a period of years) and regular short sleepers (persons who slept under six hours), and by studying them in pure culture—the subjects, who were not patients but volunteers chosen purely on the basis of their sleep patterns, had no sleep complaints, no serious illnesses that affected their sleep—we were able to distinguish some very interesting characteristics differentiating long and short sleepers (Hartmann et al. 1971, 1972, Spinweber and Hartmann 1977).

Similarly, in approaching the nightmare sufferers, we attempted to find an extreme group and a group that had nightmares in relatively pure culture. We sought persons who regularly experienced a nightmare at least once a week as adults and had no night terrors. My impression from preliminary trials was that this occurred in not more than one in two hundred adults,* so the group would definitely be an extreme group.

We chose persons on the basis of the single fact that they reported nightmares. Rather than seeking out a patient population, we placed advertisements in the newspapers, asking for persons who frequently had nightmares. We planned to study people chosen only because they reported frequent nightmares, who we would then compare with control groups, obtained from the same newspapers, who did not report nightmares.

A Description of Two Studies of Nightmare Sufferers

In the first study, we placed advertisements in several Boston newspapers simply asking that persons who had frequent nightmares call us to take part in a medical psychological study. The persons who called were first screened by telephone. They were asked a number of questions to determine as closely as possible that they

---

* The criterion we used was a definite report of at least one nightmare per week for at least the past six months, described in a telephone interview and confirmed in a face-to-face interview. Persons meeting this criterion are rarer than persons simply checking off on a questionnaire that they have nightmares once per week, as in chapter 3.

had nightmares as opposed to night terrors. We accepted for the study only persons who reported at least one definite nightmare per week for a period of at least the past six months, and who reported no night terrors.

Persons who were acceptable on the basis of the telephone interview then came to the laboratory for a series of personal evaluations. From these, we eliminated a few more subjects who had misunderstood and apparently did not have nightmares, did not have sufficient nightmares (one per week), or who had night terrors in addition to nightmares.

The first study involved a total sample of thirty-eight adults, most of them in their twenties, a few older; twenty-seven were women and eleven, men (Hartmann and Russ 1979, Hartmann et al. 1981b). It turned out that these were almost all people who had suffered from nightmares as long as they could remember or at least since childhood; there were two possible exceptions, but even these said their nightmares probably began at age ten or twelve and that they might have had nightmares earlier. Each of the thirty-eight subjects had at least one long interview with a psychiatrist (myself) and half of the subjects had an additional interview with another psychiatrist so that we would be able to compare notes later. The interviews focused first on the nightmares themselves—what they were like, when they had begun, what conditions increased or reduced their frequency. Examples of nightmare content were obtained. Specific questions were asked as to whether stressful or traumatic events influenced the nightmares, and whether medications, drugs, alcohol, or anything else of a physical nature had an effect. Then we went on to discuss the person's dreams and his or her sleep pattern in general. The interview continued with a detailed discussion of the subject's present life, occupation, interests, relationships, life style, use of alcohol, nicotine, marijuana, and other drugs. We focused also on any medical or mental illness. We talked in detail about difficult periods, including depressions and suicide attempts, and periods of psychiatric treatment. We then discussed the person's adolescence and childhood in some detail, including questions of medical illness, mental problems, family relationships, and traumatic events. The interviewer also attempted to obtain a family history to determine whether any members of the patient's family had nightmares, other sleep problems, specific medical or mental illnesses.

In addition to the interview, each person took several psychological tests to enable us to describe personality characteristics in a more quantified way. All subjects took the Minnesota Multiphasic Personality Inventory (MMPI), an "objective" personality measure, often used by psychiatrists and psychologists. The test consists of 585 statements to be marked true or false. Many of the statements are straightforward, for example, "I like mechanics magazines." Some of them refer to disturbing experiences, such as, "I believe I am being followed," or "I feel weak all over much of the time." The test was put together in final form after initially having been given to a large number of apparently normal persons as well as large numbers of persons with clearly diagnosed mental illnesses and personality problems. The MMPI cannot be used clinically by itself to make a valid diagnosis. If someone scores high on D (Depression scale), one should not conclude from the test score alone that the person is depressed; one can only say that this person's pattern of responses is similar to that of persons who are clinically depressed. Although the MMPI must be interpreted cautiously in individual instances, its well-tested, quantitative clinical scales terms are very useful in comparing one group of persons with another or with a "standard" population (Dahlstrom, Schlager, and Dahlstrom 1960*a*, 1960*b*).

All our subjects also took a Cornell Index (Weider et al. 1944), a questionnaire in which a person states that he does or does not have 101 different medical, psycho-somatic, and psychological symptoms. In addition, all subjects took the Rotter Locus of Control test (Rotter 1966), a brief questionnaire that reveals to what extent a person feels his life is controlled by external forces. Most of the subjects had a complete Rorschach test, the well-known "projective" test based on ten standardized inkblots: The subject simply relates what he sees in the inkblots; since the inkblots are objectively the same for everyone, differences in what people see are assumed to be due to the internal makeup of the person taking the test, "projected" out onto the inkblots. Approximately half of the subjects also took the Fear Survey Schedule (Geer 1965)—a questionnaire asking simply whether the person is afraid (and how afraid on a 1–4 scale) of a variety of different items—diverse items ranging from bugs, to knives, to marriage.

Although this was not basically a sleep laboratory study, we were able to study eleven of the subjects for four nights each in the sleep laboratory. Whenever a nightmare was reported in the laboratory, it arose from out of D-sleep (REM-sleep), thus confirming our assumption that we were indeed studying persons with true nightmares (Hartmann et al. 1978).

In the first study of thirty-eight subjects, we were able to compare our nightmare group with population norms for the various psychological tests, as well as with results of past studies of subjects recruited by newspaper advertisements. But there was no formal control group obtained and studied at the same time. Thus, we could not absolutely disprove the objection that we might be studying characteristics of persons answering advertisements in Boston area newspapers, rather than characteristics of nightmare sufferers. Therefore, we continued with a second, more formal study.

In the second study, we compared nightmare sufferers with two matched control groups all recruited by similar newspaper advertisements. We studied a total of thirty-six subjects—three groups of twelve, with six men and six women in each group, all between twenty and thirty-five years of age. Twelve subjects were chosen on the basis that they reported at least one nightmare per week, as before. This time we made a lifelong history of nightmares a condition of selection; in other words, we included only persons who stated that they had had nightmares "lifelong" or "since childhood." One control group comprised twelve persons who reported frequent vivid dreams but no nightmares. The second control group comprised those who had neither nightmares nor vivid dreams (Hartmann et al. 1981a). We felt it was important to use these two groups, since our earlier study had shown that nightmare sufferers were invariably persons with vivid, lifelike dreams. Therefore there existed the possibility of gradations of dreams—ordinary, vivid, and nightmare—with nightmares being simply a more extreme form of vivid dreams, and that the personalities of the three groups would likewise form a continuum.

All subjects underwent procedures and tests similar to those of the first study. The interviews, or other material were scored on a blind basis; that is, the scorer did not know to which group a subject belonged. First, each had a psychiatric interview, which was videotaped for later review. The interview (by myself) usually took one and a half hours and focused on all the same areas as in the first study. Second, another interviewer spent a half to one hour concentrating on the individual's complete family history including a carefully mapped pedigree diagram (family tree). Questions were asked about each person on the diagram: whether, as far as the subject knew, the particular person had had a history of nightmares, any other sleep problem, any serious mental or medical illness. Whenever there was a positive response, the subject was asked to elaborate on it. The family history interviews were always conducted by the same person—a woman—and were also videotaped whenever possible. Thus, in addition to family history information, we obtained an impression of whether the subject acted differently in an interview with a female than with a male.

Each subject took the MMPI, the Cornell Index, the Rotter Locus of Control test, and a complete Rorschach test. In addition, each person also took a portion (five cards) of the Thematic Apperception Test (TAT), a projective test in which the person is shown, instead of inkblots, a series of silhouette figures in various interpersonal situations and is asked to invent a story about them. This test is especially sensitive to issues of relations between people.

Each person also took a Pendulum Tracking Test developed by Holzman and associates (1973) that detects minor abnormalities of eye movements while the subject watches a pendulum; we used it because it had been found to be abnormal in certain mental patients (schizophrenics) as well as sometimes in their relatives.

This study was carried out on a blind basis insofar as possible, although the psychiatric interviewer could not help knowing which group a subject belonged to, since a portion of the interview dealt with nightmares and non-nightmare dreams. Portions of this interview were later viewed by others who rated various items without knowing to which group the subject belonged. Likewise, the person administering the family history interview, the psychologist administering the Rorschach and the TAT, and the scorers for all tests made judgments and ratings without knowing which subjects were which.*

* Our approach of studying groups of extreme nightmare sufferers in "pure culture" avoids many problems involved in generalizing from a few patients. However, this approach still has some problems. We cannot say that we are obtaining a completely random sample of all persons with nightmares. We obtain information only from those who are willing to come and talk about their nightmares. There is no way this selectivity problem can be totally eliminated. One can legitimately ask however whether the groups we studied were very unusual subgroups skewed in some particular direction—exhibitionists who wanted to show off their nightmares or persons desperately asking for help by coming in as research subjects and using the nightmare as a way to obtain help; some might even suggest we obtained a group of liars who like to make up interesting symptoms with which to fascinate and befuddle investigators.

It is conceivable that a few unusual persons did join our group. However, I spent considerable time with each person in this group, and I have spent many years as a clinician seeing psychiatric patients and as a researcher interviewing volunteer subjects—frequently obtained from newspaper adver-

Who Has Nightmares?

Results of the Studies

In the second study we found that on most measures the twelve nightmare sufferers differed greatly from the vivid and nonvivid dreamers, but resembled very closely the thirty-eight nightmare sufferers in the original uncontrolled study. This suggests that we were indeed sampling from the same population of nightmare sufferers and confirms our assumption that the first group of nightmare sufferers did not simply represent people who answer newspaper advertisements. I will present below the results of test material obtained from each study, but because of the similarities I will also feel free to look at the entire group of fifty nightmare sufferers and try to draw some overall conclusions. When I speak simply of "the nightmare sufferers" or "subjects with nightmares" this usually refers to the entire group of fifty from the two studies.

---

tisements similar to these—for various studies. I can state with confidence that the subjects described here were by and large honest persons who did experience nightmares and whose motivations, though somewhat different in every case, were generally along the lines of an interest in their nightmares and a genuine interest in talking with someone, sharing knowledge, helping science. In some cases, the subjects were also obtaining assurance that they were not unique; that our studies showed there indeed were other people who experienced frequent nightmares. They very rarely asked for help in dealing with their problems, no more frequently than other research subjects. Other clinicians who interviewed some of the subjects themselves or saw my interviews on videotape agree with this assessment, and the MMPI validity scores confirm the impression that these were honest, open persons.

The Nightmare and the Nightmare Sufferer

Among the nightmare sufferers, the nightmares were of course dreams—long, frightening dreams. The themes varied considerably, the most common simply that of being chased. Typically, a subject would recall childhood nightmares in which he or she was chased by a monster, something big, strange, or unknown. Later on, the chaser was more likely to be a large unidentified man, a group of frightening people, a gang, or a troop of Nazis. Often, the dreamer was not only chased, but attacked, or hurt in some way. Sometimes there was only a threat that something would happen and the dreamer awakened in fright. However, in many cases the dreamer was actually caught, beaten, stabbed, shot, or mutilated.

The nightmares are described as very vivid, frightening, and "real." For instance, one woman reported:

> I was swimming along in cool blue water. A strange man swam after me and started slicing me with a knife. It was all in brilliant color and I could feel everything. I felt the cool water and the hot pain of the knife slashing into my arm; I saw my blood spreading out in the water and I could see slices of my flesh drifting off away from me. It was very real. I could definitely feel the knife and feel the pain in this dream.

Not only did frightening events occur, but the entire background scene was sometimes eerie and frightening: "I was out in the street with a friend and it was raining blood." Other themes involved the dreamer taking part in or watching scenes of war, catastrophe, or torture. There was almost always a sense of an awful scene—either an individual attack or a general war, riot, catastrophe in which the dreamer is helpless. Even when the dreamer described taking part in the war, hurting, killing, and mutilating others, there was a sense of helplessness and terror. On occasion the nightmare contained non-nightmare features as well. Thus, the dreamer was helpless in one part of the dream, but then was able to fight back and on rare occasions even vanquished the threatening figures. In a few cases (but only among the women in this sample), the nightmares had an altruistic character; it was not the dreamer herself but her mother or her children who were in danger and the dreamer was trying in vain to help them.

It is also interesting to note some aspects that did *not* characterize these nightmares. First of all, among these civilians with a lifelong history of nightmares—the nightmares were not repetitive: each was different, although the themes were often similar. Some of the subjects described having had "some form of this nightmare" or "something like this" many times. These nightmares were not the repetitive replayings of an actual experience that occurred among veterans with post-traumatic stress disorders (see chapter 8). Explicit sexual content was not prominent in the nightmares. A few of the women when describing being chased by a frightening man or creature said something like, "I was afraid I was going to be killed, or raped." One man had a sexual torture scene in some of his nightmares, but most nightmares had no manifest sexual content. Violence directed at others was also rare, occurring only under two conditions. One involved the dreamer occasionally "fighting back" against the attacker; the other involved the dreamer "being forced" to beat or hurt someone else.

It was striking how often the nightmares involved generalized fears—probably childhood fears—such as being chased, being attacked, the body coming apart or being cut apart, even though there was no history of any specific traumatic event related to these themes. However, there is no question that events in a dreamer's recent life entered into nightmares and were superimposed on these generalized fears. Thus, when a disturbing event did occur—for instance, a number of the subjects actually had been attacked, mugged, or raped—this event then entered into the nightmares in different ways for a period of a few weeks or months. The nightmares would usually combine elements of the recent attack with some of the old themes: "Some men were chasing me, I was trying desperately to escape down an alley. The scene was very much like what actually happened to me last month, except that in the dream there were several huge men—not just two teenagers—involved." Thus, in these persons, although having nightmares was not initiated by a traumatic event, as far as we can tell, recent traumatic events definitely entered into the content of the nightmares.

FACTORS THAT INFLUENCED THE NIGHTMARES

Although these persons had had nightmares all their lives, the nightmares were more or less frequent at different times. The factors most consistently influencing frequency were periods of stress in many different senses: adolescence, geographical moves, difficult times at school or work, and loss or the breakup of a relationship. Traumatic events such as muggings or attacks increased the severity of nightmares in addition to their being incorporated into the nightmares' content. The persons who had had psychotic or close-to-psychotic episodes almost always described an increase in frequency or severity of nightmares at these times; often the nightmare condition became worse first, before other symptoms occurred. Periods without stress were associated with fewer nightmares, as were periods when the person was maturing, or increasingly "taking charge" of his life, or involved in a continuing solid relationship.

DREAMS OTHER THAN NIGHTMARES

Aside from having nightmares, all the nightmare sufferers had extremely vivid, lifelike, detailed dreams. In these respects, they closely resembled the "vivid dreamer" group, and both were quite different from the "ordinary dreamer" group in the controlled study. The nightmare group, as well as the vivid dream group described most of their dreams as being in color, often very bright color, and usually including sound. The nightmare group also emphasized other sensations such as touch, pain, taste, smell ("I could smell the smoke," "I felt the weight of the stone on my leg"). The dreaming experience was especially intense emotionally for the nightmare sufferers and they described more frequently than the other groups that the emotional feeling of the dream continued powerfully after awakening.

The dreams themselves were somewhat unusual in the nightmare group, even when the dreams were not nightmares. It is worth keeping in mind that although many of our dreams are in some ways crazy, uninhibited or bizarre, they mostly follow certain patterns. For instance, we are usually ourselves in a dream. We either take part in a story or watch a story unfold in front of us. The dream may have some shifts in scene, but usually we know pretty well when a dream is over and when we have awakened; we do not awaken into another dream.

However, in all these respects, the nightmare subjects were somewhat different from most of us and from the two control study groups. For instance, a number of them described dreams in which they were not themselves but someone else. Several of the women had dreams in which they were men. Several had dreams in which they were animals. One had a long dream in which she was a butterfly flying over fields—quite a happy dream. And a number of the nightmare subjects had dreams within dreams (a very rare phenomenon in most of us). They experienced a long, emotional, perhaps frightening dream, waking up thinking "Whew, I'm glad that's over, now it's time to go about my business" only to find, as they tried to go about their business, that they were still dreaming and had to wake up again to get to their real waking lives.

SLEEP PATTERNS

Aside from the nightmares and the dream characteristics mentioned, these persons with frequent nightmares did not have any particular sleep problems or abnormalities. They could be described as having a degree of insomnia in that they awakened a lot from nightmares, but they were not persons who took an especially long time falling asleep; they did not complain of inability to return to sleep or of not getting enough sleep; they did not have episodic events such as bed-wetting, sleepwalking, or sleep talking, though a few had had such episodes in childhood. (Of course, they did not suffer from night terrors since that had been one condition for inclusion in the nightmare-sufferer group).

The only unusual feature of their sleep pattern was that they were frequently unable to tell whether they were asleep or awake for some time after awakening in the morning. This may be related to their unusually lifelike emotional dreams and the fact that they sometimes awakened from one dream into another dream. It may simply be considered an exaggeration of the situation we all encounter occasionally of waking up slowly and not being quite certain we are awake, but in these subjects this condition lasted sometimes for half-an-hour or an hour.

PERSONALITY: ADULT ADJUSTMENT

Nightmare sufferers had some problems and some psychopathology, as we shall see, but as a group they were persons living in society, working to support themselves, or in school—usually as graduate students—or both. A few were unemployed. One striking feature was that none of those who were employed held ordinary blue- or white-collar jobs. A number were musicians (both composers and performers), painters, poets, writers, craftspersons, teachers, and therapists. Those who were teachers frequently taught art or music. One of the therapists was a music therapist and another a body therapist. Many saw themselves as rebels or "outsiders" to a greater or lesser extent. Some of them actively rejected society—materialism, mediocrity, bourgeois values, and so on—while others saw themselves more as rejected by society. Most, as we shall see, felt from childhood on that they were a little different from other people.

Their sexual identities could be described as somewhat fluid. Two of the fifty thought of themselves as definitely homosexual; some had had sexual relationships with persons of both sexes; others frequently fantasied experiences with both sexes. The majority were basically heterosexual, but they tended not to identify themselves intensely with their own sex; they did not fit society's "sexual stereotypes": among the fifty nightmare subjects in the two studies, there was not a single man who could be considered an old-fashioned, tough, macho-type male; and there was not a single woman who thought of her role in life as pleasing a man, marrying him, and having children. (In case anyone believes such people are becoming extinct, I should mention that these descriptions did fit at least five of the twenty-four men and women in the control groups.)

Their relationships—marital, sexual, and also friend-ship—could be described as being variable and changeable, often stormy and unsettled. There was a tendency to become overinvolved in relationships quickly, with difficult painful separations, and in some cases, a secondary tendency to avoid relationships completely because they could be so painful.

Many had gone through difficult and stormy adolescent years. Some of the same factors mentioned under adult relationships had been present in adolescence, but even more painfully so since coping skills had been less developed. Thus, almost all the nightmare sufferers had found their adolescent years difficult. One-third of the group had attempted suicide or had thought very seriously about suicide. Others had been depressed without having had suicidal thoughts. Two-thirds had been in psychotherapy at some time (table 4–1). Almost all had experimented with alcohol and drugs but were not present drug users. Most had had bad experiences with street drugs at some time during adolescence or early adulthood. Quite typically, they described having had very uncomfortable feelings or even "bad trips"—including paranoid feelings and feelings of isolation or alienation—even after smoking small quantities of marijuana.

CHILDHOOD HISTORY

We questioned each person in great detail about his or her childhood in an attempt to find any unusual characteristics, including the possibility of any traumatic events or unusual family relationships or dynamics that might have led to the onset of nightmares.

It did not appear that these nightmare sufferers had had obvious traumatic events in childhood. They remembered their childhoods unusually well. Many of them were intensely introspective, interested in themselves, and had spoken to their parents about many aspects of their childhood. So it is quite likely that at least some of them would have been aware of it if there had been a serious traumatic event. We were not able to interview any parents directly, but several subjects became very interested in their childhoods in connection with our study and asked their parents for additional information. No traumatic events were unearthed in this way.

Nor could we find any regular family constellation

TABLE 4–1
Characteristics of Our Four Study Groups

	Study 1 Nightmare Subjects N = 38	Study 2 Nightmare Subjects N = 12	Study 2 Vivid Dreamers N = 12	Study 2 Ordinary Dreamers N = 12
Mean number of nightmares reported per week	4.0	3.5	0	0
Percent who remember having nightmares in childhood	100	100	67	50
Percent who describe "vivid," "totally real" dreams	100	100	100	0
Percent who spend a great deal of time "daydreaming"	77	75	67	25
Percent who experienced "daymares"	n.o.	67	8	8
Percent who have definite or possible "dreams within dreams"	55	67	25	25
Percent who had (or experienced) known traumatic events (attacks, rapes, violent deaths of someone close to them)	68	83	33	17
Percent who had traumatic events occurring *before* the onset of nightmares	0	0	n.a.	n.a.
Percent of those with traumatic events in whom the events influenced content of nightmares	100	100	n.a.	n.a.
Percent who described themselves as very sensitive children in some sense	74	75	8	0
Percent who experience precognitive dreams, out-of-the-body experiences, or other such experiences	68	67	50	17
Percent who have a history of psychiatric hospitalization	11	17	0	0
Percent who had psychotherapy (short- or long-term) at some time	76	67	17	17

TABLE 4–1 *(continued)*

	Study 1 Nightmare Subjects N = 38	Study 2 Nightmare Subjects N = 12	Study 2 Vivid Dreamers N = 12	Study 2 Ordinary Dreamers N = 12
Percent who have first- or second-degree relatives known to have been hospitalized for mental illness	37	33	8	16
Percent who have thought seriously of suicide	39	50	0	8
Percent who have made a suicide attempt (not necessarily life-threatening)	18	33	0	8
Percent who described periods of serious depression (usually in adolescence)	53	50	8	8
Percent who described their childhood as "happy" or "very happy"	n.o.	33	67	58
Percent who described at least one "unusual reaction to drugs" (usually marijuana or alcohol)	n.o.	42	17	17
Mean score on childhood "Indicators of Vulnerability to Schizophrenia"*	n.o.	5.6	2.1	2.1
Percent scoring over 2 on childhood "Indicators of Vulnerability to Schizophrenia"* (1–2 is average)	n.o.	100	25	17

n.a. = not applicable
n.o. = not obtained (the data were not obtained in this form)
* This refers to a score on a group of possible indicators of vulnerability to schizophrenia which we have used in other studies (Hartmann et al. 1984a). In the form mentioned here, the scores range from 0 to 8.

occurring in these persons that might have been related to the nightmare: the nightmare sufferers had not been family scapegoats; nor had they been Cinderellas suffering hardships while their siblings were better loved and better treated. They had not been, as far as we could tell, loved intensely and then "deserted." Many did have a younger sibling born one to three years after their own birth and they did appear to have taken the birth of the sibling unusually hard. However, there is nothing externally very exceptional in these events—the birth of a younger sibling when one is one to three years old is obviously a common occurrence. (It was, in fact, as common in the two control groups as it was in the nightmare groups.) It seemed rather that the psychological makeup of the nightmare sufferers was perhaps already somewhat unusual, even at the age of one to three, so that the birth of a sibling was especially painful or traumatic to them.

The one recurring theme in the interviews about childhood was that the nightmare sufferer saw him- or herself as unusual, even in childhood. "Unusual" generally meant "different from the others," often more sensitive, more artistic, more easily hurt, more fragile. The word sensitive occurred frequently: referring sometimes to perceptual sensitivity—to light and sound, for instance; sometimes to interpersonal sensitivity—empathy, awareness of others' feelings; and almost always to being themselves emotionally sensitive—easily hurt by others. They saw this personality characteristic as having been present more or less from birth.

I was intrigued by hearing, in four different subjects, of family grouping by personality type. For instance,

Who Has Nightmares?

"Yes, I was always very sensitive, everything got to me, I cried easily, I felt easily hurt, I also felt I could sympathize really well with other people; and I was always more of an artist than my brothers. This is interesting because my father is just like me. On the other hand, my mother and my two brothers are completely different. They are solid-citizen types. Stone walls. Nothing bothers them." This description—wherein several members of a family are described as definitely having a characteristic (such as sensitivity) throughout life while others lack it—suggests the possibility of a genetic transmission of something akin to "sensitivity." ("Sensitivity" and "stone-wall character" appear to be distributed among family members in the same way blue and brown eyes sometimes are.) The data are not sufficient to confirm this however. Sensitivity is not as easy to identify as blue eyes; and psychological processes such as identification can influence judgments; someone whose image of herself is "I'm just like father" may insist that the two of them are sensitive, while mother and the brothers are not. But my impression was that such identification or wishes did not satisfactorily explain the descriptions. The subjects did not describe their looks or interests or feelings as being "just like father" but only the quality of extreme sensitivity.

MEDICAL HISTORY

The subjects were young and, as a group, were not severely ill medically. Nor had there been serious long-term illnesses in childhood. They had not spent months or years sick in bed, nor did they seem to have experienced more than the usual number of febrile childhood illnesses. However, comparing the nightmare subjects to the non-nightmare subjects and comparing the overall group of nightmare subjects from both studies with other groups of volunteers, I was struck by the tendency of the nightmare subjects to report more allergies, more unusual drug reactions, and more accidents than the other groups. Unfortunately, I do not have these data in clear numerical form for statistical analysis.

PSYCHOPATHOLOGY

Even though the nightmare subjects and the control groups came to the study as volunteers and not as patients, there was considerable psychopathology in the nightmare group and it was consistent with the psychological test results described below. We attempted to give a psychiatric diagnosis whenever possible (using DSM-III, the American Psychiatric Association's official *Diagnostic and Statistical Manual of Mental Disorders* [1980]). None of the vivid dreamers and ordinary dreamers could be given a clear DSM-III diagnosis. There was no case among the twenty-four for whom one could even consider a diagnosis of schizophrenia, schizoid personality, schizotypal personality, or borderline personality.

Among the nightmare sufferers, it was possible to make a DSM-III diagnosis in some cases. Among the twelve in the controlled study, we diagnosed two as schizophrenic, three as schizotypal personality disorder, and one as borderline personality disorder. Likewise, in the thirty-eight of the first study, twelve could definitely be given one of these diagnoses and several others less definitely (we are less certain here since less information was available, and we had not originally planned to make formal DSM-III diagnoses).*

In addition to the fact that a sizable number of these "normal volunteer" nightmare sufferers could be diagnosed as schizophrenic, schizotypal, or borderline, most of the others (for whom no definite diagnosis could be made) nonetheless had a few of the characteristics of schizophrenic or schizotypal persons. For instance, they were a bit loose and tangential in their thinking but not so markedly that one could speak of a "thought disorder"; many had experienced occasional paranoid feelings though they had had no paranoid delusions, and so on.

The nightmare sufferers very strikingly did *not* have the characteristics of neurotics. None of them could be diagnosed as having anxiety states, phobic states, dissociative states, conversion states, or obsessive-compulsive disorder. (Or, in older terminology, none of them had anxiety, hysterical, or obsessional neuroses, nor could they be characterized as having clearly hysterical or obsessional personalities.) In psychodynamic terms, it was striking that these persons—although most were intelligent and many were students or teachers—did not

* For those who are not familiar with current psychiatric diagnoses, schizophrenia refers to a serious mental illness involving thought disorder, affect or emotional disorder, and usually psychotic episodes with loss of contact with reality. Schizotypal and borderline personality disorders refer not to major psychotic illnesses, but to long-standing personality problems. Specifically, schizotypal refers to eccentricity, suspiciousness, etc. in persons who have some characteristics of schizophrenia but who generally stay in touch with reality and are able to function quite well. Borderline refers to instability in interpersonal relations, in mood, and in self-image. Many psychiatrists feel that these conditions are interrelated. It is possible that schizophrenia and schizotypal personality (plus schizoid personality, a diagnosis we did not make in our group), and perhaps also borderline personality, share a common genetic or biological background.

use typical, relatively mature defenses such as isolation, intellectualization, repression, or undoing which one commonly sees in such groups. I saw these subjects as "defenseless" or unusually vulnerable. When there were manifestations of defenses, they were of a primitive kind, such as projection.

FAMILY HISTORY

Among the thirty-eight subjects of the first study, I was struck that although not many mentioned relatives afflicted with sleep disorders or serious physical illnesses, twenty-eight described close relatives who were mentally ill; from the descriptions, the relatives appeared most often to be schizophrenic. In the controlled study, we attempted to examine the family histories more systematically. An interviewer drew a detailed family tree for each subject and asked him or her questions about each of the persons represented, emphasizing especially the presence of any nightmares or other sleep problems and any physical or mental illness. The information was then coded and a "familial fraction" was constructed for each kind of problem, in which the number of relatives having a particular problem was divided by the total number of relatives about whom the subject had information, first degree relatives carrying more weight than second degree relatives.

The groups did not differ in terms of sleep problems or physical illnesses among relatives. However, there appeared to be a higher incidence of nightmares, of serious psychological problems, and perhaps of psychiatric hospitalization among the relatives of the nightmare

Who Has Nightmares?

sufferers than among the relatives of the other groups (table 4–2). Nine of the twelve subjects with nightmares described at least one relative with "serious psychological problems" and four described at least one relative with a known psychiatric hospitalization. This high proportion of psychological problems and psychiatric hospitalization in the families of the nightmare sufferers confirms our impression from the first study. However, we must remember that we are relying on the memories of the subjects. It is possible that the nightmare subjects who were in many ways more sensitive to other people might have been more interested in the peculiarities of their relatives, and might perhaps have seen mental illness where others would have ignored it or even actively denied it. Precise diagnoses for the relatives were, of course, not available. Among the descriptions were: "He had a nervous breakdown three or four times," "She spent many years in a mental hospital," or "He was hospitalized several times and always had ideas of persecution." In the cases where detailed descriptions were given, it appears quite certain to me that the predominant diagnoses were schizophrenia and schizophrenia spectrum disorders. There was some mention of alcoholism in relatives but the difference between the nightmare groups and the other groups is not clear in this respect. It definitely did not seem that the nightmare subjects were describing depression, mania, mental retardation, or organic psychoses as the forms of mental illnesses in their families. It was only these variables, relating to nightmares and mental illness in the family, that differentiated nightmare sufferers from the other groups.

TABLE 4-2
"Family History" Ratings (Familial Fractions)

	Males	Females	
1. *Family History of Nightmares*			Significant difference
Nightmare Group	.096 (±.05)	.108 (±.05)	between groups:
Vivid Dream Group	.037 (±.04)	.036 (±.07)	Nightmare higher
Ordinary Dream Group	.014 (±.02)	.020 (±.05)	than Vivid,
			Ordinary p < .01
			(Analysis of
			Variance)
2. *Family History of Serious Psychological Problems*			
Nightmare Group	.128 (±.11)	.166 (±.16)	Significant difference
Vivid Dream Group	.056 (±.04)	.064 (±.10)	between groups:
Ordinary Dream Group	.054 (±.09)	.042 (±.07)	Nightmare higher
			than Vivid,
			Ordinary p < .05
			(Analysis of
			Variance)
3. *Family History of Known Psychiatric Hospitalization*			
Nightmare Group	.034 (±.05)	.042 (±.05)	No significant
Vivid Dream Group	.018 (±.04)	0 (±0)	difference. A trend
Ordinary Dream Group	0 (±0)	.035 (±.06)	to higher values in
			the Nightmare
			Group (Analysis of
			Variance)

NOTES: The numbers are "familial fractions" (FF) calculated as

$$FF = \frac{(\text{No. of affected } 1° \text{ relatives}) + \frac{1}{2}(\text{No. of affected } 2° \text{ relatives})}{\text{Total no. of } 1° \text{ and } 2° \text{ relatives}}$$

The numbers presented are means (± standard deviation). "Affected" means relatives reported to have the condition (nightmares, serious psychological problems, or psychiatric hospitalization). These numbers may be useful in comparing the groups. However, the fractions represent a very rough measure, and in retrospect, they could have been calculated in other, preferable ways. They cannot be considered estimates of actual frequency of the conditions; they are in fact certain to be underestimates since numerous relatives—especially second-degree relatives—may have had these "conditions" without the awareness of our subjects. First degree (1°) relatives are those who share one-half of one's genetic material: parents, full siblings, children. Second degree (2°) relatives share one-quarter of one's genetic material.

Who Has Nightmares?

PSYCHOLOGICAL TESTS

Minnesota Multiphasic Personality Inventory. The MMPI, as described earlier, is a standardized objective test and we hoped to use it to examine in more quantitative terms the conclusions about personality and psychopathology arrived at on the basis of the interviews.

Figures 4–1, 4–2, and 4–3 present the MMPI profiles in our second study; table 4–3 summarizes the results. The most clearcut findings are the following: First, the ordinary dreamers and vivid dreamers had almost identical mean profiles; there were no significant differences between them on any MMPI scales. In other words, the two groups had almost identical personalities as measured by the MMPI. And the mean scale values for these two groups were all well within the normal range. This lack of difference between the control groups makes the results in the nightmare group, which differed distinctly from the two other groups, even more striking. First, the nightmare sufferers scored significantly higher than the other groups on the so-called "psychotic" scales—paranoia, psychasthenia, and schizophrenia.* The higher scores were especially prominent on the schizophrenia and paranoia scales. This means that the nightmare sufferers answered the whole group of questions more in the way schizophrenic patients or paranoid patients would than did the other two groups. The male nightmare sufferers scored even higher on these scales than the females.

Second, the three groups did *not* differ significantly on

* The MMPI is scored on three "validity scales" and on ten "clinical scales": Hypochondriasis (Hs), Depression (D), Hysteria (Hy), Psychopathic Deviate (Pd), Masculinity-Femininity (Mf), Paranoia (Pa), Psychasthenia (Pt), Schizophrenia (Sc), Mania (Ma), Social Introversion (Si).

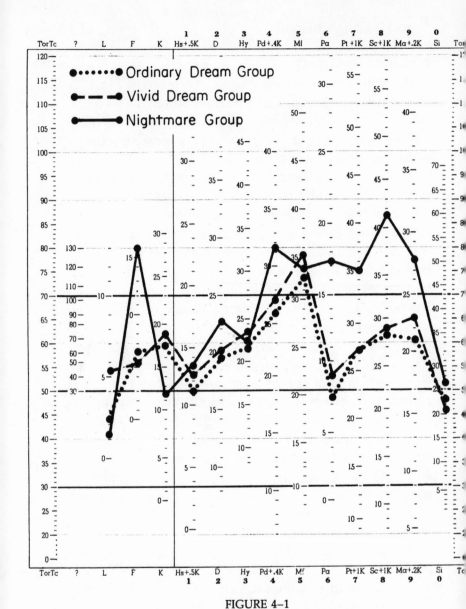

FIGURE 4–1

Mean MMPI Profiles in Study 2: Male Subjects

NOTE: Copyright © 1948, renewed 1984 by the University of Minnesota. Reprinted by permission.

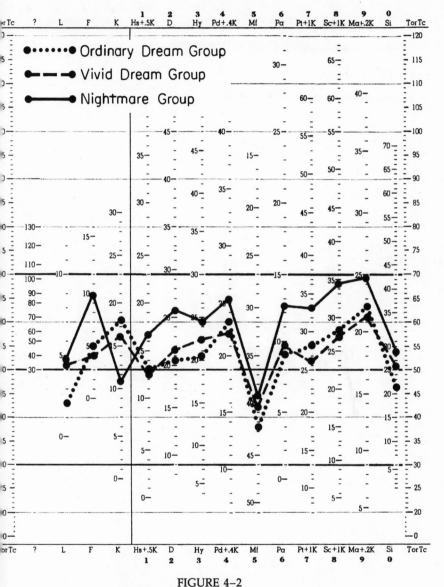

FIGURE 4–2

Mean MMPI Profiles in Study 2: Female Subjects

Note: Copyright © 1948, renewed 1984 by the University of Minnesota. Reprinted by permission.

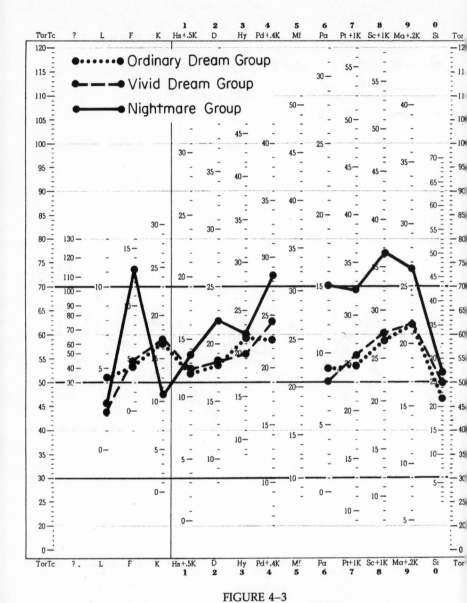

FIGURE 4–3
Mean MMPI Profiles in Study 2: Male and Female Subjects
NOTE: Copyright © 1948, renewed 1984 by the University of Minnesota. Reprinted by permission.

Who Has Nightmares?

TABLE 4–3
MMPI Scales: Difference Between Groups and Between
the Sexes (Two-Way Analysis of Variance)

Scale	Group Effect (NM, V, O)	Sex Effect (M, F)	Interaction
L	n.s.	n.s.	n.s.
F	NM > V, O (p < .01)	n.s.	n.s.
K	NM < V, O (p < .01)	n.s.	n.s.
Hs	n.s.	n.s.	n.s.
D	n.s.	n.s.	n.s.
Hy	n.s.	n.s.	n.s.
Pd	n.s.	M > F (p < .01)	n.s.
Pa	NM > V, O (p < .01)	n.s.	n.s.
Pt	NM > V, O (p < .01)	n.s.	n.s.
Sc	NM > V, O (p < .01)	n.s.	n.s.
Ma	n.s.	n.s.	n.s.
Si	n.s.	n.s.	n.s.
ES	NM < V, O (p < .01)	n.s.	n.s.

NM = Nightmare Group
V = Vivid Dream Group
O = Ordinary Dream Group
M = Male
F = Female
ES = Barron's Ego Strength Scale
n.s. = not significant
NOTE: Only differences significant at p < .01 (two-tailed) are reported.

the "neurotic" scales—hypochondriasis, depression, and hysteria. In other words, the nightmare sufferers scored higher on the psychotic scales *without* scoring higher than the others on the neurotic scales. This differentiates them from most patient and subject groups. For instance, many laboratories including ours have studied groups of persons with insomnia and other sleep problems. Insomniac subjects almost always have elevated scores on many MMPI scales—especially on the "neurotic" scales (Coursey 1975; Kales et al. 1976; Beutler, Thornby, and Karacan 1978). The group of nightmare sufferers were

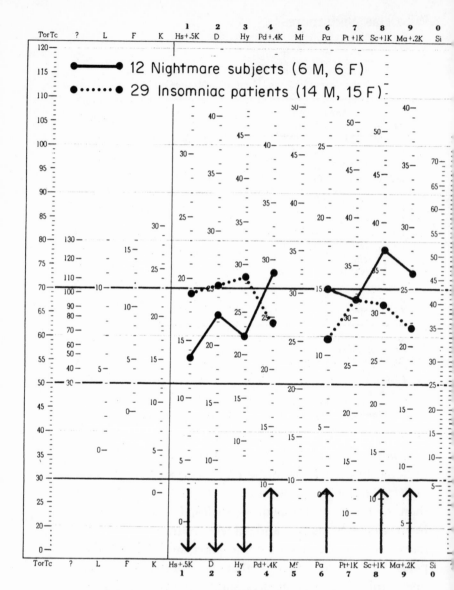

FIGURE 4-4

Nightmare Subjects Compared to Patients with Insomnia
NOTE: Copyright © 1948, renewed 1984 by the University of Minnesota. Reprinted by permission.

obviously quite different. In fact, we did a comparison of the twelve nightmare sufferers in our controlled study with twenty-nine insomniacs in a recent study (Smitson, Walsh, and Kramer, 1981). The nightmare sufferers scored significantly *higher* than the insomniacs on the psychotic scales, Sc, Pd, and Ma, but significantly *lower* than the insomniacs on the neurotic scales, Hs, D, and Hy (figure 4-4).

Our conclusions are strengthened by the fact that the mean MMPI profiles for nightmare subjects in our first study produced results very similar to those for the second study (figure 4-5).

Similarly, the MMPIs can be used to compare our nightmare subjects with various groups of anxious subjects, and anxious patients (Lanyon 1968). Such groups show high values on the scales Hs, Hy, Pt, usually without elevated values on the scales Sc, Pa, Ma. Our nightmare subjects obviously have very different profiles from these groups. The only groups with mean profiles somewhat similar to our nightmare group are schizophrenic patients, borderline patients, schizotypal patients, and to a certain extent, groups of art students (Lanyon 1968).

Perhaps also of importance are the high F scale scores—significantly higher in the nightmare group than in the two other groups.* A high F score combined with a relatively low K score, characteristic of our subjects, is taken as a measure of openness or willingness to admit

---

* A high F score means that the subject answers true or false to many statements that are rarely (less than 10 percent) answered in that direction by the whole population of "normals." The statements included are a miscellaneous group, for instance, an answer of "true" to the following, and many others, would increase one's score on the F-scale:

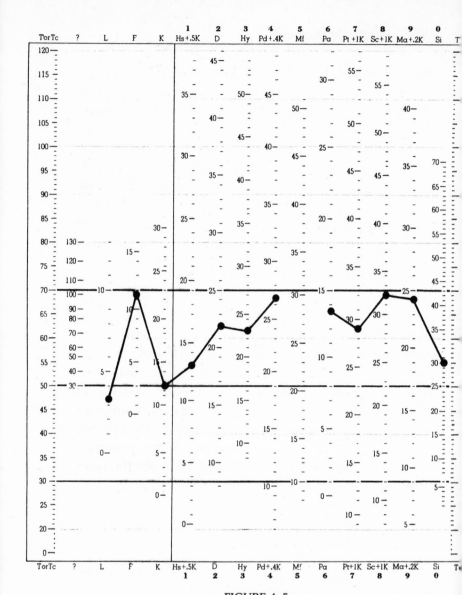

FIGURE 4–5

Mean MMPI Profiles: Male and Female Subjects with Frequent Nightmares in Study 1 (N = 38)

Note: Copyright © 1948, renewed 1984 by the University of Minnesota. Reprinted by permission.

to problems, to quirks, to unusual experiences. In this sense, the nightmare subjects as a group are "unusual," more open to suffering, more willing to admit to problems than are the two comparison groups.

In addition to providing data on individual scales, the MMPI can also be used to diagnose personality in an overall clinical sense. However, this should be done with care, by clinicians experienced in the use of the MMPI. For this purpose, I submitted the six mean profiles in the controlled study (males and females of each of the three groups), on a blind basis, to three experts who had had many years of experience in scoring and interpreting the MMPI. They were each asked to write a clinical description of a person with such a profile. All three of the experts stated that the four profiles that turned out to belong to the male and female vivid and ordinary dreamers were basically normal. All agreed that there was something unusual about the profiles that turned out to belong to the male and female nightmare sufferers. The descriptions of the three judges differed somewhat, but there are common themes, and some important points are noted. Here, slightly condensed, are the three clinical descriptions for the male nightmare group:

"I have the wanderlust and am never happy unless I am roaming or traveling about."

"Most of the time I would rather sit and daydream than do anything else."

"I have reasons for feeling jealous of one or more members of my family."

A high F score can occur in someone who does not understand the test (language problem, mental retardation), or someone who is answering questions carelessly or randomly. In subjects who are cooperative and do understand the test—this was definitely the case in the nightmare group—the F scale measures unusual characteristics—unusual answers of various kinds.

1. They generally have difficulty with interpersonal relations. They lack social skills. They avoid close personal relationships. They distrust others and are oversensitive to rejection. Sexual problems are likely.

Persons with this profile are usually diagnosed as personality disorder (antisocial, paranoid, or schizoid) or schizophrenic disorder. This profile more closely fits the personality disordered profiles. This is a chronic pattern that shows little change over time. Short-term "chaotic" circumstances are likely.

2. My clear diagnosis of this profile would be along paranoid schizophrenic lines. There is little doubt in my mind that they are excessively suspicious and distrustful to the point of ideas of reference. Their thought is quite loose and pervaded with idiosyncratic notions. They are quite unhappy and have very low self-esteem except that this may be compensated for by grandiose, unrealistic notions of themselves. There is considerable primary process thinking which it seems the person has become accustomed to and which does not overwhelm him completely. This person might be troubled by very true feelings and how to cope with them. Nonetheless, it is striking that he still seems to seek the company of others and has not withdrawn into an isolated existence. In summary, I think this profile comes from at least a schizotypic person who may or may not be clinically schizophrenic.

3. This individual* is markedly deviant, presenting himself in odd or strange ways. He is different, shy, and retiring but not self depreciative. . . .

Underlying dynamics center upon alienated feelings and disturbing experiences that frighten and puzzle him. He

---

* The judges knew that each profile they were given was the mean of six individual profiles. However, they were asked to examine the mean profile clinically—to discuss the characteristics and problems of a patient with this profile—so they speak at times of "he," "she," or "this person" rather than "they."

senses that others have pleasures and sources of enjoyment that he does not share and cannot empathize with. He finds himself to be so different and difficult to accept that he projects these same views of himself on others and anticipates rejection and misunderstanding. There is little love, affection, or tenderness in his relationships with others.

The three clinical descriptions for the female group were:

1. Individuals with this validity configuration are admitting to some psychological distress. Often individuals entering treatment will produce this overly frank self-appraisal. . . .

The MMPI profile shows a somewhat mixed range of symptoms emphasizing general discomfort in their present situation. They are experiencing some depressed mood, tension, anxiety and self-doubt. They appear to be somewhat agitated and feel rather alienated at this time.

2. This group has fairly serious psychological problems. They are quite unconventional to the point of being idiosyncratic and probably have some very strange ideas. They are not very happy and seem rebellious and angry, although the anger may be expressed indirectly, or even projected, rendering them suspicious and distrustful. They, at times, may be difficult to follow in that their ideas become very abstract, only poorly related to reality. They may be quite impulsive.

3. She has a number of enthusiasms and puts a great deal of energy in her undertakings. Those who know her only superficially consider her to be a successful and highly effective person with few hang-ups.

There is evidence in her manner, however, that conveys some tension and doubts about her true worth and merits. She harbors a number of doubts and misgivings and her competitiveness is laced with a pervasive hostility. This edge of anger and resentment is mistaken for masculinity by some but she is quite feminine in a number of areas.

She strongly resents being stereotyped in regard to these preferences, however, and makes a strong effort to establish herself as an independent and autonomous person. She has periods in which she is quite discouraged and overwhelmed with feelings that she is not able to keep up the struggle.

Although there is, of course, not perfect agreement between these judges and the clinical description—the nature of the task made it impossible and the judges approached the task somewhat differently—there are themes in common and the descriptions do appear to fit our clinical impressions. These descriptions characterize the nightmare sufferers as an unusual group with unusual openness and considerable psychopathology, including some paranoid and other psychotic-like aspects.

Rorschach. The well-known Rorschach (inkblot) test is a projective test and thus very different from the objective "true or false" MMPI. We used the Rorschach to help gain insight into the subjects' internal world, including unconscious fears and conflicts. I felt that the characteristics I noted in interviews and called "openness," "defenselessness," and "thin boundaries" (see chapter 6) might become clearer in the Rorschach responses.

The Rorschach gives primarily a rich clinical picture and only secondarily can be scored numerically so that groups can be compared. The psychologist who worked on the Rorschach tests found more indications of pathology and disturbance among the nightmare subjects compared to the other groups and she also found some of them to be quite creative, complex, and unusual in their thinking. Here are a few quotes from the two-page clinical descriptions written on a blind basis for several subjects who, when the code was broken, turned out to be the nightmare sufferers:

J.D., a female nightmare subject: Very disturbed, *in a psychotic direction:* Many confabulations and contaminations—disordered thought processes. Malevolence; *paranoid* fantasies ("He is watching everything—but you can't see his eyes."—IX; "It's alive, and it *watches* people, watches with his eyes.") *Sadistic,* parasitic responses. Merging (Siamese twins), hybrid creatures. However, some of the responses are "popular" and others, too, relatively undistorted. There are some attempts at *defense*—like using *artistic context.* Also, *form* responses are accurate, indicating some capacity at reality-adherence. Maybe a borderline person, who, under the stress of projective testing, "yields" a very psychotic picture—unable to control her impulsive, malevolent fantasies.

F.A., a female nightmare subject: A sense of vulnerability (transparent body in card III, bleeding uterus in card II). Some *hysterical* quality in movement responses, when flooded with anxiety—some contaminatory tendency (cards III and X). Unsuccessful handling of affect, relatively few color responses. High M% [movement responses]—possible *early trauma. Defensiveness* manifest in some long reaction times, and by *intellectualization*—attempt to use the context of *art* works. Some resourceful and *creative* handling of the test—possibly an ability on which better functioning depends.

I.F., a female nightmare subject: A well elaborated record, without very problematic issues. . . . Some *immaturity,* as manifest in many A vs. H responses and, correspondingly, many FM vs. M. Some *oral* preoccupation—several "food" responses. No strong conflict, nor overt *anxiety*—no malevolence, paranoia, or gross penetration. Indirectly, anxiety can be inferred from high sensitivity (shading responses), some cross-section views, revealing vulnerability (anatomy). *Markedly low percentage of human responses and human movement*—attributable more to a generally *immature* personality than to hostile or schizoid-avoidant tendencies.

F.I., a male nightmare subject: Thought disorder very marked—many confabulations and contaminations. Very vivid *fantasies of violence,* destruction, mutilation; some aggressiveness combined with sexual fantasies. People hostile and sadistic! Fear of "falling apart"; general sense of danger and vulnerability. Some primitive fantasies of merging and amorphousness. Poor, schizoid object relations. Some attempt at defense by rather long and elaborate "explanations" in the inquiry phase. But, since the *"card-reality"* is accepted as *actual reality,* attempts at "distancing" are unsuccessful.

I.S., a male nightmare subject: A very *"vulnerable"* person, expressing *helplessness fantasies* ("bird falling out of nest into space") and preoccupation with anatomy and sex. *High anxiety* and low coping capacity (very low whole-card responses % = 10%), poor *interpersonal* quality (only one human response, on card III, without interaction between the figures).

Most, but not all of the nightmare subjects, had clinical descriptions of this kind. Only one or two of the subjects in the other two groups were described in similar fashion. However, hardly anyone looks completely normal and ordinary on a Rorschach test. Here are two typical subjects from the other groups:

I.L., a male in the "ordinary dreams" group: This person has marked difficulty in dealing with emotional experience— no use of color whatsoever, which may indicate *very strong defensiveness,* but also some *dullness,* and perhaps *depression* (the low R also points to depression). A rather *dull* and *constricted* functioning, very *defended*—many *profile* views

Who Has Nightmares?

(which "inflate" the H% [human responses]). Humans are "distanced" into quasi-human *cartoon* characters ("Li'l' Abner"). Some profiles have a well-differentiated and elaborated approach—seen as specific personalities ("Richard Nixon"; "Alfred Hitchcock"). One slightly malevolent response on X ("medieval drawing of demons"). Otherwise, no expression of any *anxiety,* sex or aggression. *Very strongly repressed!*

C.F., a female in the "vivid dreams" group: Seems a rather "normal" person: *not very anxious and not overly defended,* not too controlled. Some *avoidance* of male sexuality (human response on card IV seen only as "additional"; phallic part is excluded: "that's nothing—pretend it's not there . . ."). Some *depressive* response especially on card IV (sad, limp . . . wilting tree . . .)—perhaps as *denial* of sexual impulses. Otherwise, good reality testing, some infantile tendencies (more animals than humans; some *"humanized" animals;* or cartoons). A generally well-balanced person, rather resourceful, not too anxious or conflictual, effectively defended, perhaps somewhat immature—but no serious disturbance.

We had expected the vivid dreamers to be somehow more "vivid"—perhaps more emotional—in their Rorschach responses than the ordinary dreamers, and possibly that the vivid dreamers would fall halfway between the ordinary dreamers and the nightmare group. But, somewhat to our surprise, we could find no differences between the vivid and ordinary dream groups.

The Rorschach test is most often used in a clinical descriptive way, as above. However, one can use formal scoring systems categorizing each subject as to total number of response to the cards, number of responses involving humans, animals, color, etc. For instance, R is simply the number of responses produced; F are well-formed responses, and so on. There are about twenty-five such measures on the standard Exner scale. In the controlled study of thirty-six subjects, no measure was significantly different between groups. Thus, the nightmare group was no different from the other groups in the quantity of responses, the formal types of responses, or the cues used in responses.

We developed one additional scoring system. Because of our developing interest in boundaries and my impression that the nightmare subjects had something open or thin about their sense of boundary,* Ilana Sivan, the clinical psychologist in our group, developed a new, detailed scoring system for boundary responses (unpublished) on the Rorschach, derived partly from the work of Bernard Landis (1970), Seymour Fisher and Sidney Cleveland (1958), and Sidney Blatt (1976). After testing these scoring categories on a number of other subjects, she scored each of our thirty-six subjects on a blind basis.

The results are in table 4–4. In this system, each response dealing with boundaries in any sense is scored as B+ (Boundary Defense) or as B− (Boundary Deficit) (B+ and B− each has several subcategories). B+ responses involve *firmness* ("This looks like two sculptures, carved out of stone"); *armor*, or *clothing* ("two butlers wearing black coats," "a football helmet," "a sea-urchin with a hard-shelled body"). B− responses include *amorphousness* ("This is amoeba-like"); *loss of shape* ("Here's a face; it's melting or dripping"); *merging* ("This is two women merged together"); and *penetration* ("a frog that's been

---

* I mean boundaries in many senses including ego boundaries, interpersonal boundaries, fantasy vs. reality boundaries, even sleep-wake boundaries, which will be discussed in detail in chapter 6.

Who Has Nightmares?

TABLE 4-4
"Boundary Scores" on the Rorschach Test

	Group Means (± Standard Deviation)	
	Females	*Males*
B− (Boundary Deficit Score)		
Nightmare Group	40.2 (±9.9)	41.9 (±24.0)
Vivid Dream Group	30.3 (±19.3)	29.4 (±7.0)
Ordinary Dream Group	26.1 (±6.5)	25.0 (±10.8)

Significant differences between groups, NM > V, O (p < .01)
No significant difference between sexes (Analysis of Variance)

All Nightmare Subjects (N = 12)	41.1 (± 18.0)	
All Others (N = 24)	27.7 (± 11.5)	p < .01 (t-test)

B+ (Boundary Defense Score)		
Nightmare Group	22.8 (± 10.1)	17.5 (± 8.3)
Vivid Dream Group	21.8 (±9.5)	14.6 (±7.5)
Ordinary Dream Group	19.8 (±7.2)	30.1 (±8.7)

No significant difference between groups or between sexes. (There is a barely significant interaction: male ordinary dreamers score higher than all other groups, p < .05.) (Analyses of Variance)

All Nightmare Subjects (N = 12)	20.2 (±9.2)	
All Others (N = 24)	22.6 (±8.9)	No significant difference (t-test)

dissected," "a torso being torn apart"). On these measures, the results were clearcut: there was little difference between vivid and ordinary dreamers; the nightmare group scored significantly higher than the other groups on boundary deficit (B−), but not on boundary defense (B+). Apparently, the nightmare subjects saw in the inkblots more amorphousness, loss of shape, merging and penetration, without seeing more protective features such as clothing, armor, firmness.

We also examined the differences between boundary defense (B+) and boundary deficit (B−) in each individual. In the ordinary and vivid dreamers, the differences between a person's B+ and B− scores are not large—those who have a large number of boundary deficit responses usually also have a large number of boundary defense scores. The mean difference is only 5.1: five more B− than B+ scores. Most subjects in the nightmare group, however, have large difference scores. The mean difference is 20.9: boundary deficit greatly exceeds boundary defense (Hartmann et al. 1984d).

Overall, the Rorschach test tells us that the nightmare subjects are an unusual group. The clinical summaries, done on a blind basis, describe most of the nightmare subjects as more pathological, more primitive, more vulnerable than the controls. The nightmare subjects do not differ from the non-nightmare subjects on the formal scoring categories, but they do differ on a scale measuring boundary defense (Hartmann et al. 1984d).

Thematic Apperception Test (TAT). We were also interested in the interpersonal relationships of our subjects. Since the nightmare sufferers are so frequently chased, or hurt, or mutilated by others in their nightmares, we were interested to know whether their fantasies of interpersonal relations would involve a great deal of frightening or aggressive material. To find out that we used the Thematic Apperception Test (TAT), which allows people to project their interpersonal fantasies onto the pictures. Time constraints allowed us to use only a partial version of the TAT consisting of five cards for each subject.

TABLE 4–5
Mean Scores on the TAT Aggressive Content Scale

	Nightmare Group	Vivid Dream Group	Ordinary Dream Group
Female	4.5	2.5	2.8
Male	3.8	2.8	7.0
Analysis of Variance			
Group	F = 3.08	no significant difference	
Sex	F = 2.87	no significant difference	
Interaction	F = 3.82	p < .03 (male ordinary dreamers score higher than other groups)	

Dr. Steven Cooper, a clinician experienced in TAT interpretation examined the results on a blind basis and wrote a few paragraphs on each subject. Words that came up much more prominently in the clinical descriptions of the TATs of the nightmare sufferers than in those of the other groups were: active fantasy life; withdrawn; suspicious; overwhelmed; feels coerced. However, the stories made up by the nightmare subjects did not demonstrate preoccupation with aggressive activity, violence, or death. A specific quantitative scale for aggression has been developed by Dr. Cooper and his associates who worked with us on this project; this was an adaptation of the TAT Aggressive Content Scale of Harold Stone (1956). The interrater reliability on this scale was excellent. Two scorers, blind as to treatment group, gave each TAT protocol a score for aggression (see table 4–5). The nightmare group did not differ from the two other groups in terms of aggression score; there was no overall difference between groups. In fact, when we compared the six groups (examining males and females separately in each group), it was the male ordinary dreamers who scored the highest. This could be of interest and is worth trying to replicate; the male ordinary dreamers were interesting in that they also had the highest B+ scores (boundary defense, or "thick boundaries" on the Rorschach [table 4–4]). But for our present discussion, the main point is that on the TAT the nightmare group did not show more aggression than did the others.

Other Tests. We relied principally on the results of the MMPI, the Rorschach, and the TAT, but additional information was available from other tests. For instance, we used the Cornell Index, described earlier, as a general measure of symptoms or illnesses. On this test, the mean score for the nightmare group was 20.0, whereas the vivid dreamers had a mean of 7.8 and the ordinary dreamers 5.0. (A score of eight or less is usually considered within the normal range.) These results were not very specific and simply confirmed our impression that the nightmare subjects had more symptoms and problems than the other groups.

The Cornell Index can be divided into a number of subscales; the nightmare sufferers scored somewhat higher on all subscales. Considering the individual items in the Cornell Index, they scored significantly higher than the other groups on only a few items. In addition to two questions dealing specifically with sleep and awakenings at night, the following were more frequently checked by the nightmare subjects: they were "scared of some movement or noises at night"; they did *not* "usually feel cheerful and happy"; they did "have very disturbing or frightening thoughts that keep coming back into your mind"; and they "get spells of exhaustion and fatigue."

The Rotter Locus of Control test consists of twenty-nine statements framed in the form of "beliefs about society" that the subject simply answers "true" or "false." The test is meant to distinguish between persons who feel in charge of their lives, feel that they can influence the world and the way things come out (this is called "internal locus of control" and is represented by a low score) as opposed to those who feel that the environment determines their lives, that they are pushed around by the world (this is called "external locus of control" and is represented by a high score). We included this test because some of our research group predicted the scores might be unusually high for the nightmare group: perhaps persons with nightmares are those who feel unusually helpless or powerless or pushed around. This turned out not to be the case. The mean score of the nightmare subjects was twelve and of the other subjects was ten. These are both in the middle range. The difference was not significant and suggested that as a group, the nightmare subjects did not feel excessively helpless in their then-current waking lives.

In the first study of thirty-eight subjects, each also took the Fear Survey Schedule. This test asks a subject to rate on a scale of one to four, "How scared are you?" of eighty very different things of which people are sometimes scared. The test was basically developed to study persons with phobias. One might expect that persons with nightmares would be especially phobic and would have a large number of serious fears. This did not turn out to be the case. The nightmare subjects did express a number of fears on this scale, but when we checked the results against groups of students and hospital staff, we found almost exactly the same scores. Thus, almost everyone has some fears rated on the Fear Survey Schedule, but the nightmare subjects were not characterized by especially many or especially severe fears.

In an attempt to follow up our interest in whether these nightmare sufferers—who appeared to have schizophrenic relatives—had other characteristics found in schizophrenics and their relatives, we administered to each of the thirty-six subjects in the formal study the Pendulum Tracking Test (developed by Philip Holzman and associates 1973, 1977). Holzman's group has shown that many schizophrenic patients have slightly rough or unusual tracking movements as they look at a pendulum swinging back and forth in front of them. The finding was that over 65 percent of schizophrenic patients and 45 percent of first-degree relatives of schizophrenics had a certain abnormal tracking pattern, whereas only 7 percent of the normal control subjects had it. With the help of Dr. Holzman's group, we obtained this measure in twenty of the thirty-eight nightmare subjects in the first study, and in each of our thirty-six subjects in our controlled study. On this measure the results were unclear: 25 percent of the first group of nightmare subjects showed abnormal tracking, but in the second study none of the nightmare subjects, or of the control subjects, showed definite abnormal tracking. We can draw no conclusion from this test.

Who Has Nightmares?

We have already discussed the fact that overall the report of nightmares appears to be somewhat more common among adult women than among adult men (but not more so among girls than among boys), and that this distribution may be deceptive and may relate to the greater willingness of women than men to discuss frightening experiences such as nightmares. We can now examine the groups we have studied—especially the second controlled study in which equal numbers of men and women were investigated—to determine whether there were any striking differences between the sexes in these groups.

One way of examining male-female differences is by psychological testing. The MMPI profiles (figures 4–1 and 4–2) show that the male nightmare sufferers in the controlled study tended to have higher scores than the females on the psychotic scales, Pa (paranoia), Pt (psychasthenia), and Sc (schizophrenia). Thus, the males could be considered slightly more disturbed on the average than the females. Again, one must be careful to state that maybe only men who were willing to talk about their nightmares were more disturbed than women who were willing to talk about them.

On the Rorschach tests, males and females did not differ on the boundary scores, the scores that separated nightmare subjects from other groups. The clinical descriptions suggested somewhat more thought disorder or psychotic thinking among males; descriptions of four of the six males included such comments as "psychotic elements" or "very disturbed." However, two females in the nightmare group also had descriptions including such

99

comments, as did two of the twenty-four subjects in the other groups. (It has to be kept in mind that the Rorschach is especially sensitive in this way, and detects bits of "psychotic elements" in persons who do not appear psychotic otherwise.) It is interesting that the TAT—sensitive to interpersonal relations—did not detect clear male-female differences in the nightmare group: males and females did not differ on the quantified aggression score derived from the TAT.

Our interviews did suggest some differences between men and women in the nightmare group. Diagnosable psychopathology was more frequent in the men. The openness and defenselessness I have described were traits more prominent among the women than among the men. The mystical or extrasensory experiences of various kinds as well as periods of depression and suicidal thoughts were more frequent among the women. A tendency toward paranoid thinking was definitely more prominent among the men. These male-female differences were specific to the nightmare groups. Our sample of non-nightmare subjects (the vivid and ordinary dreamers) showed so little evidence of these characteristics that we could not look for a sex difference. It is of interest that these differences roughly parallel findings about mental illness in general population statistics: paranoia and paranoid schizophrenia are more common in men, and depression is more common in women.

An additional clinical impression of sex differences is worth noting. Among the eleven men in the first study, there were two very young men (ages eighteen and nineteen); these two definitely exhibited more openness, artistic sensitivity, and vulnerability than the older men.

Who Has Nightmares?

The somewhat older men (ages around thirty to thirty-five) most clearly exhibited paranoid tendencies. My hypothesis, based on these cases and on the material on childhood and adolescence, is that all the nightmare subjects may initially have had traits of vulnerability, openness, or defenselessness. But in our society, these traits are easier for women to exhibit than men. It is difficult for adult males to live as open, undefended people. Thus, as they get older, men more than women have used the "paranoid mechanisms," one of which is to blame society or other people to compensate for their feelings of helplessness and vulnerability as they try to make sense of a painful world.

There were also a few differences between men and women in the content of the nightmares: two women, but no men, had altruistic nightmares in which the terrifying element was danger to someone else (a child, for instance) rather than to the dreamer. And several women, but no men, mentioned fear of being raped by someone in a nightmare; however, rape was always one of several fears: "I was afraid I would be beaten, or raped, or killed."

In this connection, several of us also reviewed the videotapes of interviews with a male and female interviewer that the subjects had undergone. There are many people who for reasons related to their sexual identity, sexual role model(s), or the sexual image they wish to portray, act very differently during an interview depending on whether the interviewer is male or female. In reviewing our material, there were certainly persons in each of the groups who showed this tendency, but to no greater degree among the nightmare sufferers than among the control groups.

The lack of sexual themes in the nightmares, the lack of pronounced sex difference in the nightmares, and the lack of difference in relating to male and female interviewers suggest that nightmares may have their origin in early childhood experiences and involve early primitive fears, vulnerabilities, and boundary problems from a time before definite sexual identity was formed.

Frequent Nightmare Sufferers: Conclusions

One clear finding is that the nightmare subjects are different from ordinary and vivid dreamers. There is *not* a continuum (e.g., ordinary dreamer → vivid dreamer → nightmare subject) in which the vivid dreamers differ from the ordinary dreamers on various measures and the nightmare sufferers differ even more in the same direction. Somewhat to our surprise, the vivid dreamers and ordinary dreamers turned out to be quite similar on almost all our tests and interviews while the nightmare subjects clearly differed from those two groups. Each person in the study is a unique individual yet we have been able to outline a number of systematic differences between the groups. Is there an overall description that we can use to characterize these people with frequent nightmares?

First, there is evidently more pathology or mental illness in the nightmare group. The pathology is in the direction of schizophrenia, though most of the subjects at the time of the study could not be diagnosed as such and, in fact, many did not fit into any diagnostic group. The pathology is strikingly *not* in the direction of ordinary neurosis. The most striking finding is not the formal psychopathology of some, but rather the *openness* and *defenselessness* of almost all the nightmare sufferers. They have not developed the usual defenses and protections that most persons have. They are not "armored"; they are vulnerable in many respects. The exceptions are a few older males in the sample, and my impression is that these men were overly open or defenseless when they were younger, but then developed primitive paranoid defenses belatedly in an attempt to deal with their vulnerability in a "dangerous" world; they appear to be wearing an ill-fitting suit of armor. Most, especially the women, have continued to live with their open and defenseless styles. In someone with other strengths and talents, such a posture may be useful: openness with themselves and others can perhaps make them especially good artists, teachers, and therapists. But it also has its dangers. For instance, they were often overly trusting in relationships; quite a few were actually physically attacked (mugged, beaten, raped). My impression is that this was a consequence of being overly open and trusting—walking alone in dangerous parts of the city, for instance.

Another term that comes to mind is *sensitive*. Nightmare sufferers appear to be unusually sensitive in a number of different meanings of the term. A few of them described themselves as being perceptually sensitive—unusually aware of and disturbed by noise, light, etc. that others were less affected by.* Almost all described themselves also as sensitive in the sense of being easily hurt and emotionally fragile—letting things "get to them" easily. Many subjects also described themselves as being very sensitive to the feelings of others. This was usually put in terms of emotional empathy, of knowing when others were hurting. In a few, this sensitivity took more extreme forms such as being able to sense auras or emanations from others.

Finally, the most accurate way I can sum up the characteristics of these persons is to say that they have *thin boundaries* or *permeable boundaries.* They do not keep things pigeonholed between rigid partitions; they "let things through." I use boundaries in many different senses (see chapter 6). Their dreams are not bounded in the usual sense: the nightmares themselves can be seen as a failure to keep dangerous and frightening material out of dreams in a way that most of us are able to do. They can be animals in their dreams; they wake from dreams into other dreams. Their sleep-wake boundaries can be considered permeable in that they often are not certain they are awake for quite a while upon waking. Ego boundaries can be considered thin in that these people allow sexual and aggressive material to enter into consciousness more than most of us. Interpersonal boundaries are thin in that they sometimes become very involved in overly close, merging relationships with others. And sometimes, as we have seen, they have trouble due to excessive openness and trustingness (oc-

---

* This aspect of their makeup is reminiscent of children with unusual sensitivities studied by Paul Bergman and Sybille Escalona (1949), though the latter were more extreme in their sensitivities and showed psychotic features.

casionally, they react by forming temporary and very primitively hard boundaries as in paranoia). These observations are supported by the high "boundary deficit" scores on the Rorschach.

Using this concept of thin boundaries, I am now in a better position to answer several questions alluded to briefly, inherent in the work of others as well as our work on nightmares. First, are persons who suffer from nightmares those who have an excess of aggression, hostility, or anger? We have seen in the earlier chapters on childhood nightmares that fear of retaliation for one's angry impulses may produce nightmares. Along these lines one might suggest that nightmares in general involve projecting onto others one's own angry impulses. However, the data summarized here on the adult nightmare sufferers do not support this conclusion. From the negative findings on the Rorschach and on the TAT Aggressive Content Scale, and the openness and defenselessness rather than aggression manifest in their behavior, my conclusion is that these are not persons with an excess of aggressive drive or of hostility, but rather persons with thin boundaries such that normal fears and angers "get through" more and become more vivid and frightening for them than for most of us (see chapter 6).

Second, are these nightmare sufferers persons who have experienced serious trauma in early childhood? We know that trauma can be followed by nightmares and it would be reasonable to suppose that very early trauma when the child is more helpless might be followed by more severe or longer-lasting nightmares. However, as mentioned, I was not able to obtain a history of serious trauma from any member of the frequent nightmare group. It is true that we tend to forget or repress most events of the first four or five years of life; but I and other interviewers were impressed that these nightmare sufferers, like many schizophrenic or borderline patients, exhibited less such repression than most of us. In other words, they were sometimes able to remember quite vividly scenes from their second, third, and fourth years. Could there have been serious trauma—a sexual attack, a physical attack, or witnessing a death or other catastrophe extremely early, say in the first and second year of life, completely forgotten or repressed by these subjects? None of the fifty frequent nightmare sufferers reported such a trauma, but out of twenty patients with nightmares whom I have seen in psychotherapy one did experience a serious trauma—the death of her father and older brother in an automobile accident when she was seven months old. Though it is possible, I cannot believe that serious trauma of this kind could have occurred in many of the subjects without their knowing and telling us of it. I say this because the other interviewers and I were struck by how interested, introspective, and honest these subjects were; they were interested in learning about their nightmares and themselves; most had questioned their parents in detail about their childhood. At least some of them would have heard second hand about a serious traumatic event from their parents or from someone else if such an event were a part of their histories.

Thus, although traumatic etiology cannot completely be ruled out, the available evidence suggests to me that these are persons who are vulnerable and have thin boundaries, possibly from birth. Then a relatively ordinary event, such as the birth of a younger sibling, could have been felt to be especially painful and traumatic; most of them may indeed have had a series of "traumas" of this kind during childhood. But I do not believe we require a postulate of gross or unusual traumatic events. The nightmare content is consistent with this conclusion. The content involved a variety of chases, violent scenes, attacks and so on, but it varied from nightmare to nightmare. None of the fifty subjects displayed in their nightmares anything resembling the repetitive replay of an actual traumatic event such as occurs in typical post-traumatic nightmares (chapter 8).

My conclusion is reinforced by the fact that I, and most psychiatrists, have seen patients who have suffered serious obvious trauma as children—patients who had repeatedly witnessed beatings or attacks, been severely beaten and abused themselves, or completely neglected by alcoholic or uncaring parents. One would certainly expect that such trauma would increase the sense of helplessness and of the nightmarishness of the world. Yet these persons, though they may have developed a variety of problems, do not as adults suffer from nightmares once a week; and no person with an obviously traumatic childhood of this kind was found in our sizable group of nightmare sufferers.

I believe that the frequent nightmare sufferers—vulnerable, open, and sensitive persons with thin boundaries—constitute a group specifically vulnerable to schizophrenic illness. Genetic studies and adoption studies make it almost certain that there is a biological, probably genetic, predisposition or vulnerability to schizophrenia, but that environmental factors are important as well

(Kety et al. 1968, 1975). There is no question that there are many persons with this genetic predisposition who do not develop schizophrenia and there is some evidence that these may include interesting, unusual, artistic individuals. I suggest that the frequent nightmare sufferers fall into this group—persons who are biologically vulnerable to schizophrenia. They have thin boundaries in the senses we have discussed, leaving them open to being easily hurt and traumatized by events not usually seen as traumatic. I would suggest that frequent nightmares, continuing after the ages of eight or ten, might be considered a danger sign that a child is vulnerable to schizophrenia and may need special help.

I also believe that the nightmare subjects we studied have definite artistic and creative tendencies and energies, although they may not necessarily have the specific talent required of a great artist. Still, several in our group were on the way to becoming at least locally recognized artists. I am suggesting that one important aspect of what makes a person an artist is having a psychological makeup of thin boundaries, which include the ability to experience and take in a great deal from inside and outside, to experience one's own inner life in a very direct fashion, and an ability (sometimes an unwanted ability) to experience the world more directly, more painfully than others.

In this chapter, we have discussed an extreme group—persons experiencing nightmares at least once per week as adults with a lifelong history of nightmares. Does this mean that people who are somewhat less extreme—who have nightmares but not as frequently as this group—would have the same personality characteristics but to a lesser degree? Is there a continuum of people with no nightmares at all to people with nightmares every day and would the personality patterns alter along such a continuum? We have no solid research data supporting this conclusion; however, on the basis of my experience in treating patients who had nightmares perhaps once a month or so, I would say that quite a few are persons who have some degree of the vulnerability, sensitivity, and thin boundary conditions I have described. In the next chapter, we examine other related groups—persons with nightmares of different kinds, persons with a less severe history of nightmares, and also groups of artists and mental patients—to examine whether our findings hold up in such populations.

CHAPTER 5

Stress, Creativity, and Madness: Studies of Other Nightmare Sufferers

IN this chapter, I explore some implications of the findings about the personalities and lives of nightmare sufferers described in the last chapter. If the findings in our extreme "pure culture" group are true, we would expect to find confirmation of them in other populations of nightmare sufferers. For instance, would we find similar personality characteristics among veterans who have a history of longterm nightmares? And in other groups of less extreme nightmare sufferers, are the findings at least somewhat similar? In surveys of nightmare frequency in large groups (students or others), do we find more nightmare experiences among those who have artistic or creative interests? If we examine artists as a group, do they turn out to have a high frequency of nightmares? And finally, if we begin with patients identified as schizophrenic, do we find that they also have a high incidence of nightmares?

A War Veterans Group

It is well known that one group suffering from frequent nightmares consists of war veterans, whose stressful wartime experiences may be responsible for the condition. We studied a group of veterans selected on the basis of questionnaires returned by 1,572 Veterans Administration (VA) clinic patients, followed by interviews and detailed studies of subgroups, in an attempt to examine the personality of veterans with nightmares and to determine where similarities and differences could be noted between these veterans and the civilian population of nightmare sufferers we have previously described.

As expected, we found that an outpatient veterans administration clinic included many men for whom nightmares were a problem. Thirty-five percent reported one or more nightmares per month. In the majority, the nightmares indeed appeared to have begun with a traumatic event in wartime; results from our study of this group (van der Kolk et al. 1980) will be discussed in chapter 8. However, one finding that interested us greatly was that a sizable group turned out to have had night-mares as a lifetime condition. Among those veterans who reported a then-current incidence of one nightmare or more per month, one-third (34 percent) reported when they were interviewed that the nightmares had not begun with traumatic events in wartime but had been a lifetime condition, or had begun at some time in child-hood. We studied in detail twenty-five veterans who reported having nightmares more than once per month including a subgroup of ten for whom the nightmare had not begun with traumatic experiences but were described as beginning in childhood and continuing more or less through the veteran's life (van der Kolk et al. 1984).

This group of ten consisted of males about thirty years old; they were all Vietnam veterans, although they had seen no actual combat in Vietnam. They had not expe-rienced major trauma of the kind experienced by those with post-traumatic nightmares. Despite this, the content of their nightmares frequently involved frightening war-time scenes, sometimes based on combat experiences of friends or combat scenes they had read about; the content was variable, however, and was not the replay of a single traumatic event. These men also had non-combat nightmares involving being chased, being unable to escape, being in catastrophes, etc., similar to the themes of the civilians with lifelong histories of night-mares. Sometimes the combat and noncombat themes merged in a single nightmare. We were not able to obtain all-night sleep laboratory studies for these men.

However, the nightmares were described by them as long, frightening dreams occurring in the second half of the night—very similar to the nightmares of our civilian group. We had little doubt that these men had true nightmares (D-nightmares), as opposed to night terrors. Each of the ten received two psychiatric interviews, one specifically aimed at making a psychiatric diagnosis and one exploring a variety of factors in his current and post life. Each also took an MMPI and a Rorschach test.

Overall, the group with a history of lifelong nightmares was definitely functioning poorly—worse than the groups of veterans suffering from pure post-traumatic nightmares and worse than a control group of no-nightmare veterans. Of these ten thirty-year-old veterans, only three were married; none held a steady job. Eight of the ten received a DSM-III diagnosis of either schizotypal personality disorder, schizoid personality disorder, or borderline personality disorder.

The MMPI results were quite dramatic. The mean profile for the group had a huge elevation on the schizophrenic (Sc) scale, but the scores were also elevated on most other psychotic and neurotic scales (figure 5–1). (Several control groups of veterans we used did not show these unusual patterns.) On the Rorschach test, also, the lifelong nightmare group definitely had the most unusual results. There were a large number of responses; the responses were often rich and varied, but very pathological with many responses called "contaminations" and "fabulized combinations"; for instance, "This is a man with a dragon's head." The Rorschach testers interpreted such responses in most cases as "poor reality testing" and possibly indicating a schizophrenic

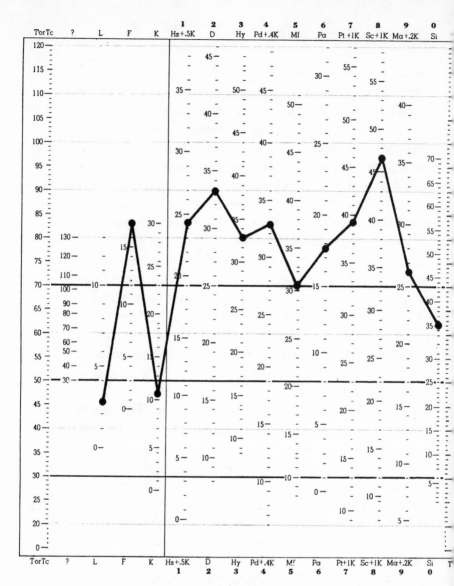

FIGURE 5–1

*MMPI (Mean Profile) of Ten Veterans with
Lifelong History of Nightmares*

NOTE: Copyright © 1948, renewed 1984 by the University of Minnesota. Reprinted by permission.

process. On a thought disorder index for the Rorschach (Johnston and Holzman 1979), veterans without nightmares scored between zero and one (in the normal range); the group with clear post-traumatic nightmares had a mean score of seven; the lifelong nightmare group had an extremely elevated mean score of twenty-six, which suggests thought disorder and possible psychotic process.

Our conclusion was that the subgroup of veterans characterized by lifelong nightmares was quite different psychologically from veterans with post-traumatic nightmares but was qualitatively similar to the group of civilian nightmare sufferers (chapter 4) except that the veterans were more troubled and had more psychopathology. It was reasonable to believe the two groups were samples coming from essentially the same population except that there was more pathology in the veterans group since they had been chosen from among a group already obtaining treatment at a VA outpatient facility whereas the civilian groups studied in chapter 4 had come to the laboratory as volunteer subjects. It appears likely that these veterans are persons with a lifetime vulnerability and thin boundaries for whom the Vietnam War constituted a period of stress that may well have increased the frequency and severity of their nightmares, as stressful periods and events usually do.

A Civilian Group

Anthony Kales and associates (1980) reported on a group of thirty adults suffering frequent nightmares—a group in some ways similar to the groups we described in chapter 4. However, their aim was not to study nightmares in "pure culture"; they chose rather to include all persons with nightmares and then determine whether those subjects had other problems as well, including night terrors. Also, the group was not as extreme as our two groups of nightmare sufferers: Kales and associates chose persons who reported "twelve or more nightmares within the previous year," but not necessarily anytime before then. Also, the gender composition of the group differed considerably: there were twenty-seven women and only three men. Thus, the groups differed in several respects yet were similar enough to warrant a comparison of their results with ours.

In their nightmare group, MMPI scores were elevated on almost all the clinical scales, with especially high elevations found in the Pd and Sc scales (table 5–1). Kales and associates did not use the Rorschach test, but the MMPI was administered to all nightmare subjects. There were no formal control groups. Kales and associates interpret the personality results as follows: "Suggests long-term schizoidness and perhaps what Meehl termed 'schizotypy'; however, there was no indication of any overt psychoticism." Overall their nightmare subjects were also found to complain of more symptoms than the control subjects on the basis of a symptom checklist.

TABLE 5–1

MMPI Findings of Subjects with Nightmares (twelve per year)
and Normal Control Subjects

	Subjects with Nightmares		Normal Control Subjects	
MMPI Scale	*Mean*	*SE*	*Mean*	*SE*
Hypochondriasis (Hs)*	63.0	2.1	48.5	1.4
Depression (D)*	63.8	2.2	49.2	1.9
Hysteria (Hy)*	66.2	1.8	54.0	1.7
Psychopathic deviate (Pd)*	69.1	2.4	55.2	1.8
Paranoia (Pa)*	63.4	1.8	55.2	1.2
Psychasthenia (Pt)*	65.3	2.4	50.3	1.4
Schizophrenia (Sc)*	68.8	2.7	52.8	1.7
Mania (Ma)	59.0	2.0	55.6	1.7

* The difference between the groups was significant by Student's t-test ($p < .01$).
NOTES: The MMPI scales are as described in chapter 4. T-scores refer to standardized scores such that for each scale 50 is the population mean and 10 the standard deviation. Thus, a score of 70 is two standard deviations above the mean.
NOTE: Reprinted with permission from A. Kales et al., "Nightmares: Clinical Characteristics and Personality Patterns," *American Journal of Psychiatry* 137 (1980): 1197–1201.

These results, including the MMPIs, are basically consistent with the findings from our groups. The authors did not report the artistic careers or artistic talents and sensitivities that were so prominent in our subjects, but since their study involved a highly structured interview, this area may not have been explored.

The results also emphasize some differences between their group and ours. First, Kales and associates reported that half of their subjects had experienced the onset of nightmares by age ten and half after age ten. In addition to nightmares, 43 percent of their group described current or past insomnia, 33 percent sleeptalking, 17 percent sleepwalking, 13 percent enuresis (bedwetting), and 7 percent night terrors. Further, they stated that "the occurrences of a major life event preceding the onset of the disorder (nightmares) was reported by 60 percent of the subjects." It is not clear whether the events were traumas, and whether some of their subjects had post-traumatic nightmares, making them more similar to subjects we discuss in chapter 8 rather than our lifelong nightmare group.

Overall, the Kales group had many findings similar to ours, primarily a high MMPI Sc scale, and schizoid and schizotypal characteristics. In fact, their MMPI profiles especially resembled those of the females in our group, which is consistent with the fact that their group was 90 percent female. Overall, the personality findings were less pronounced and less specific in their group (high scores on "neurotic" as well as on "psychotic" scales of the MMPI, for instance). This is consistent with the fact that their group was composed of less specific and less extreme nightmare sufferers.

Students with Artistic or Creative Interests

In a survey in which 314 college students were asked to fill out a questionnaire, Belicky and Belicky (1982) found that students majoring in art tended to report the most nightmares, while students majoring in physical education had the fewest (see table 5–2, survey 1). Those majoring in science or math were intermediate. In a second survey by the same authors (1983), the major fields of study were divided in a slightly different way. Survey 2 in table 5–2 presents these results, in which only the two

TABLE 5–2
Nightmare Frequency and Majors of College Students

Survey 1 Frequency of Nightmares	College Major			
	Arts	Sciences	Math/ Engineering	Phys. Ed
Number of students with no nightmares (less than one per year)	18	15	31	13
Occasional nightmares (one to twelve per year)	71	41	63	27
Frequent nightmares (more than twelve per year)	15	7	11	2

Survey 2 Frequency of Nightmares	College Major		
	Arts	Science	Math/ Engineering
Number of students with no nightmares (less than one per year)	47	17	30
Frequent nightmares (more than twelve per year)	25	1	7

NOTES: Survey 1: Arts major vs. other majors $X^2 = 4.4$, p = .036 ($X^2 = 3.5$, p = .061 with continuity correction). Survey 2: Arts major vs. other majors $X^2 = 6.6$, p = .010 ($X^2 = 5.6$, p = .018 with continuity correction).
SOURCE: Data for this table were adapted from D. Belicky and K. Belicky, "Nightmares in a University Population," *Sleep Research* 11 (1982): 116, and from a personal communication with Belicky and Belicky, 1983.

extremes are compared: students who reported no nightmares at all (less than one per year) and students who
reported more than one nightmare per month. Clearly,
a greater proportion of students majoring in the arts
reported frequent nightmares than students majoring in

science, math, or engineering; there were no physical education majors in the second survey. These authors also compared the frequent nightmare students with the no-nightmare students on a number of other dimensions besides the major field of study. They found that students with frequent nightmares tended to have more visual imagery during waking, scored higher on an absorption scale (tendency to become absorbed in aesthetic stimuli), and scored higher on a hypnotizability scale. Obviously, we would like to know a great deal more about the students than was learned in this survey. However, the relationship between field of study and nightmare frequency is certainly in the direction we would expect on the basis of results from our groups of nightmare sufferers.

Artists

As we have seen in chapter 4, persons with frequent nightmares often turn out to be creative people or at least persons with artistic tendencies who want to become artists. If this is true, one should be able to find the same relationship applicable in the reverse direction—that is, we should be able to find that recognized artists and creative persons have more nightmares than most people. This is not the kind of issue that has been investigated in controlled scientific studies. Nevertheless, there is one study of a small group of creative persons conducted over a number of years and, in addition, there are many individual case studies and biographies that may help us.

Dr. Albert Rothenberg (1971) has for some years been following a group of about twenty "established" artists who have had their creativity formally recognized by society; the group includes winners of the Pulitzer Prize or other awards. Rothenberg reports few nightmares among this group. He writes, "My highly creative subjects do not report nightmares, neither in their youth nor in adult life. Even more surprising is that very few actively remember their dreams as a general rule; in most cases, they only started remembering dreams after I asked about them systematically and after we had met for several sessions. There is also no obvious pattern or relationship between dreams and creativity" (Rothenberg 1981).

This is important information. From the results of this small group, we cannot conclude that artists in general have no nightmares and remember few dreams. However, I believe Rothenberg's information is significant in that it at least disproves the opposite generalization: it is clearly *not* true that *all* creative persons have nightmares. One explanation—the one preferred by Rothenberg (1981)—is that nightmares may be frequent in a "middle group of artists who have some talent but are limited by psychopathology," whereas nightmares do not occur in the truly successful artists who are not so constrained. This explanation is ultimately unsatisfying, conflicting with the many accounts of well-known artists and other creative persons who have suffered from serious nightmares. Although there is no single index and no systematic way to conduct a study of such people, an informal survey of biographies and letters is revealing.

Robert Louis Stevenson is well known to have had frequent nightmares and reported using them in his work. *Dr. Jekyll and Mr. Hyde* was based on a nightmare in which Stevenson saw a man change from a good-looking, upper-class Englishman into a hideous monster (Hammerton 1903). Mary Shelley is reported to have had nightmares frequently and to have based her best-known work, *Frankenstein,* on a nightmare (Shelley 1831). In a similar (jugular) vein, Bram Stoker, who wrote *Dracula,* is reported to have had frequent nightmares and to have used them in his work (Wolf 1972).* Samuel Taylor Coleridge reported a large number of nightmares, though there is some question as to whether these were ordinary nightmares occurring in sleep or opium-induced reveries (Coleridge 1912). André Gide (1948) reports having had horrible dreams and nightmares especially as a child. Both Richard Wagner and his wife Cosima Wagner were disturbed by frequent nightmares, according to their biographers (Skelton 1982). Theodore Dreiser, according to his recently published autobiographical sketches (1983), often spoke of his nightmares. The American author Edgar Lucas White (1866–1934) pro-

---

* Although this is not our chief focus here, one cannot help being intrigued by the immense and worldwide popularity of works such as *Frankenstein* and *Dracula.* Obviously, these works tap our basic childhood fears and helplessness. These stories, and especially the movies made from them, almost always place the reader or viewer in the position of the helpless victim—the dreamer's position in the nightmare. It is not surprising that at least some of these works were derived consciously from nightmares; and their resonance comes from all or most of us having had nightmares with the same themes. The half-human–half-animal, or half-human–half-something-else tears apart the center of our cognitive world: of what can I be certain if I can't be sure the face looming above me is mother rather than some "other" that might eat me alive, or suck my blood. Other horrifying images such as those of Hell probably are drawn from our nightmares as well (see chapter 7).

vides descriptions of his frequent nightmares in great detail (White 1919). The poet Louise Bogan (1920–70) suffered from frequent nightmares as described in biographical pieces by Elizabeth Perlmutter (1979). I also have heard reports of nightmares suffered by a number of other famous authors and artists, though I have not as yet found documented confirmation: this list includes Nathaniel Hawthorne, Mark Twain, Rimbaud, Lautréamont, Dostoyevsky, Jack Kerouac, Goya, Henry James, Edgar Allan Poe, and Peter Ilyich Tchaikovsky. In these cases, even if the reports are true, there is no way of course to establish frequency of nightmares. These artists were simply reported as "often" or "frequently" being awakened from sleep by a nightmare.

A number of dramatic nightmares reported by well-known creative people are collected in a marvelous conglomeration of dreams, *Das Buch der Träume*, by Ignaz Ježower (1928). The earliest is that of the sixteenth-century Italian mathematician and philosopher, Girolamo Cardano (Ježower, p. 89):

> In my dream it was early morning and I was climbing a huge mountain together with a great mob of people of every age and sex. I asked someone where we were all going and one of them said, "To death." I shrank back. Now that the mountain was on my left, I wandered around so that I again had the mountain on my right side. The mountain up to there was covered with vines, but all hard and dry without grapes as one sees them in late fall. The people began to climb the mountain. It was a difficult uphill climb on a steep path. I climbed up using the broken vines to help me. When I got up towards the top of the mountain and wanted to use my energy to run forward, suddenly there appeared stark, broken cliffs straight in front of me

and it would not have taken much for me to fall into a horrible deep and dark gorge which opened before me. I still, after 40 years, remember clearly with fear and shivering the images of this dream. Then in the dream I turned to the right towards something overhung with heather. I ran there in my fright not knowing where the path was going. I suddenly found myself under the door of a straw- and rush-covered peasant hut and on the right there was a boy, perhaps 12 years old, wearing an ash colored costume. At that point I awoke.

This is obviously a REM-nightmare or dream with nightmarish elements, interesting in its very formal literary symbolism dealing with aging and death.

A brief nightmare by the eighteenth-century philosopher Hedwig Swedenborg is packed with symbolism and contains familiar nightmare themes: "I saw a man with a long sword coming towards me. I thought I also had a sword, one with a silver handle, but as the man came closer, I had no sword left, only a broken stick. The man jumped on my back and bit me. I kept calling for help, but no help came."

Nightmares of many seventeenth- and eighteenth-century thinkers and scholars also appear in this collection—those of René Descartes, Hippolyte Taine, Camille Flammarion, Madame Jullien of the French Revolution, German philosopher Friedrich Hebbel, Swiss novelist Gottfried Keller. Dramatic nightmares are reported by authors and poets of the nineteenth century including Fyodor Dostoyevsky, August Strindberg, Maurus Jókai, Richard Dehmel, Detlev von Liliencron, Max Dauthendey, Friedrich Huch, and by the composer Hugo Wolf.

Obviously, the list is a long one. We know nothing of the frequency of nightmares experienced by these artists and other creative people. It is possible that the artists mentioned had had only a few nightmares in their whole lives but remembered them and recorded them because they were so dramatic or because they fit into something the artists were working on. This might make us over-estimate the incidences of nightmares. However, from talking to many present-day artists, I conclude that there may be a bias in the opposite direction and that night-mares among artists may be more frequent than we think. Many people, artists included, do not like to talk about having nightmares; as we have seen, this is especially true of adult males (a segment of the population well represented among famous artists!). Thus, in many cases, nightmares may never have come to the attention of biographers, unless they had been an extremely serious problem. My impression is that a good many artists may have had nightmares but chose not to make a particular issue of it.

In trying to pursue the possible correlation between artistic creativity and nightmares, I placed a note under "Author's Queries" in *The New York Times Book Review:*

> For a psychological study of nightmares, we would appreciate documentation from letters or diaries about any author or creative artist known to have suffered from them. We will be happy to correspond with individuals and provide them with information concerning our more general findings about nightmares.

My expectation was that I would hear from scholars and biographers working on the lives of well-known artists who might know of nightmares suffered by their subjects. I received a total of thirty-five replies. Four of them were of the kind I had expected and led me to look further into the biography of several artists. The other replies were more or less as follows: "You may not have heard of me, but I myself am quite a well-known poet (writer, painter) in my area and I have frequent nightmares." A number of them went on to describe their nightmares in great detail. The descriptions made it clear that these artists were describing long, frightening dreams that woke them up—in other words, that they had nightmares (D-nightmares) and not night terrors or post-traumatic nightmares.

A number of them expressed interest in my work, and I sent them a brief summary of the findings I had already collected on frequent nightmare sufferers. Several then wrote back to say that the pattern I described fit them quite closely. For instance, "I have always been sensitive to lights, sounds, and colors. I am easily hurt; I have always been very sensitive and feel I am sensitive to the feelings of others. I have also been 'sensitive' in the parapsychological sense ever since childhood." Another, "I am very easily hurt . . . definitely a nervous type. I came very close to a nervous breakdown six years ago, but decided to become a writer instead of having a nervous breakdown. Rather than talking to a psychiatrist, I talked to the typewriter and worked my problems out in this way. . . . I have identity problems, which may be what you describe as flexible ego boundaries." One respondent also brought up a point that I had heard from my frequent nightmare sufferers, that perhaps the nightmares were performing a useful function. She described meeting with several friends, writers and painters, all of whom suffered from either insomnia or nightmares: "We agreed that sleeping pills were very bad for us. We would rather be exhausted than take medications that prevent dreaming. Even if the dreams are nightmares, they are what we work out of, and are essential to us."

Two of the writers also said, "It has always seemed to me that most creative people have nightmares," and "I can't imagine creative people who do not have nightmares." Obviously, the relationship is one that has been thought of before, at least among artists who themselves have nightmares. I can add one bit of anecdotal evidence. Both Dr. Bessel van der Kolk, who worked with me on some of these studies, and I have had the experience of finding ourselves in a room full of artists and writers and asking whether anyone there had nightmares. We were immediately overwhelmed with descriptions of nightmares, and we obtained the impression that over half of the group had them. When I asked the same question in rooms full of hospital staff or engineers, there was little response.

It is difficult of course to draw solid conclusions from these not-very-solid data. I am left with the impression that at least a sizable subgroup of creative artists frequently experience nightmares and that there is some relationship between nightmares and creativity. And it is clear from the descriptions that the type of phenomenon found in artists is the D-nightmare (REM-nightmare), not the night terror or the repetitive post-traumatic nightmare. Obviously, not all creative artists have nightmares and not all creative artists are good recallers of dreams of any kind. It would be interesting to obtain more information on exactly which artists have nightmares and which do not. I do not believe Rothenberg's suggestion that it is a matter of slightly crazy artistic people who do not accomplish much having nightmares while great artists do not. Rather, the pattern I would suggest is that those artists who have nightmares might be especially those whose art depends on thin boundaries—on sensitivity to their own inner worlds and sensitivity to other persons. Presumably this category would include tortured romantic poets and painters and the "confessional poets" of our times who explore the recesses of the human soul. On the other hand, I would expect fewer nightmares or none in those whose greatness is in exceptional craftsmanship or mastery of already developed techniques and styles.

Creativity and Madness

We are now touching upon the difficult area of the relationship between creativity and madness. Plato described the artist as infused with a divine madness, and over the centuries there has been consistent interest if not much solid research work relating to the possible madness or at least bizarre characteristics of creative artists. An impressive catalog by Wilhelm Lange-Eichbaum (1928) lists over a thousand persons he calls "geniuses" with notes as to possible mental illness suffered by them or close family members; of course, the exact nature of the mental illness is not usually specified. Although this cannot be considered a scientific study, the data are quite convincing, especially with regard to the number of close relatives of "geniuses" who had serious mental illnesses.

Some recent works attempt to trace a link between creativity and more specific forms of mental illness, not only schizophrenia but manic depressive illness. However, this is a vast and difficult area that I cannot analyze in detail here. Overall, I believe there probably is some link between creativity and mental illness; I believe new light is shed on it by our studies of nightmares and that the unifying concept can be expressed as "thin boundaries" (see chapter 6). Thin boundaries are important to the work of creative people who have to be open to new ways and be able sometimes to see things in two ways at once. They must be especially sensitive and open to their inner world and often the outer world as well. This concept of thin boundaries in artistically or scientifically creative people is compatible with much of what has been written about creativity. For instance, Arthur Koestler (1964) emphasized "bissociation" (the intersection of different modes of thought) as necessary to creation; a creative person cannot be rigidly bound to one way of doing things.

Artists have been called the "mine canaries" of civilization—those who go in first and sense a dangerous atmosphere before other people can experience it. This pioneering aspect of creativity again suggests thin boundaries as they break new ground, and sensitivity as they feel their way to merge the old with their vision of the new. The artist must be capable of "regression in the service of the ego" (Kris 1952), which means ability to shift, to be open to one's own past, one's childhood, one's earlier ways of doing things. What the artist above all cannot be is rigid, armored, set in his ways. All this is, of course, not true of all artists all the time, but is especially true of soul-searching discoverers of the new.

Thin boundaries also characterize people vulnerable to a certain kind of "madness"—or schizophrenia. These people have many types of thin boundaries: they may be overwhelmed by their own aggressive and sexual feelings; they may have trouble telling reality from fantasy and dreams; they may have difficulty in relationships because they may tend to merge with others. They are unable to filter incoming stimuli—to decide which are important and which are unimportant so that they experience too much all at once. In any case, I believe that formation of unusually thin boundaries, starting in early childhood, is an important predisposing factor in the development of frequent nightmares, schizophrenia, and certain kinds of artistic or scientific creativity.

Schizophrenic Patients

If persons chosen simply on the basis of their having frequent nightmares turn out sometimes to be schizophrenic or to have schizophrenic relatives, or to be vulnerable to schizophrenia, one would expect that patients diagnosed as schizophrenic would also turn out to have more nightmares than most people. There have been only a few studies relating to this question. Michael Hersen (1972) surveyed nightmare frequency in one thousand hospitalized psychiatric patients and reported increased nightmare frequency with increased anxiety. He did not report specifically on the diagnoses of the patients, but experience with patients in various hospital settings suggests that the more anxious patients would certainly have included a large number of schizophrenics. Van der Kolk and Goldberg (1983) have reported that most chronic schizophrenic patients have at least one nightmare per month during periods of remission even when they are taking medication that appears to reduce nightmare frequency. And, as we have discussed in chapter 3, there is considerable evidence that nightmares are frequent in schizophrenic patients in the period when they are becoming psychotic and before they take anti-psychotic medication. Some textbooks of psychiatry (Detre and Jarecki 1971) consider this correlation of nightmare frequency with onset of psychosis so well established that they make it a diagnostic point: One can sometimes suspect the onset of an acute schizophrenic episode especially early by noting nightmares as a symptom. I have seen a number of clinical instances of this kind myself.

My conclusion, based on clinical experience as much as on the research studies mentioned, is that nightmares are found to a certain extent in *all* or almost all schizo-phrenic patients; however, there are many reasons why nightmares may often not be reported or recognized in such patients. First, an acutely psychotic patient has a breakdown in the ability to test reality; he often has waking hallucinations and delusions, and may not be able to differentiate nightmares clearly from frightening daytime experiences. Second, even when the patient is able to differentiate them clearly, nightmares usually represent a relatively minor problem among a host of problems and thus escape mention unless they are specifically asked about. Third, among patients who were not so acutely ill, I have seen cases in which they were hesitant to talk about their nightmares, even to their psychotherapists, because the nightmares seemed to represent the more fearful and sick part of themselves and they were afraid of appearing sicker than they were. Finally, most psychotherapists and other professionals working with seriously ill patients tend to concentrate on restructuring reality, on important day-to-day concerns, current interpersonal relations, and so on. They are thus much less likely to ask about dreams and nightmares than are therapists working with less ill patients in psychotherapy or psychoanalysis. In recent months, I have had the experience at two different hospitals of having a schizophrenic patient presented to me at a conference. In each case a therapist had worked for several years with the patient who had had no known history of nightmares. Aware of my interest in the subject, the therapists asked the patients about nightmares before the conference presentation; in both cases, it turned out that the patients had had a long history of nightmares but had never mentioned them to the therapists for a variety of reasons, but chiefly because they simply had not previously been asked about them. This is probably a common situation. I believe that most therapists working for a long period of time with a schizophrenic patient will eventually hear about the presence of nightmares if they ask about them. This is the case with schizophrenic patients but to a much lesser extent with others. I have frequently asked patients with various neuroses and character disorders about dreams and nightmares and heard that they never had a nightmare or that they have not had a nightmare since childhood; I cannot recall hearing this from any schizophrenic patient.

Children Vulnerable to Schizophrenia

In chapter 4 I suggested on the basis of our studies that children who continue to have frequent nightmares after age four to eight may be vulnerable to schizophrenia. Is there any evidence that persons considered vulnerable to schizophrenia on other grounds actually have nightmares? Several groups of investigators are studying "high-risk" children—children thought to be vulnerable on the basis that they have one or sometimes two schizophrenic parents. One of these studies has now continued for over fifteen years, and early results are already available showing which children later developed schizophrenia (Erlenmeyer-Kimling 1975). The overall results are as yet unpublished, but one of the investigators has noted that a complaint of nightmares was a frequent symptom among the children who later developed schizophrenia (Kestenbaum 1982).

We have examined childhood data of large numbers of people, including some assumed to have been vulnerable to schizophrenia since they later developed schizophrenia as adults. In two recent studies, we searched a large group of childhood records (obtained thirty to forty years ago) on a blind basis—not knowing which ones had which outcome—for a whole group of possible "indicators of vulnerability to schizophrenia." The presence of frequent nightmares in late childhood and adolescence was one item among many making up the "indicators of vulnerability" (Hartmann et al. 1984a,b). Our total group of indicators was able to "predict" schizophrenia fairly accurately, even though information was often not available on specific items of interest, including presence of nightmares. Nonetheless, in the study in which some data were available, they showed a significant positive relationship between reports of nightmares in late childhood and later schizophrenia (Hartmann et al. 1984b,c).

Other Groups with Nightmares: Conclusions

Overall, the results of the various studies summarized in this chapter support our findings described in the previous chapter. Veterans with lifelong nightmares were similar to our civilians with lifelong nightmare histories; as expected they showed more psychopathology since they were drawn from a patient population rather than from a normal volunteer population. A group of subjects with nightmares chosen in a manner somewhat similar to ours—a civilian population chosen for having frequent nightmares but defined somewhat differently from ours— turned out to have personality characteristics similar to those of our group, although less prominent and less differentiated from other sleep disorder groups; this is entirely consistent with our findings since this group resembled ours in many respects, though they were not as extreme (nightmares once per month rather than once per week and not necessarily lifelong) nor were they studied in pure culture as they had other sleep problems as well.

Two surveys of student populations showed that those in more artistic or creative fields tended to have more nightmares than those entering fields such as engineering or physical education. Finally, available evidence indicates that more artists suffer nightmares; that schizophrenic patients have more nightmares than most persons; and that persons thought to be vulnerable to schizophrenia often have nightmares in late childhood or adolescence.

All of the groups examined here overlap the more specific and extreme group we described in chapter 4. The findings appear compatible with the hypothesis we developed there, that having nightmares is associated with sensitivity and artistic or creative tendencies, with psychopathology including schizophrenia, and in general with thin boundaries. The concept of boundaries which has been mentioned several times but not explored in depth forms the topic of the next chapter.

CHAPTER 6

Nightmares and
Boundaries in the Mind

IN the previous chapters, I suggested that artists, on the one hand, and schizophrenics, on the other, have thin boundaries and that persons with frequent nightmares can be characterized as persons having unusually thin boundaries in a number of senses. In this chapter, I shall discuss in more detail what I mean by boundaries in the mind, and the ways thin boundaries are found in people with nightmares; I shall investigate what insights we can gain into boundaries in general from the data acquired from studies of persons with nightmares.

The formation of boundaries is part of a child's development of mental structures. Partly as a simple matter of neurological maturation and partly as a result of interaction with the environment, a child learns to distinguish between himself and others, between fantasy and reality, between dreaming and waking, between men and women and so on. Each of these distinctions implies mental realms with boundaries around them. Boundaries of many kinds are built up and all of them can vary from very "thin," "fluid," or "permeable," to "thick," "solid," or "rigid." In every sense, as we shall see, people with frequent nightmares appear to me to have "thin" or "permeable" boundaries.

I am using the term "boundary" in a very inclusive form. I include straightforward boundaries such as those between sleeping and waking. But I also mean to include among others the *Reitzschutz* (or boundary protection against irritation) described by Freud (1920), the conceptual boundaries discussed by Eugen Bleuler (1950), the topological boundaries around the self of Kurt Lewin (1936), ego boundaries discussed by many psychoanalysts such as Paul Federn (1952a, 1952b) and more recently by Bernard Landis (1970), heavy boundaries called "character armor" described by Wilhelm Reich (1933), and the "boundary-related" measures derived from projective tests—usually Rorschach responses involving contaminations, confabulation, and fabulized combination (Zucker 1958, Jortner 1966, Blatt and Ritzler 1974, Blatt et al. 1976). My assumption is that these many uses of the term boundary are not simply unrelated analogies but that there is an important structural-developmental concept underlying the term's many uses. Obviously, we do not yet know much about such an underlying basic boundary structure. The present discussion is a preliminary exploration, undertaken because empirical data, such as that persons reporting frequent nightmares appeared to have problems touching on *all* these types of boundaries, pointed to the legitimacy of a search for a basic boundary structure embracing diverse types of mental demarcations.

Types of Boundaries

The term boundary has been used in a variety of ways (see table 6–1). Clearly, many boundaries are interrelated and some could be called subtypes of others. I have not attempted a complete systematic classification but I have listed the types separately to emphasize their great number, their diversity, and their ubiquity in our lives.

Waking versus Sleep. This is one of the simpler uses of the term since we tend to divide our lives into waking versus sleep, and there is for most of us a clear boundary between them; we are either in one state or the other. However, for the nightmare subjects, boundaries are less firm even in this simple sense. Many of us sometimes spend a few seconds or even minutes not quite certain if we are awake, but among the nightmare subjects, this indeterminate period often lasted half an hour or an hour, or longer. Especially after a vivid dream, not necessarily a nightmare, they were often unsure whether they were awake or asleep for a considerable amount of time.

Waking versus Dreaming. Most people wake up from a

TABLE 6–1
Some Major Types of Boundaries

Waking versus Sleep
Waking versus Dreaming
Waking Reality versus Dream Reality
Fantasy versus Reality: Daydreams
Play versus Reality
Interpersonal Boundaries
  • open versus closed
  • sharing versus not sharing
  • unguarded versus guarded
  • topological boundaries
Territorial Boundaries
  • group, community, nation
Sexual Identity
Sexual Preference
Adult versus Child
Human versus Animal
Animate versus Inanimate
Body Surface
Self in the World
Memory
  • familiar versus unfamiliar
  • primal repression
Physical Dimensions
  • size constancy
Temporality (Sense of Time)
Ego Boundaries (Ego versus Id)
Defense Mechanisms
  • isolation
  • character armor
Ordinary Sensory versus Extrasensory Experience

dream and know they are clearly awake. The nightmare subjects—more than half of them—report sometimes waking from a dream into another dream. They are having a dream—perhaps a nightmare; they wake up; or rather they have the experience of waking up, apparently getting out of bed, doing something else, and then notice that they are still in a dream and that they have to wake up again. In other words, they have dreams within dreams.

Waking Reality versus Dream Reality. Many people do not remember dreams clearly and remember them as a bit vague, indistinct, and different from waking perception. Even those who dream clearly and consider them important nonetheless place a kind of boundary around them—"It was powerful, but it was just a dream." Dreams are kept separate from waking reality, and there is an emphasis made of their difference from waking reality. The nightmare subjects in many cases describe all their dreams, not just their nightmares, as "extremely real," "just as real as waking."

Fantasy versus Reality: Daydreams. Most people have daydreams to a varying extent, but these are usually very much under the person's control. Frequently our daydreams are simple, undisguised wish fulfillments— we're rich, we're famous, we're making love to our favorite movie stars. We daydream of things the way we would like them to be, but we are aware it's "only a daydream." The nightmare subjects, much more than most of us, get lost and caught up in their daydreams to such a degree that sometimes they are not sure whether the daydreams are real or not. And related to this, the daydreams sometimes run away with them, go out of control, and turn into "daymares." When I asked the ordinary dreamers or vivid dreamers whether they had "daymares," they said without exception either, "no" or more frequently "I don't know what you mean." The

Nightmares and Boundaries in the Mind

nightmare sufferers always knew what I meant and some of them described vivid "daymares."

Play versus Reality. Children differ a great deal in the degree to which they get caught up in play, lose themselves in play, and have trouble coming out of it into ordinary reality. Among adults, too, some completely "lose themselves" in a book or a piece of music much more than others. The subjects with frequent nightmares were definitely at the high end of the continuum on this measure of "losing oneself in play" and had been that way as children, too. This characteristic or ability is obviously found in other groups, especially creative people.

Interpersonal Boundaries. We differ greatly in the extent to which we are willing to open up, share with others, share secrets with friends, fall in love, and, in general, let others into our lives. The nightmare sufferers were extremely open and tended to let others in and to merge with others very easily. This was clear in their relationships where often they rapidly became intimate and very involved and sometimes found themselves enmeshed in disturbing relationships from which they had problems extricating themselves.

In interviews, the nightmare subjects were unusually open and unguarded in many senses. What I mean is this: a patient in psychoanalysis is specifically asked to say whatever comes to mind and is highly motivated to do so, or to try his best. Even under these conditions, this is not an easy task. It often takes patients a long time to be willing to share shameful secrets—material consciously suppressed—not to mention material that is not accessible to the patient because it is repressed by various unconscious mechanisms. A subject volunteering for a research study is in a very different position. He expects to be asked questions and, generally speaking, is prepared to answer honestly. At the same time, most subjects maintain a certain guardedness. Their position is, "All right, I'm in this study; I'm interested; I'm helping science; maybe I'll learn something about myself; I'm being paid for it; I want to cooperate and I'll try to answer questions; however, I am certainly not going to bare every dark secret, and I am not going to volunteer really painful or embarrassing information unless it is specifically asked for, or it seems essential." The subjects with nightmares were extreme in that most of them did not maintain this guardedness. Within five or ten minutes into an interview, they were telling me intimate family problems, sexual problems, interpersonal problems. They pulled skeletons out of the closet in answering open-ended questions such as "What was your childhood like?" or "What important things have happened to you in the last few years?" There were a few exceptions that occurred among the two or three subjects who had paranoid features; but in these, I felt a tendency to openness, too—they would begin to open up and share a lot, and then become suspicious and "clam up." Those were the ones who had learned that it can be painful or dangerous to be too open or trusting; they suddenly and somewhat clumsily erected a wall. There was not the usual sense of modulated defense or guardedness, gradually decreasing as an interview progresses. These interpersonal boundaries form much of what Kurt Lewin

(1936) meant by "topological boundaries" around the self.

Another related aspect is the boundary around one's family, a group of friends, one's own neighborhood group or ethnic group. Without thinking about it, most of us tend to share information and to be open with certain people, to be less open with others, to be much more guarded with strangers. The nightmare sufferers made little use of this sort of group boundary. They seldom saw themselves as firmly part of a group; they were "liberal" with their friendship and made little distinction between members of their group or neighborhood and others. The nightmare sufferers were not people who placed great emphasis on their being part of an ethnic or national group.

Territorial Boundaries ("Turf"). Most people who live in urban settings know that there are certain areas where they can feel safe and walk freely and other places where they have to be careful. There are places where they tend not to go at all, or to be very much on their guard if they do find themselves there. Again, the nightmare subjects did not have this sense of territorial boundary. They were overly trusting; they walked alone in parts of town where most others would fear to tread; they did not "put up their guard" when in potentially dangerous territory. This characteristic may help account for the high incidences of muggings and rapes reported by the nightmare sufferer group.

Sexual Identity. Some people have an extremely firm or rigid sense of themselves as male or female: "Men do things this way. Women do things that way. I am a man and I do things the man's way." Others are much more inclined to think of themselves as a mixture of masculine and feminine. The nightmare subjects were clearly in the latter group. Among the many men with nightmares I have interviewed, there was not a single one who came anywhere near the typical macho male image. Among the women there were none who adopted the stereotyped feminine role. Several women in the nightmare group reported they often had dreams in which they were men; this did not occur in the other groups.

Sexual Preference. Most people draw a very firm boundary line around their sexual preferences. They are heterosexual and do not allow themselves the least hint of homosexual behavior or even homosexual fantasy or thought. Some homosexuals are equally strict about their preference. The nightmare subjects were much less strict. A few were actively homosexual, most were heterosexual, but several had had sexual relations with both sexes and most experienced fantasies or thoughts about sexual relations with both sexes.

Adult versus Child. Some persons maintain this kind of boundary with great rigidity. "I was a child. Now I am grown up. Certain things are appropriate for children. Other things are appropriate for adults, and that's it." Again, there is a great variation in the extent to which people maintain this "generational" boundary, but the nightmare sufferers were definitely on the side of fluid boundaries. Many of them, although young adults, thought of themselves in some ways as children. They spoke with pride of not having lost their childhood wonder and naiveté, which they felt most adults had lost. Several were acutely aware of the loss of wonder and magic involved in no longer being a child and seemed to be fighting against it. Their statements about childhood were paraphrases of Wordsworth's "Intimations of Immortality."* Two who were teachers felt that an especially important part of their job was to maintain in their pupils a childhood wonder and excitement about the world and not allow them to be pigeonholed or their feelings to be blunted by society.

Human versus Animal and *Animate versus Inanimate*. Most people maintain very strict boundaries between these categories. Again, the nightmare subjects seemed to be more flexible or loose in this way, at least in their

---

* Especially stanzas 1 and 2:

1

There was a time when meadow, grove, and stream,
The earth, and every common sight
    To me did seem
    Apparelled in celestial light,
The glory and the freshness of a dream.
It is not now as it hath been of yore;—
    Turn wheresoe'er I may,
    By night or day,
The things which I have seen I now can see no more.

2

    The Rainbow comes and goes,
    And lovely is the Rose,
    The Moon doth with delight
Look round her when the heavens are bare,
    Waters on a starry night
    Are beautiful and fair;
    The sunshine is a glorious birth;
    But yet I know, where'er I go,
That there hath past away a glory from the earth.

dreams and fantasies. Several reported dreams in which they were dogs or other animals. One reported a dream in which she was a butterfly; one reported being a leaf floating in the wind. These sorts of images sometimes occurred in their daydreams as well. Most people may be capable of this sort of fantasy; for instance, creative writing teachers (who presumably can do it themselves) sometimes assign themes in which the student is supposed to imagine himself to be a dog or a butterfly. For many people this is not an easy task and for some with rigid boundaries the task may be impossible. The nightmare subjects have no trouble with such an assignment; they find it easy and enjoyable.

Body Surface. Most of us think of our bodies as a whole. In our dreams and daydreams, as well as in our thoughts, our bodies are intact. The body surface—our skin—is an important boundary. For many it is not only painful but actually difficult to imagine their body torn, or to imagine isolated fragments of a body. The nightmare sufferers in their nightmares, in their other dreams, in their daydreams, and in Rorschach tests, saw their own bodies and other bodies as torn, broken, or penetrated. A frequent nightmare theme involved being cut, or stabbed, or something of the kind. Pieces of flesh, or whole arms, legs, and lips were described as cut off. The Rorschach responses which led to the high "boundary deficit" scores (chapter 4) are responses involving thin or torn clothing, torn skin, stab wounds, etc.

Self in the World. Along related lines, there is the background sense most people have of being a solid self in a solid world. This sense was less firm in the nightmare subjects, who experienced episodes of depersonalization—not quite feeling themselves, not knowing who they were, not feeling their body was their own—and derealization—not being sure the world was real, not feeling it was solid. Again, there was a continuum: many people have such experiences occasionally, especially with the assistance of alcohol or marijuana, but many of the nightmare subjects appeared to have these experiences relatively often and without chemical help.

Memory. Most of us maintain a more or less clear boundary around our memories. We make our way through the world dividing it smoothly into familiar places—"Yes, I've been here before"—and unfamiliar, new places; likewise, people we know and people we don't know, familiar and unfamiliar faces. Once in a long while, we are struck by an odd experience such as *déjà vu*, in which we feel certain we have been here before, although we know we haven't; or *jamais vu*, in which a place we knew well suddenly seems unfamiliar. The nightmare subjects had frequent episodes of *déjà vu* and *jamais vu*. For some of them, these experiences were not just isolated instances; they did not appear to have the usual reassuring division of the world into "familiar" and "unfamiliar."

There is another kind of memory boundary. The average person remembers almost nothing of the first three or four years of his or her life and only isolated bits and pieces of the subsequent two or three years. Freud suggested an active repression of early material, and called it "primal repression." Others explain the same facts by suggesting that early memories are not stored, or stored in poorly retrievable ways by an immature nervous system. In any case, there is a boundary between this childhood period of no memory or isolated memory and the later period of clear and connected memory. In some persons this forgetting or repression is especially massive and they can remember nothing of their first eight or ten years. The nightmare sufferers were at the other extreme: they remembered a great deal from before the age of three, sometimes even from before the age of two.

Physical Dimensions. Most people without really thinking about it keep things in their proper size. Our bodies are a certain size; our houses are a certain size; objects and people generally maintain their size even in our fantasies and dreams, though there are occasional exceptions. However, again, the nightmare subjects shifted sizes more; they reported many dreams and daydreams in which objects, people, faces became larger and smaller and their own bodies lengthened and shortened. This is somewhat similar to what often occurs in an LSD experience.

I have heard dream reports from quite a few patients and others involving faces that become larger or frightening; usually, there were no associations to recent events. I suspect that these images may have been related to very early memories of being a child, perhaps still in the crib, and having an adult face suddenly come close. This sort of report was found to a varying degree among many persons, but was especially frequent among the nightmare subjects.

Nightmares and Boundaries in the Mind

Temporality (Sense of Time). Everyone organizes his life in time, but there are great differences in the degree of rigidity versus flexibility. Some maintain a rigid schedule throughout their day; some have a definite exact sense of how long any given task should take. Others, including the nightmare subjects, are looser or more casual about time. This was especially striking in the interviews. Most subjects, when asked a specific question such as, "How long do you usually sleep?" gave an answer lasting only a few seconds. When asked an open-ended question such as: "What were things like in high school?" gave a longer answer lasting perhaps up to two minutes; they had a sense of social time limits. The nightmare subjects did not have such boundaries—they frequently went on for five or ten minutes or more answering a single question. Also, in terms of longer epochs of time, the nightmare subjects did not tend to put their plans in terms of specific time frames. Thus, they hardly ever said, "I am planning to go to graduate school for the next two years and then I'll take a job in such and such a field for the next year or two."

Ego Boundaries (Ego versus Id).* Ego boundaries are thinner in nightmare sufferers. Most people have quite firm boundaries between their ego and their id—the impersonal, often rejected "It" consisting of those forces, impulses, desires which they do not really acknowledge as being part of themselves. Usually, the sexual and aggressive wishes of the id are kept out of awareness or are dimly, indirectly perceived. In fact, in a typical

---

* I refer here to ego boundaries in the narrow sense, between ego and id. The term ego boundaries is sometimes enlarged to include many of the other boundaries discussed. See, for instance, Landis (1970).

psychoanalysis of a neurotic patient, the patient's ego boundaries are often seen as too tight or too rigid; during a successful analysis the boundaries of the ego loosen and expand so that more and more of the dangerous id material is eventually taken in by the ego. "Where id was, ego shall be" (Freud 1939). This neurotic problem clearly was not the problem of the nightmare sufferers. On the contrary, they were very aware of id impulses; they seemed to either accept them or sometimes used primitive coping mechanisms such as projection, attributing their feelings or wishes to someone else.

Defense Mechanisms. I have already mentioned repression. Some of the other well-known mechanisms of defense can also be seen in terms of boundaries—for instance, the mechanism of isolation. Basically, isolation consists of not allowing a thought and its associated emotion to come into consciousness at the same time. Some people are very adept at thinking about something disturbing, but protecting themselves by keeping the emotion out of consciousness. A very obsessional person who likes to keep things pigeonholed (bounded) and not let anything get out of hand often employs the mechanism of isolation. Again, the nightmare subjects tended *not* to do this. In fact, in many senses, the nightmare subjects had characteristics opposite to those of the obsessional character.

Related to this is the heavy boundary known as character armor (Reich 1933). This implies a use of some characteristic pattern of behavior and defense in a solid, constant manner that prevents any change or any influence from outside. I was struck by how little such defense or armor the nightmare subjects had. Again, there is a continuum; but with a few exceptions (those with paranoid features), the nightmare subjects were among those who did not armor themselves against the world.

Ordinary Sensory versus Extrasensory Experience. Almost half of the nightmare sufferers interviewed reported some unusual or paranormal experiences such as telepathy, out-of-the-body experiences, clairvoyance, or precognition. Again, many persons who are not frequent nightmare sufferers have some such experiences. In our study the nightmare sufferers had these experiences much more frequently and dramatically, although several of the twenty-four vivid dreamers and ordinary dreamers also reported such experiences. However, the nightmare sufferers were not firm believers in the occult. None that I spoke to felt absolutely convinced that he or she had special powers; none had put on shows or demonstrations or tried to make use of such powers commercially. Usually, they took a noncommittal attitude—they believed they were different and more sensitive than most people, and they more-or-less believed in extrasensory phenomena. Some believed that there are unknown energies and influences around and that they were just a bit more sensitive than most people to such "influences." However they were not certain; and some had a very reasonable scientific scepticism about their experiences.

This is an intriguing area that deserves further investigation, but is almost impossible to study. The most parsimonious explanation is that the nightmare sufferers are sensitive in many ways, often have vivid imaginations, and are not too concerned with boundaries of reality. Thus they may interpret some of their vivid memories or daydreams, or feelings of depersonalization, as extra-sensory or parapsychological. On the other hand, it is possible that forces of forms of energy exist that science does not yet fully understand. For that matter, there are well-understood forces for which we have no recognized sensory receptors; for instance, we live in a network of magnetic fields including the earth's but apparently are unable to sense these fields. Yet recently some animals have been shown to have a kind of receptor for magnetic fields and to be able to use the information in guiding their travels. It is conceivable that humans have some form of rudimentary receptors for such forces or others, and there might be great variation in the degree to which people have any awareness of such dim sensations. If so, it might not be surprising that the nightmare sufferers who are sensitive in so many other ways might also be sensitive to such unusual sensations and be more aware of them than most.

Under either assumption, we are dealing with an aspect of thin or permeable boundaries. If the phenomena are nothing other than ordinary psychological ones, the nightmare subjects demonstrate poor reality testing—indistinct boundaries between what is coming from inside themselves and from outside. Alternatively, if there are indeed forces or receptors yet to be understood, these persons have a thin boundary or thin skin in a very interesting new sense.

Nightmares and Boundaries in the Mind

Boundaries in Schizophrenia and Other Conditions

The list of boundaries just summarized is not complete, and the types of boundaries have not been organized and classified in a systematic manner. Rather, the list is meant primarily to emphasize the multiplicity of boundaries in the mind and the fact that the nightmare sufferers appear to have thin boundaries in all the categories we considered. It is important to note, however, that thin boundaries are not unique to our group. A number of the aspects of thin boundaries we have discussed can be found in schizophrenic patients. Indeed, boundary disturbances may be an important aspect of the pathology of schizophrenia especially as they relate to problems in ego boundaries and boundaries between fantasy and reality. Bleuler (1950) and others were especially struck by differences in concept boundaries, leading to studies of overinclusiveness—including too many items within a given conceptual category (see, for instance, Cameron and Margaret 1951; Chapman 1961). David Shakow's (1963) well-known formulation of the cognitive problem in schizophrenia as "inability to maintain a major segmental set" is a boundary concept; Harold Searles (1960) emphasized the schizophrenic's problem with the boundaries between human and nonhuman, and between animate and inanimate. In some schizophrenics the boundary problems are prominent features, in others less so. There is no question but that we can find evidence of thin or permeable boundaries in many patients with schizophrenia, but often the boundary problems are not so apparent because there is so much flagrant symptomatology. In the nightmare subjects, who are not psychotic, we were looking at boundary problems without being distracted by other associated problems and issues.

Is this thin boundary condition found also in persons with a variety of psychiatric illnesses, or persons with sleep problems other than nightmares? Clinical experience and research studies of depressed patients, anxious patients, patients with insomnia, narcolepsy, sleepwalking, or night terrors do not reveal, in any of them, the boundary problems or the personality characteristics of the frequent nightmare group. For instance, patients with various kinds of insomnia have been studied in some detail in my laboratory and others. It turns out that there are many medical causes for insomnia: some insomniacs have painful medical or surgical conditions; some have sleep apnea, nocturnal myoclonus, or other sleep-related illnesses.* But even among those who do not have clear medical reasons for their insomnia—those who have "psychophysiological" types of insomnia—MMPI profiles and other test results are quite different from those of the nightmare sufferers (Coursey 1975; Kales et al. 1976; Beutler, Thornby, and Karacan 1978). Insomniacs tend to have elevations in depression, hypochondriasis, and hysteria on the MMPI—the so-called neurotic scales— more than on the psychotic scales that are elevated in the nightmare subjects. Also, my hundreds of interviews with such patients do not reveal the thin-boundary characteristics of the nightmare sufferers.

---

* Sleep apnea refers to a serious condition in which breathing (air flow) ceases numerous times each night. Nocturnal myoclonus is a condition characterized by frequent muscle jerks during sleep.

TABLE 6–2
MMPI Scores in Night Terror Sufferers
Compared to Nightmare Sufferers

	L	F	K	Hs	D	Hy	Pd	Pa	Pt	Sc	Ma	Si

MMPI T-scores (mean values)

	L	F	K	Hs	D	Hy	Pd	Pa	Pt	Sc	Ma	Si
Night Terrors												
Males												
N = 7	48	58	53	59	56	59	67	58	64	63	69	52
Females												
N = 11	49	55	58	54	51	58	59	60	53	57	55	48
All Subjects												
N = 18	48	56	56	56	53	58	62	59	57	59	60	49
Nightmares												
Male and												
Female												
N = 12	46	73	48	57	63	60	72	70	69	77	74	52

NOTE: The MMPI scales are as described in chapter 4. T-scores refer to standardized scores such that for each scale the population mean is 50 and the standard deviation is 10. Thus, a score of 70 is two standard deviations above the mean.

As we said before, night terrors are a severe, and sometimes extremely disturbing phenomena and had previously been thought of as being simply worse forms of nightmares. However, I have studied many subjects with severe night terrors in pure culture and their MMPI profiles do not show the elevated psychotic scales of the nightmare subjects (Hartmann, Greenwald, and Brune 1982); most had quite normal profiles (table 6–2). In fact, the two patients with the most severe night terror conditions I have seen—one of them caused several deaths during a night terror episode—were totally different from the nightmare sufferers. Neither of these men had any of the aspects of thin boundaries we have listed. Both were solid citizens with no hint of schizophrenia or artistic tendencies. Both were somewhat rigid, obsessional, and well defended; in most senses discussed, they were characterized by very thick boundaries. These are obviously very different people from the nightmare sufferers.

Scanning MMPI profiles of groups with a wide variety of medical and psychiatric illnesses and problems (Lanyon 1968) leads to the same conclusion: there are no groups with mean profiles similar to those of nightmare sufferers except for a few patient groups with schizophrenic and related conditions, and possibly groups of artists. Individual patients who do have similar profiles are usually schizophrenic patients or persons who may be diagnosed as "schizoid," "schizotypal," or "borderline." These are individuals who may be considered vulnerable to schizophrenia. I believe there is a true relationship between these groups and the nightmare sufferers; and that persons with frequent nightmares form part of the population of persons vulnerable to schizophrenia. Conversely, we have noted (chapter 5) that persons who have demonstrated such a vulnerability by actually becoming schizophrenic have a history of nightmares far more commonly than has been thought.

Development of Thin Boundaries

If thin boundaries are a basic structural characteristic in persons with frequent nightmares, it is crucial to our understanding of nightmares to know how these thin boundaries come about. Since nightmares are already present in childhood, we are not dealing with boundaries somehow being torn by a traumatic event in adolescence or adulthood: obviously, the condition (of thin boundaries) started very early. As I said earlier, we failed to find evidence of obvious traumatic events in early life. We even asked about traumatic births, or obstetrical complications without finding anything striking. Yet, the possibility of undetected perinatal trauma or even intra-uterine trauma cannot be completely ruled out. On the basis of the data we have discussed, I suggest that a predisposition to thin boundaries may well be present from birth, perhaps on a genetic basis (based in part on the family histories described in chapter 4).

Persons with this biological predisposition can be seen as having a vulnerability to later developing schizophrenia, developing in an artistic direction if they have appropriate talents, having frequent nightmares, or various combinations of these tendencies. Environmental factors probably determine the path followed, and presumably particular environmental factors may induce longterm frequent nightmares in some children with thin-boundary conditions. If there is such an environmental component, I suspect from data on a few subjects that it may be related to a lack of support by the mother in the first two years of life. In a few cases, though there was no clear trauma, the mother was definitely depressed and unavailable to the child; in others, although the mother was not obviously depressed or physically unavailable, the child was not given support and encouragement to master age-appropriate tasks and to overcome the fears and terrors associated with early development. In some the birth of a younger sibling at age one to two, accompanied by the relative unavailability of the mother for a time, appeared to be especially traumatic and they later developed lifelong nightmares. In all these situations the child was left alone with his or her impulses and fears, with insufficient support, or insufficient amounts of what Gerald Adler and Daniel Buie (1979) have called "soothing."

If persons with frequent nightmares are born with a genetic/biologic tendency to thin boundaries, perhaps compounded by lack of early support, how does this thin-boundary condition affect their development? The tendency to form thin boundaries probably has a pervasive effect: They may form less firm ego boundaries, less solid boundaries around their feeling of self, and less firm interpersonal boundaries among others. These people are painfully sensitive to, and in danger from, their own wishes and impulses as well as demands or threats from the world outside. Indeed, the childhood histories obtained from the nightmare sufferers are those of persons who were always unusually sensitive, unusually open and vulnerable, and thus to some extent felt different from others. They often have had a painful and sometimes lonely childhood followed by a stormy and difficult adolescence. As they became adults, some of them—and this is more true of women—were able to maintain the openness inherent in a thin-boundary condition and were able to apply it in their work as artists, teachers, or therapists, but it was a difficult state to maintain and they were sometimes vulnerable to psychosis and also to physical injury, as we have seen. Some of them (often males), as they became older, found they could not live in this open way and desperately tried to develop boundaries, defenses against the world outside. But, deficient in the ability to develop the usual firm and sometimes flexible boundaries, they then tended to develop a massive sense of alienation from the world, and paranoid tendencies. If we look at these paranoid tendencies in terms of boundaries, we see a desperate effort to escape the vulnerable thin-boundary condition by differentiating "I" firmly from "you people," "them," and "society." In this effort, the "others" of course are given negative qualities. Persons who take this path can be considered to have belatedly built themselves a thick boundary or armor. But it is hastily constructed, cumbersome, and interferes with their lives as much as it protects them.

Thin Boundaries and Alternative Concepts in Nightmare Sufferers

I have found that the term thin or permeable boundaries is the clearest and most basic way to describe the mental structure of persons with frequent nightmares; it fits my clinical experience in psychotherapy and psychoanalysis with patients who have occasional nightmares as well as with those who have frequent nightmares. However, it will be worthwhile to examine some alternative formulations that have been proposed or may be proposed on the basis of the facts and theories discussed.

Are persons with nightmares anxiety neurotics or phobic patients? In other words, are they persons in whom intrapsychic conflicts, fear of their own wishes or fear of their own conscience, produce these nighttime symptoms? It would not be unreasonable to suppose that someone constantly frightened at night by nightmares might have a variety of daytime fears as well; and we have discussed the role of guilt in at least some nightmares. However, the nightmare sufferers definitely did not appear to be phobic or anxiety neurotics, on the basis of clinical interviews or psychological tests as discussed in chapter 4. They scored high on psychotic rather than neurotic scales of the MMPI. They did not describe especially many fears on the Fear Survey Schedule. They did not appear to have the well-formed psychic structures, good reality perception, and definite intrapsychic conflicts characteristic of neurotic patients, but rather had problems with reality and structure formation. Also, they were not, as far as we could determine, persons who had a powerful sexual wish met by a powerful inhibition, in Jones's phrase. There was little evidence that sexuality and sexual conflicts played an unusually important part in their symptoms or in their lives, although many of them certainly had problems with sexual identity and sexual relationships.*

Another formulation, already discussed, is that these are persons who had had terrible traumatic experiences early in childhood and were now suffering from long-term, post-traumatic nightmares. As we have seen, there

---

* It can be argued that the tests and the two or three hours of interview time spent with the fifty subjects of the frequent nightmare study may not have been sufficient to uncover powerfully repressed wishes. However, I reached the same conclusion from patients with whom I have spent hundreds of hours in psychoanalysis and psychotherapy; admittedly, the latter group had a less severe history of nightmares.

was little or no evidence for severe early trauma in the usual sense. However, it is difficult to disprove the presence of trauma completely; and I have discussed the possibility that certain environmental events not usually thought of as traumas, such as a depressed or unavailable mother, may have played a role.

Some psychiatrists have suggested that people with frequent nightmares involving violence, mutilation, and death must be unusually hostile, angry people. I found little evidence to support this idea. Most of our subjects could not be described as hostile in psychiatric interviews, either with a male or a female interviewer, or in Rorschach tests or TATs: the nightmare subjects did not have higher scores than the controls on a scale specifically designed to measure aggressive fantasy. Our impression in the interviews was that more anger and hostile feelings, like other emotions and experiences, "got through" and were perceived more readily by these people than by most (an aspect of thin boundaries). In other words, I see the problem not as an excess of hostility, fear, or anger but as an excess of awareness or perception. The nightmare sufferer is more intensely aware of fears and rages that we all possess that in most persons are more walled off, perhaps, or differently handled. The fact that nightmare content seldom refers to a particular traumatic or frightening event, but more to a general sense that something is dangerous, something is chasing him or her, etc. suggests that persons with nightmares are especially sensitive to or aware of their helplessness in childhood—a helplessness that is part of reality for all of us.

Another possible formulation, relating to Freud's view

of superego wishes and punishment dreams, is that persons with frequent nightmares might be persons with unusually strong and punitive superegos. However, I saw no evidence for this supposition based on interviews with the frequent nightmare sufferer subjects and clinical experience with patients. The nightmare sufferers did not appear to be feeling especially guilty in the daytime; they did not "undo" or take back their actions or words on the basis of conscious or unconscious guilt as many patients do; they did not have an inappropriately poor opinion of themselves or their abilities; they did not enter into a project (or relationship) and then unconsciously sabotage the project and make it collapse. Some of them described guilt feelings, but fairly appropriately, not in a hidden, distorted way. They seemed often quite open and conscious of guilty feelings, as of so much else. Their superego functions related to moral or ethical beliefs were certainly not powerful and punitive. The nightmare sufferers were quite flexible and relativistic in terms of their value judgments and ethical beliefs. In other words, if they had an excessively punitive superego, it was strangely selective, punishing them only during their dreams.

A number of other formulations or descriptions were considered as we worked with the frequent nightmare sufferers. For instance, we often spoke of them as basically "open" and this is still my impression; it is true of many of the patients I have seen, as well as the research subjects. But as I have discussed, I would consider this "openness" part of the thin boundary condition. Likewise, we often have spoken of frequent nightmare sufferers as being "defenseless." This is true in the sense that they did not have well-developed neurotic or mature defenses. They were either defenseless, excessively open, or used relatively primitive defense mechanisms such as projection. Again, I believe "defenseless" is a valid description, but it is one way of saying that they did not have ordinary, carefully formed, or bounded psychic structures, but rather were too open and perhaps let too much in.

I have been asked by some associates whether the persons with nightmares I am talking about were not simply "a little crazy": were they simply pre-schizophrenic patients, some of whom had not yet become manifestly ill? A few could have been described in this way, as we have seen, but I would insist that many could not have been. I believe they may have had a vulnerability to schizophrenia, which I see as a lack of boundaries, including defenselessness, making it possible for them to develop schizophrenia. But many were obviously improving at the time I saw them, usually in the direction of developing a life based on their artistic or empathic talents; they could have been called "a little unusual" in that they were so open, empathic, sensitive or artistic, but they were certainly not "crazy" in the sense of being headed for a life of constant or intermittent hospitalization for mental illness.

Awareness of Thin Boundaries

Did the concept of thin boundaries make sense to the nightmare sufferers themselves? Were they aware that they had thin boundaries along the lines discussed? In many ways I believe they were. They did not think of themselves as violent people, but as being fragile or sensitive, often as teachers and artists having special abilities in terms of insight and communication. They had insight into the fact that they were somewhat unusual people and many accepted that they perhaps were unusually vulnerable to mental illness or at least to unhappiness and difficulty though they may not have thought of it as mental illness. One of them expressed it as "if you remain alive and open, the way I am, you eventually get hurt." Many of them had sought help in the form of various kinds of therapy or counseling. Interestingly, they had seldom sought psychotherapy specifically for their nightmare problem. Their nightmares had been accepted as being part of the way they were, perhaps even as being helpful at some time along the way. Most recognized that they had unusual perceptions and often unusual reactions: for instance, most had experimented with street drugs but almost all had given them up. They either had experienced some disturbing effects—perhaps further loosening or paranoid reactions—or expressed the feeling that they had not "needed" psychedelic drugs such as LSD as other people did. Several of them said something like this: "I have had people describe LSD trips to me, how vivid and bright the colors are, how meaningful everything is, etc., but for me it's that way all the time. I don't need LSD."

Nightmares and Boundaries in the Mind

Thick and Thin Boundaries

If one accepts the concept of boundaries, one cannot help being struck by the fact that the nightmare group has thin boundaries in a great many senses. There may be others who have thick boundaries in all senses. I believe these would be persons such as severe obsessional characters who "pigeonhole everything" and keep feelings and thoughts, as well as material objects, clearly in their places; but there may be a number of other "thick-boundary" types as well.

There are many kinds of boundaries and it is not necessary that any one person have totally thin or totally thick boundaries. In fact, we have discussed some possible combinations. Thus, someone who initially has very thin ego boundaries and is very open to and perhaps scared of his own impulses and desires may sometimes become suspicious and paranoid, and thus secondarily develops thick boundaries or armor. In an extreme case, a person who develops a definite paranoid system takes one section of reality and projects onto it his own unacceptable impulses; certain persons become the "persecutors"; this part of reality is strikingly impermeable to any change or to connections with the rest of reality; it is walled off. In this way, a person who has very thin boundaries "inside" may have one very thick boundary of this kind for protection; I have seen this developing in two of the male subjects with nightmares as they became older.

Some neuroses can be conceptualized in terms of boundaries where only a specific boundary is thickened, corresponding to a specific defense. Repression is a kind of walling off. Thus, a person with a hysterical character may have walled off a whole region of the mind relating to frightening sexual thoughts, impulses, or experiences so that they became inaccessible to ordinary consciousness. However, this same person, once he or she has walled off these dangerous areas, may be open and unguarded and have apparently very thin boundaries in interpersonal relations or in other areas. Or an obsessional neurotic, who uses the defense mechanism of isolation of thought from emotion, may appear to have a very thick boundary or wall in this one area. When something happens that might be expected to make him or her angry, sad, or happy, thoughts are readily forthcoming, but the emotional aspect is walled off and inaccessible. However, despite this specific thick boundary, the same person may have thin boundaries in other senses.

A Clinical View of Thin Boundaries

The concept of thin boundaries has many clinical implications. For example, because persons with thin boundaries are unusually sensitive to the pains of life and feel their own impulses and fears unusually intensely, we might suspect that they would be unusually prone to suicidal thoughts and to suicide itself. With this concern in mind, I reread the records of ten patients with nightmares I had treated clinically. In each patient, there was a record of suicide attempts or at least suicidal

TABLE 6–3
Number of Subjects Answering Two Suicide-Related
MMPI Questions "True" (Suicide-prone Direction)

	Question 139[a]	Question 339[b]
Ordinary Dreamers (N = 12)	0	0
Vivid Dreamers (N = 12)	2	0
Nightmare Sufferers (N = 12)	5	1
Nightmare Sufferers from the earlier study (N = 38)	14	5
Or, considering all nightmare versus all non-nightmare subjects:		
Non-Nightmare Subjects (N = 24)	2 (8%)	0 (0%)
Nightmare Subjects (N = 50)	19 (38%)	6 (12%)

[a] Question 139: "Sometimes I feel as if I must injure either myself or someone else."
[b] Question 339: "Most of the time I wish I were dead."

thoughts, though none had actually killed him- or herself. This led me to review once more the records of the subjects described in chapter 4. Even though these subjects had been seen only a few hours each, and thus there had been less opportunity to talk of suicide, twenty-one of the fifty subjects mentioned that they had thought seriously of suicide at some time, and eleven had attempted it. I also re-examined the MMPI data looking especially at the answers to two items sometimes considered to be suicide warnings.* I found the two questions answered in the suicide-prone direction far more frequently in the nightmare group than in the other group (table 6–3). I then attempted to find as many of the subjects as possible for a follow-up study; unfortunately, the population had been a transient one and I

* These are item 139—"Sometimes I feel as if I must injure either myself or someone else"; and item 339—"Most of the time I wish I were dead."

was able to locate only a very few. Those I was able to locate—about one-fourth of the total—were on the whole doing better than they had been at the time of the original study several years before. But this was only partly reassuring. Facilities not having been available for a more thorough follow-up study, I could not know of any actual deaths in the group. But I cannot help being concerned that a number of them may have encountered too much pain or too little support and may have killed themselves.

Our studies also suggest that those who have continuing nightmares, or other signs of thin boundaries in childhood, may be vulnerable to developing schizophrenia. If we can identify these at-risk people, we may be able to help them—in structuring reality, in developing a particular artistic talent, in bearing pain without losing touch with reality and people, and perhaps help in the form of medication. Help in these various forms may prevent a schizophrenic outcome and allow positive potential to emerge.

Thin boundaries can be a valuable and useful characteristic if associated with the right combination of intelligence, talent in some particular direction, and interpersonal support. Having thin boundaries can be an advantage in allowing insight into one's own mental content and mental processes, and presumably those of others, making one a better writer, painter, teacher, therapist, negotiator. Scientific as well as artistic creativity requires "regression in the service of the ego" implying an ability to regress to a point where different realms of thought are merged, to temporarily ignore boundaries in order to put things together in a new way. This regression may be easier for people with a tendency to thin boundaries. On the other hand, keeping regression in the service of the ego may be more difficult for them than it is for others.

The Biology of Boundaries

Finally, if we accept that thin boundaries may be a useful psychological concept, can we say anything about the underlying biology—about what aspects of brain function or structure underlie thin boundaries? Nothing is conclusively established. However, in chapter 10 we discuss in detail the biology and especially the chemistry of the nightmare. If nightmares are an indication of thin boundaries, and an indication of a certain kind of vulnerability, as we have suggested, perhaps the chemistry of the nightmare also forms part of the chemistry of thin boundaries in the mind and the chemistry of these vulnerabilities. I propose that there is a basic structural concept of thin or thick boundaries underlying our many uses of the word and that this structure must have a brain biology. Furthermore, I believe a concept such as boundaries may be one psychological concept that lends itself especially readily to a search for an underlying biology. For instance, it is not impossible that thickness of boundary could refer to "insulation" or resistance to spread of excitation from one part of the forebrain to another, though the situation will probably turn out not to be quite so simple. There is already evidence that some of the brain substances—serotonin, norepinephrine, and dopamine—which we suggest in chapter 10 are involved in the chemistry underlying dreams and nightmares, can act as "neuromodulators" increasing or decreasing the conductivity or resistance to conductivity of certain synapses in the brain (Weight and Swenberg 1981, Descarries, Watkins, and Lapierre 1977).

Conclusion

In any case, whether or not it leads to a relevant biology, I am suggesting that boundaries in the mind, the ability to form boundaries, and the types of boundaries formed are among the most important human psychological variables. And persons who have frequent nightmares, continuing since childhood, appear to be among those who have thin boundaries in a great many senses.

I have now completed my attempt to answer the question "Who has nightmares?" This issue, along with the relation of nightmares to schizophrenia and creativity, and the development of the concept of thin boundaries, represents the principal conclusions of this book. In my focus on the development of this thesis, I have necessarily omitted a number of important aspects of the study of nightmares that have practical as well as theoretical importance. In the following chapters I consider the more clinical aspects of the nightmare that lead us in several new directions but also lead us back a number of times to the material just discussed.

PART II

Clinical and Biological Aspects of Nightmares

CHAPTER 7

Interpreting Nightmares

WHEN we talk about true nightmares as opposed to night terrors, we are, of course, talking about dreams, which lend themselves to interpretation just as other dreams do. The typical REM-nightmare, a long, frightening dream with many elements, is often unusually vivid and intense, and one can obtain associations to its elements and attempt to arrive at underlying thoughts, wishes, fears (latent content) as one can with any other dream.

Obviously, each person is different and will have his or her own individual associations to the elements of a nightmare. The earlier elements of the dream, before the frightening "ending" are most like those of other dreams, referring often to day residues from the dreamer's recent experiences, as well as containing hints of childhood patterns and wishes. However, my experience is that associations to the frightening "nightmarish elements" most often lead back very quickly to childhood fears: common statements are "I really was scared in just that way" or "I used to be really scared that monsters would come into the room just the way they did in this nightmare," "I felt helpless just like this whenever my parents left on their long trips." These often lead to pervasive feelings of fear and helplessness in childhood that are sometimes difficult to analyze in detail.

These clinical impressions are consistent with research findings in the sleep laboratory concerning the content reported after awakenings at different times of night and at different points within a dream period (REM-period). Dream contents of awakenings during the first REM-period of the night or early within a REM-period (say one to five minutes after the start of the period) are predominantly straightforward material referring to events that took place the day of the dream or the few days before. Dream contents of awakenings later during the night and later during a REM-period are more "dreamlike" and contain elements from earlier in the dreamer's life—often from childhood (Verdone 1965, Foulkes 1966). The typical nightmare, as we have seen, occurs late during the night (4:00 to 7:00 A.M.) and from a long REM-period—in my experience, the awakening is often twenty to forty minutes or more after the start of a REM-period. Thus, the last part of the nightmare, which is almost always the frightening part just before awakening, comes exactly when one would expect the elements from the dreamer's childhood to emerge.

When the fears in the nightmare can be analyzed further, they turn out to be almost always the basic fears of childhood—the fear of completely dissolving or being destroyed; loss of the mother's breast (loss of sustenance); loss of mother or loss of a beloved person (abandonment); loss of mother's love; and fears of mutilation, castration, or loss of body parts. All children have such fears, which may be activated or reactivated in adulthood when they feel helpless or out of control or when they feel guilty about their own hostile impulses. Each of these basic feared events is sometimes seen as a punishment for something done or wished by the child. For instance, a child of three or four will sometimes describe nightmares after the birth of a sibling. In the nightmare, the dreamer is being chased or beaten or killed by a monster, or sometimes left alone on a desert island. The context often makes it clear that these are punishments for the child's wish to kill his younger sibling. For instance, Harry (chapter 3, pp. 45–46), had nightmares in which he was hurt or killed that appeared to be a result of his extremely hostile feelings towards his recently born baby brother.

But these are children's dreams. Aren't these fears resolved and mastered as the child grows older? To some extent they usually are and, as we know, nightmares become less frequent in most children after the age of five or six. However, these fears appear in some way to be still active in those who continue to have nightmares and to be reactivated in those who have nightmares occasionally.

One might think that adults would have nightmares about more adult fears and concerns, and indeed, the cast of characters in the nightmare world does "grow up" a bit: fewer monsters and tigers appear; there are more thugs, gangs, and armies. However, the most frightening nightmares in adults seem to relate to the same basic childhood fears. Even when adult nightmares appear to express the hostile impulses of adults and frightened reactions to them, there is a link to childhood fears. For instance, a patient I treated in psychoanalysis, who had recently had a child and was basically very happy with the child, dreamed "I was frying my baby in a frying pan." Associations led quickly to suppressed angry feelings toward the baby: she loved the baby but there were times when it got in the way, woke her at night, etc., and she obviously had occasional wishes to be rid of the baby that she did not like to acknowledge. Almost all mothers have such feelings at times more or less consciously; these are adult feelings that may be disturbing, but I do not believe such feelings are sufficient in themselves to produce a nightmare. This woman's further associations to this dream and others also led back to her early childhood and her rage at her own mother. Her mother had been depressed for long periods and had not given her the comfort, structure, and support she had needed; she (the daughter) had gone through difficult frightening periods of impulsivity, temper tantrums, inability to control her feelings. A good description of her own state in childhood was that her mother had left her "frying in a frying pan."

In fact, "frying in a frying pan" is an excellent somewhat nightmarish description of the helplessness that may lead to nightmares. It describes the state of the child's ego, helpless among large environmental forces surrounding it, and equally or even more helpless among powerful internal drives and pressures: the child is being "heated up" by forces he or she is unable to control and from which he or she is unable to escape. We have all been in this state to some extent, but those who have relatively solid internal structures, well developed egos, nurtured perhaps by ideal ever-present parents have probably suffered from it rather little. Those who suffer most are those who have thin boundaries so that they experience especially intense emotions, and those who did not have sufficient support from parents or other caregivers.

While we are at this point, I would like to suggest a thought on the origins of hell that emerges from our discussion of nightmares. Our conceptions of hell are full of images of helplessness in the face of powerful creatures (demons) and full of images such as "frying in a frying pan." Hieronymus Bosch actually depicts one of the damned souls being fried in a pan (figure 7–1). These images obviously relate to our basic childhood fears and our fear of punishment, as discussed above, and I believe our images of hell come to us directly from our nightmares. When Clarence (chapter 3, p. 43) describes his awful nightmare and then says, "I could not believe but that I was in hell," he is making a correct connection, but he has things exactly backwards. It is hell that should remind us of nightmares and has been built around nightmares. Along these lines, Jones (1931) has already suggested that devils are creatures from our nightmares. In any case, I believe that the absolute helplessness experienced to one extent or another in childhood is an essential background to the nightmare. Superimposed on it are specific fears and concerns about specific impulses or punishment for specific wishes.

Freud emphasized that a patient should be asked to

FIGURE 7–1

Detail of "The Last Judgment," by Hieronymus Bosch

NOTE: Reprinted with permission of Gemäldegalerie der Akademie der bildenden Künste in Vienna.

associate to each element in a dream separately rather than to the dream as a whole, since each element represented the end result of an associative chain that one needs to trace backwards to its origins usually involving day residues and childhood wishes. However, not all analysts agree, and clinically a dream is often interpreted as a whole. Sometimes, a dream can be interpreted as an overall symbolic representation of the dreamer's state of mind, or the dreamer's problems, as pointed out by Thomas French and Erich Fromm (1964) and others. For instance, a patient starting psychotherapy or psychoanalysis often dreams of going on a long voyage with various dangers along the way. Along similar lines, Heinz Kohut has used the term "self-state dream" to describe an occasional dream that portrays in vivid, symbolic terms the current state of the dreamer's "self." He cites the case of a woman who dreamed of being in a satellite or comet sweeping through outer space that returned to the light and warmth of the sun only once in many years; apparently, this was an accurate symbolic description of the way the woman saw her life at the time (Kohut 1977).

There is no question that a nightmare sometimes can be interpreted in this way as a very vivid depiction of the state of a person's "self" or state of mind. A patient I saw who was painfully aware of being different from others and unable to get along well socially had a very vivid frightening dream of being in a lucite box from which she could see everything that was going on, but could not talk to or communicate with anyone. This image is almost exactly the one used by Sylvia Plath (*The Bell Jar*, 1971) describing her state during portions of a psychotic episode. Even more dramatically, the neurological patient mentioned previously who was actually developing the immobility of Parkinsonism during an episode of acute encephalitis had a nightmare in which he was being trapped in a statue of himself (Sacks 1974). If one interprets nightmares as self-state dreams in this sense, one would have to conclude that the frequent nightmare sufferer often finds himself in a state reminiscent of his childhood helplessness. I believe that this is indeed the case in many of the nightmare sufferers I have seen who have thin boundaries and are open and easily hurt.

Along these same lines, changes in nightmares sometimes clearly reflect changes in a person's mental structure and dynamics. This can be seen especially clearly in situations when there is an opportunity to examine a person's nightmares over a prolonged period. Among the frequent nightmare sufferers whom I had a chance to interview again a few years after the study, several talked about changes in the content of their nightmares in that time. One woman told me:

> I used to be at the complete mercy of this strange monster or strange man in my nightmares. I couldn't escape. I would be knocked down and sometimes stabbed; I was totally helpless. But in the past year, I have several times managed to run away successfully. On one occasion I even picked up a club and successfully fought off the monster.

As we talked it became clear that these alterations in the nightmare occurred at a time when the dreamer was feeling better about herself and was in reality feeling much less helpless than before. At the time of the "fighting back" dream, she had obtained a steady job for the first time, and had good relationships with a boyfriend and several other friends, so that she indeed felt less at the mercy of her early fears.

A patient in psychoanalysis provided an especially clear series of nightmares and dreams reflecting her mental state. A brilliant young woman, who had had a difficult childhood and was working on problems in her relationships and her professional life, had several dreams of large frightening sharks or sharklike monsters coming out of the ocean and chasing or threatening her. In one dream she was held captive by the monsters who were going to torture or kill her. These dreams occurred several times before and during psychoanalysis when she was unsure where her life was headed and when she was re-experiencing childhood fears and childhood helplessness. As she began to understand and overcome some of her fears, and her life became more stable, she dreamt several more times of the sharklike monsters, but they looked less threatening and terrifying than before. Finally, at a time when she was finishing analysis, and when her life and work were going well, she had one final dream of a sharklike monster. It came up out of the water of a swimming pool right next to her, she patted it on the head and rubbed its fur, and it curled up at her feet like a friendly dog!

We have seen that at least half the adult population has an occasional nightmare. Should all nightmares be understood along the lines discussed above? It is hard to be certain since we do not have a chance to examine or analyze most of them. But quite possibly the experience of having an occasional nightmare is simply an indication that we still have childhood fears and that we did feel helpless in early childhood. Probably the occasions when we have these nightmares are times when we are reminded of this childhood helplessness, or are afraid we are going to be in a state of helplessness. For instance, psychoanalytic patients who do not ordinarily have nightmares often have one or two nightmares or frightening dreams around the time they begin psychoanalysis: sometimes the content includes those of childhood nightmares suggesting a fear that they will be helpless children again in analysis. Sometimes the content refers to childhood terrors or monsters that will emerge in the course of psychoanalysis: "I was walking along with someone and there were these great yawning pits on both sides of the road"; "I was supposed to enter this tunnel, but there was a huge wild animal hiding in it."

For the sake of completeness, I should mention one additional quite rare phenomenon that I have heard of but have not been able to document or study myself: a nightmare or anxiety dream sometimes appears to signal the presence of something wrong in the body that waking consciousness is not aware of yet. A number of analysts, including Freud, have mentioned such dreams; and some were related to me by other therapists, the most dramatic one being the following: A woman in her thirties, who had been in psychotherapy for some time, dreamt she was lying in the road naked when a motorcycle ran over her breast; she felt a severe pain in her left breast and woke up frightened. She and her therapist discussed this nightmare for a number of weeks in relation to the patient's feelings about children, about her femininity, and about her own mother, but it was not clear just what had produced this intense dream. A routine breast examination one month after the dream revealed a tumor in her left breast. (It was successfully removed soon afterwards.) In instances such as this, one could say that the nightmare (or other dream) was depicting the state of the body as it more commonly depicts the state of the mind.

The aspects described above represent a sketch of the points I think most salient in interpreting nightmares, and I have emphasized what I believe is specific to them rather than what pertains to dreams in general. I have not yet spoken of wish-fulfillment, which Freud considered basic to the meaning of a dream. Freud at one point explained nightmares as fulfillment of superego wishes—wishes for punishment—but at other times was not convinced of this explanation. Jones (1931) regarded the nightmare as an expression of a powerful sexual wish met by a powerful inhibition. Theodore Lidz (1946) suggested that the nightmares he was studying (traumatic nightmares) could be understood as a wish for punishment but also as an "ambivalent wish for death": the wish for death and the wish to escape death. On the basis of my clinical and research experiences, I am not convinced that the fulfillment of a wish is central to the nightmare. One can find wishes among the associations to a nightmare, and in one sense every fear can be interpreted as containing an opposite wish (for instance, a fear of being abandoned or rejected can be read as a wish to be accepted). However, these wishes are clearly not fulfilled in the nightmare; unless one speaks of wishes for death or for punishment, one cannot view the nightmare as essentially portraying a wish as fulfilled.

183

As we have seen, the intense, emotional dream that we call a nightmare lends itself to interpretation, like any other dream. Associations to the elements of the nightmare often lead to early childhood fears and helplessness and the nightmare as a whole often portrays the dreamer's state of mind. In contrast, a post-traumatic nightmare is an almost exact replay of a real event and generally cannot be interpreted directly as a dream. Nonetheless, they add to our understanding of the nightmare phenomenon. These special nightmares are the subject of the next chapter.

CHAPTER 8

Post-Traumatic
Nightmares

A CHILD who has escaped from a burning house awakens almost every night for the next few weeks with a nightmare, reliving her experiences in the fire. A war veteran who has lost most of his unit including his best friend in an especially fierce battle relives the battle scene in his sleep every night for years after his return home. These are traumatic nightmares. They are often characterized by imagery, speech, thought, and emotion, and obviously resemble dreams in many ways so that one would assume that they are nightmares and not night terrors, yet they have unusual features. The content is repetitive, more like a memory than like a dream or fantasy, a memory that is replayed over and over. And sometimes these traumatic nightmares occur within an hour or two of sleep onset, not at the typical time for nightmares, the later hours of the night.

It is well established that nightmares sometimes follow traumatic events. We will examine these nightmares here. First we will compare them with ordinary nightmares and with night terrors. We will attempt to establish what kinds of traumatic events are followed by nightmares and by what kinds of nightmares: Who has such nightmares and, just as important, who does *not* have nightmares after trauma? And can we relate these findings to our data on more ordinary nontraumatic nightmares?

What Is the Post-Traumatic Nightmare?

First, we must try to answer the question: Is a post-traumatic nightmare truly a nightmare in the sense that we have defined it? Is it instead a night terror, or is it something else again? So far there is no consensus on this issue. Some workers consider post-traumatic nightmares to be night terrors. At times the experience definitely resembles the night terror—awakening in terror early in the night, with a scream, autonomic arousal, and occasionally a sleepwalking episode. If one begins by soliciting information from persons who experience night terrors, some will report that the episodes began with a trauma or at least a period of stress. Joyce Kales and her colleagues (1980) reported that over one-third of their group of thirty-eight night terror sufferers had "major life events" that preceded and may have initiated the night terror episodes. Milton Kramer and his co-workers have recently shown that they can induce a traumatic nightmare in a veteran suffering from post-traumatic stress disorder by a partial arousal early in the night, suggesting that the traumatic nightmare may be a phenomenon of arousal (Schoen, Kramer, and Kinney 1983). In this sense, it resembles the night terror more than it does the nightmare.

On the other hand, a traumatic nightmare resembles an ordinary nightmare in many ways. In the first place, it is usually experienced as a dream; in the most common cases, it finds resolution and disappears as such in a few weeks by merging with other dream content and becoming more and more a part of the person's ordinary dream life. Among persons who regularly have nightmares, traumatic events enter almost always into the regular nightmare content for a time after the trauma. Here the traumatic nightmare certainly appears to be a nightmare too.

For a variety of reasons, sleep laboratory studies of post-traumatic nightmare sufferers have not yet been able to provide complete answers. As with ordinary nightmare sufferers, post-traumatic nightmare patients who report many nightmares at home have fewer in the sleep laboratory; and for many reasons these patients are often reluctant to be studied at all. In the small studies done, post-traumatic nightmares have sometimes been reported to arise out of REM-sleep (Greenberg, Pearlman, and Gampel 1972), sometimes chiefly out of stage 2 sleep (Schlosberg and Benjamin 1978). Sometimes the same nightmare, in terms of content, has been reported from awakenings out of different stages of sleep

(Lavie 1982). In one veteran with typical post-traumatic nightmares whom we were able to study in the laboratory, the same nightmare content occurred in REM- and in stage 2-sleep. Thus, at this point, their relationship to the stages of sleep is not certain; but it appears likely that typical traumatic nightmares can occur in several stages of sleep—perhaps any stage of sleep—which makes them distinctly different from either ordinary nightmares or night terrors.

I believe the best course for now is to consider the traumatic nightmare to be a third psychophysiological entity, not identical to either ordinary nightmares or night terrors. We can then discuss the phenomenology of the traumatic nightmare, but keep it apart for a time from studies of the ordinary nightmare.

Post-Traumatic Nightmares in Children

Post-traumatic nightmares most often make us think of veterans, and trauma experienced in combat; however, they occur in many other situations. They are extremely common in children. They may well occur to some extent after every serious traumatic event, though there is often no mention of nightmares in hospital or physician's records. It is not surprising that we frequently do not hear of the nightmares. Often the child does not feel like talking about a frightening experience; this is true especially when there are mixed feelings about the experience, sometimes including guilt that it might have been the child's fault in some way. Parents and other adults, including physicians, are often afraid to discuss anything that might be anxiety provoking with an already anxious and traumatized child. Few statistics are available on the frequency of post-traumatic nightmares among children (or adults for that matter), but whenever investigators interviewed children immediately after a severe trauma, a high incidence of nightmares was noted. For instance, Frederick Stoddard (1982), who works with severely burned children at Boston's Burn Center, has noted that post-traumatic nightmares are extremely frequent in burn victims in the preschool years and still frequent in the elementary and high school years as well. He presents several cases of young children with post-burn nightmares and an equally vivid example of a sixteen-year old after serious burns. At least half of these severely burned children report post-traumatic nightmares and there is reason to believe the actual frequency is even higher. Nightmares are also reported to occur with great frequency among children struck or almost struck by lightning (Myers, Colgan, and VanDyke 1977), and those who have been through horrible experiences such as seeing their parents executed or tortured (Cohn et al. 1980).

A few years ago, a bus full of children was kidnapped in Chowchilla, California; the thirty children were held hostage in an underground chamber for over twenty-four hours. This was obviously a frightening experience to all of them. The children were interviewed on several occasions over the following months (Terr 1981, 1983) and were reported to be experiencing a high incidence of nightmares. The content of the nightmares for the first weeks involved chiefly the kidnapping itself with hundreds of variations. The interviewers also noted that although the post-traumatic nightmares themselves usually subsided after a few weeks, the children often became depressed and sometimes scared and timid—and in certain cases these effects persisted for months or years.

In these traumatic situations, therapy in the form of allowing the child to talk about the experience as much as possible, connecting it to the remainder of his life is frequently helpful. Such therapy is not often provided; in fact, there has been little clinical concern with children's post-traumatic nightmares, since they generally, but not always, are resolved after a few weeks and children rarely develop the post-traumatic stress disorders of adults in which the same nightmare in the form of a simple replaying of the traumatic events occurs over and over for a period of years. Treatment is discussed further in the next chapter.

Post-Traumatic Nightmares in Civilian Adults

Nightmares are also common in adults—especially in young adults—after trauma such as serious automobile accidents. In a serious case of nightmares persisting after an accident, successful treatment consisted of simply encouraging the patient to talk about the accident and surrounding events as much as possible with family and physician (Walker 1981). Richard Blacher (1975), a psychiatrist specializing in work with surgical patients, described five cases of post-surgical traumatic nightmares in which the patients reported a vivid, frightening nightmare after surgery—a nightmare in which they are lying on the operating table with people holding scalpels and peering down at them. Blacher reported evidence that in these cases, the patients actually awoke or awoke partially during an accidental lightening of the anesthesia and really heard or saw the surgeons and nurses performing the operation. The patients had been given a powerful muscle relaxant (the usual procedure)—and when the anesthesia accidentally became lighter, the patient was in a truly "nightmarish" situation—able to see, hear, and feel pain to a certain extent, but unable to move a muscle. The nightmares occurring during the next few days recalled or replayed this exact experience. (This is very similar to the wartime traumatic nightmares in which specific scary events are played back repetitively later, almost unchanged.) Blacher noted that simply talking to the patients about their experiences, reassuring them that they were not crazy, that they did in fact wake up or almost wake up out of anesthesia, and did experience the scene, usually resulted in a rapid cessation of the nightmares. This sort of post-surgical nightmare may be more frequent than we think. It is seldom asked about by busy surgical staff, and patients may be reluctant to speak of their nightmares.

In the majority of traumatic nightmares, there is a fairly rapid fading of the nightmare, and this "fading" can be accelerated by giving the patient an opportunity to talk about it, to relive it in waking life in therapy sessions, and to integrate it into his or her life. From these cases, it appears that almost anyone can have a nightmare when the trauma is severe enough and when one is vulnerable enough. A typical story here is similar to those I have reported in frequent nightmare sufferers in chapter 4: After a traumatic event, the event may be dreamt almost literally a few times and then gradually other elements are included as the event becomes woven into the rest of one's dream life—"I was with some friends at this place we used to have near New York. Some kind of a party; and then those guys came in who looked like the guys who attacked me last month, except in the dream they were wearing these funny old-fashioned suits. I was kind of scared, but I kept talking to my girlfriend, and ignored them. . . ."

Post-Traumatic Nightmares in Veterans: Post-Traumatic Stress Disorder

So far, we have concluded that post-traumatic nightmares are quite frequent and that they are something other than ordinary nightmares or night terrors. We shall now consider post-traumatic nightmares in the war veteran population where they appear to be most serious and constitute an important clinical problem. The situation is usually more or less as follows: A soldier is in a battle or near the front lines. A horrible event occurs; most often, the soldier's buddy or best friend is killed or severely wounded right next to him. Sometimes several buddies are killed or wounded. The soldier himself escapes injury. Immediately following the event the soldier may have acute post-traumatic nightmares, as described previously. These usually fade somewhat after a time. Then, beginning either within a few weeks or sometimes after a considerable period of time, the soldier starts to wake up terrified and reports that he has dreamt of the horrible event exactly, or almost exactly, the way it happened. The condition may continue for years, sometimes associated with severe waking anxiety, and daytime "flashback" experiences in which the same scene is replayed.

We reviewed previous studies of post-traumatic nightmares and conducted one study ourselves in an effort to obtain answers to a number of related questions: Who has traumatic nightmares? In other words, who among the many people exposed to severe trauma in wartime, develops nightmares? When do they occur and what determines their occurrence at that particular time? Are veterans who suffer from post-traumatic nightmares different from others who do not? And are they different from the persons we have studied with frequent non-traumatic nightmares?

Post-traumatic nightmares have been studied by a number of authors. W. Ronald Fairbairn (1952) suggested that trauma which induces nightmares and other symptoms turns out always to be related to an individual's psychological makeup. In other words, only those traumatic events that relate to the individual's particular psychological conflicts will have lasting effects. Fairbairn noted that most frequently soldiers with post-traumatic neuroses and nightmares had overly dependent relationships with parents. Theodore Lidz (1946) found that nightmares often appeared subsequent to a soldier's experiencing the loss of an emotionally significant person. He cited a number of examples in which the soldier's nightmares, though the content involved stressful wartime experiences, did not begin immediately after the experience but somewhat later when a significant loss such as rejection by a girlfriend or by a family member occurred. Lidz also reported that many of the soldiers who developed nightmares had had unusual early lives and family relationships. He suggested that somehow residual conflicts or recent personal loss might have interacted with combat stress to produce the combat neurosis and nightmares. Rafael Moses (1978) also suggested a predisposing personality—though he is not specific—and he suggested that those who develop traumatic nightmares actually use repetitions of traumatic experiences as a screen for warding off similar, more painful experiences of the past. He also described a "narcissistic vulnerability based on a frail and insecure sense of self," in this regard. Kardiner and Spiegel (1947) noted the traumatic nightmare as revealing "the state of the organism" and its "inability to complete a task." Kardiner felt the basic problem was "a self-preservative crisis produced by the threat of destruction."

Summarizing his clinical experience with over one hundred Vietnam veterans, Richard Fox (1974) noted the frequent outbreak of traumatic nightmares and stress syndromes following the death of a buddy in combat. He felt that nightmares and post-traumatic stress syndrome are especially likely to follow when there is a close buddy with whom a soldier has a "mirror relationship" (Kohut 1977), and it is the loss of this particular buddy that represents an intolerable narcissistic injury.

Post-Traumatic Nightmares

Along these lines, Robert Blitz (1983), who worked with us, suggested that chronic post-traumatic nightmares are found as a result of "fragmentation of the self" occurring when there is a serious threat to a self-object relationship.

Veterans and Nightmares: A Clinical Study

In our study, under the leadership of Dr. Bessel van der Kolk of the Court Street VA Clinic in Boston, we first attempted to obtain an estimate of the frequency of nightmares among the clinic population. All patients visiting the clinic over a period of a month were asked to fill out a questionnaire that asked about combat experience and the occurrence and frequency of night-mares (van der Kolk et al. 1980). As we expected, nightmares were quite frequent in this population. Fifty-nine percent of the combat veterans and 13 percent of veterans who had not been in combat (35 percent overall) reported experiencing nightmares once a month or more. One finding (see chapter 5) was that one-third of the men interviewed actually had a history of lifelong nightmares or nightmares since childhood, rather than nightmares that began with combat trauma (although the nightmare usually revolved around the Vietnam War).

We selected for more detailed study Vietnam era veterans who had nightmares more frequently than once a month and were willing to be interviewed and to take psychological tests. We also chose a control group composed of veterans who had been in heavy combat, but had no nightmares (no nightmares was defined as reports of less than one nightmare per year) (van der Kolk et al. 1981, 1984).

Each veteran underwent a two-hour psychiatric interview, which included a detailed discussion of current and past nightmares, dreams, and sleep patterns. The interview also included an examination of the veterans' then-current adjustment, and their adjustment in childhood and adolescence prior to wartime experience. Another interviewer administered a military-experience questionnaire to determine the type and amount of combat experienced and of combat trauma endured. A third interviewer conducted a semi-structured interview to obtain a psychiatric diagnosis according to DSM-III criteria. Each veteran also took the MMPI, the Cornell Index, and the Rorschach test.

Our principal study involved a comparison of three groups: Group 1 consisted of fifteen veterans with frequent nightmares which began during or after their Vietnam combat experiences who had a clear-cut diagnosis of pure post-traumatic stress disorder without any other psychiatric diagnosis. Group 2 consisted of ten veterans who had a lifelong history of nightmares; these veterans were Vietnam veterans but it turned out they had no direct combat experience. (This is the group discussed in chapter 5.) Group 3, the "combat control" group, consisted of eleven men who had been in heavy combat in Vietnam but had had no nightmares in the past eight years. A number of veterans who did not fit clearly into one of these groups are not considered in this comparison.

There were many important differences between the groups (summarized in tables 8–1, 8–2, and 8–3). The nightmare and dream characteristics showed clear differ-

Post-Traumatic Nightmares

TABLE 8–1

Nightmares in Veterans: Differences in Nightmare Characteristics—
Post-Traumatic Stress Disorder Group Compared with
Lifelong Nightmare Group

		Group 1[a] PTSD (N = 15)	Group 2[b] LL (N = 10)	p
When nightmare occurs in sleep cycle				
Beginning (11:00 A.M. to 2:00 A.M.)		4	1	
Middle (2:00 A.M. to 4:30 A.M.)		11	3	
End (4:30 A.M. to 8:00 A.M.)		0	4	<.05
Nightmare replicates	Yes	11	0	
an actual event	No	4	10	.0003
Nightmare is repetitive,	Yes	15	3	
almost exactly same content	No	0	6	.0006
Body movements	Yes	15	0	.0001
concurrent with nightmare	No	0	8	
Positive effect of medication	Yes	8	2	n.s.
on nightmares	No	4	7	
Positive effect of psychotherapy	Yes	6	2	n.s.
on nightmares	No	2	5	

[a] Group 1 (PTSD)—Frequent nightmares began during or after combat experience; diagnosed as suffering from post-traumatic stress disorder.
[b] Group 2 (LL)—Lifelong history of nightmares; no combat experience.
n.s.—not significant
NOTE: Where numbers do not add up to the total N in a group, information was not available.

ences. The lifelong nightmare group (Group 2) had long, frightening dreams with varying content, sometimes including Vietnam War combat scenes that were *not* scenes actually experienced by these veterans. These dreams woke them during the second half of the night. From all we have discussed, these appeared to be typical nightmares (D-nightmares). The veterans with the most serious

TABLE 8-2
Nightmares in Veterans: Personality Variables

	Group 1[a] PTSD (N = 15)	Group 2[b] LL (N = 10)	Group 3[c] CC (N = 11)	PTSD vs LL (p level)	PTSD vs CC (p level)
Typical current relationship					
Longterm relationship	14	2	11	.0003	n.s.
No relationship, changeable, or mainly fantasy	1	8	0		
Still lives with members of family or origin					
Yes	0	4	0	.017	n.s.
No	15	6	11		
Affective disorder (depression)					
None or slight	3	1	7	n.s.	.032
Moderate or high	12	9	4		
Tangential speech or running on					
None	10	1	8	.007	n.s.
Slight to high	5	9	3		
Unusual openness					
None or slight	12	5	10	n.s.	n.s.
Moderate or high	3	5	1		
Denial					
None or slight	10	2	10	.028	n.s.
Moderate or high	5	8	1		
Projection					
None or slight	15	4	9	.001	n.s.
Moderate or high	0	6	2		

	Group 1[a] PTSD (N = 15)	Group 2[b] LL (N = 10)	Group 3[c] CC (N = 11)	PTSD vs LL (p level)	PTSD vs CC (p level)
Obsessive compulsive defenses					
None or slight	9	8	2	n.s.	n.s.
Moderate or high	6	2	9		
Hysterical defenses					
None or slight	6	5	10	n.s.	.011
Moderate or high	9	4	1		
Psychotic symptoms					
None	15	1	10	.0001	n.s.
Slight to high	0	9	1		
Extreme avoidance of expression of aggression					
None or slight	4	8	11	.013	.0002
Moderate or high	11	2	0		
Flat affect					
None or slight	8	5	11	n.s.	.01
Moderate or high	7	5	0		
Passivity					
None or slight	12	0	11	.0001	n.s.
Moderate or high	3	10	0		
Preoccupation with mystical, philosophical, or religious ideas					
None	10	0	5	.001	n.s.
Slight to high	5	10	6		
Sense of control over destiny					
None or slight	13	10	1	n.s.	.0001
Moderate or high	2	0	10		

[a] Group 1 (PTSD)—Frequent nightmares began during or after combat experience; diagnosed as suffering from post-traumatic stress disorder.
[b] Group 2 (LL)—Lifelong history of nightmares; no combat experience.
[c] Group 3 (CC)—No nightmares in past eight years; heavy combat experience.

n.s.—not significant
See legend, Table 8-1.

TABLE 8–3
Nightmares in Veterans: Childhood and Adolescent Adjustment

	Group 1[a] PTSD (N = 15)	Group 2[b] LL (N = 10)	Group 3[c] CC (N = 11)	PTSD vs LL (p level)	PTSD vs CC (p level)
Appropriate relationships with girlfriends prior to Vietnam					
None or slight	3	10	3	.0001	n.s.
Moderate or high	11	0	8		
Close friends in adolescence					
None or slight	5	7	4	.045	n.s.
Moderate or high	10	2	6		
Enjoyed academics					
No or slightly	6	9	5	.016	n.s.
Moderately or highly	9	1	5		
Member of organization or group					
None or slight	4	9	3	.003	n.s.
Moderate or high	11	1	6		
Participation in athletics					
None or slight	4	6	3	.02	n.s.
Moderate or high	10	1	6		

[a] Group 1 (PTSD)—Frequent nightmares began during or after combat experience; diagnosed as suffering from post-traumatic stress disorder.
[b] Group 2 (LL)—Lifelong history of nightmares; no combat experience.
[c] Group 3 (CC)—No nightmares in past eight years; heavy combat experience.
n.s.—not significant
See legend, Table 8-1.

and clear-cut post-traumatic stress disorder (Group 1), had nightmares that were quite different: they were most often exact or almost exact replays of actual traumatic combat events. The nightmares were accompanied by considerable body movement and occurred throughout the night, sometimes even quite early in the sleep cycle. Within Group 1, the soldiers who had the most serious and clearest post-traumatic stress disorder were the ones whose nightmares were the most exact memories.

Post-Traumatic Nightmares

In terms of post-war adjustment, many of these men were functioning quite poorly. Group 2, the group with a lifelong history of nightmares, had the most definite psychopathology: eight of the ten received diagnoses of schizotypal, schizoid, or borderline personality disorder by our raters and some received additional psychiatric diagnoses as well. They were functioning only marginally in society. None had a steady job; only three had ever been married; four were living with their parents. Group 1 (the post-traumatic nightmare sufferers) was functioning somewhat better. All of these men were or had been married, but many had unstable marriages characterized by emotional withdrawal alternating with outbursts of aggression. Those who had steady employment frequently reported problems with authority (van der Kolk et al. 1984). The veterans in the control group with heavy combat background but no nightmares (Group 3) had experienced difficulty in adjusting to society after Vietnam, but were now functioning well in relatively stable marriages and jobs. Table 8–2 rates the groups on a number of personality and lifestyle variables.

Their past histories indicated that the post-traumatic stress group as well as the combat control group appeared to have been fairly normal as children and adolescents; the lifelong nightmare group included some who had been sensitive, artistic, and somewhat unusual children (similar to our finding for the civilian lifelong nightmare group). Their histories also indicated difficulties in interpersonal relations in childhood and adolescence (table 8–3).

On the Cornell Index, described in chapter 4 as a rather nonspecific index of complaints and pathology, the lifelong nightmare group scored highest and the combat control group lowest, with the post-traumatic stress group in between. The MMPI results were quite dramatic (figures 8–1, 8–2, and 8–3). The combat control group had a basically normal mean profile. The veteran lifelong nightmare group had unusual profiles resembling those of the civilian lifelong nightmare subjects discussed in chapter 4, except that the clinical scales were even more elevated, consistent with the clinical diagnoses of severe pathology in this group. The MMPIs of the veterans with post-traumatic stress disorder were somewhat less abnormal, but had high scores on Sc, D, and Pa. There were very few normal or close-to-normal profiles for any of the subjects in the two groups of nightmare sufferers.

The Rorschachs of the combat control group were not remarkable and can be called relatively normal. The lifelong nightmare group had the most unusual Rorschachs. They were characterized by a very large number of responses (as high as 88), rich and varied, but very pathological (many "contaminations" and "fabulized combinations") suggesting poor reality testing and a possible schizophrenic process. The post-traumatic stress disorder group did not demonstrate as much pathology as the lifelong group, but there were some unusual features in their responses: the reports in many cases suggested poorly integrated cognitive processes. The pattern of movement and color responses was interpreted as showing strong external responses to affective stimuli, with a lack of developmentally mature response; this suggested to the psychologists that they may have lacked the internal mechanisms needed for resolution of trauma (van der Kolk et al. 1982). Each Rorschach test was also

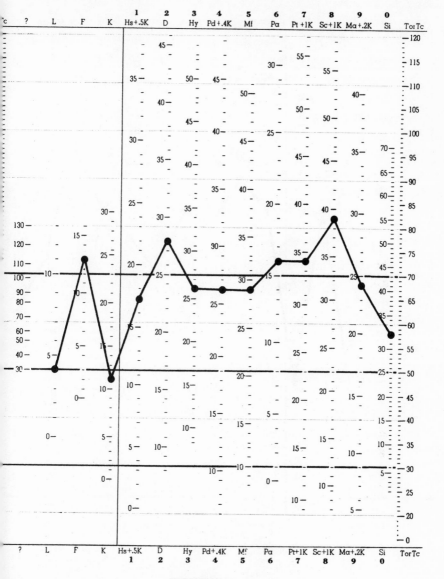

FIGURE 8–1

Mean MMPI Profile: Group 1—Post-Traumatic Stress Disorder Group
(N = 15)

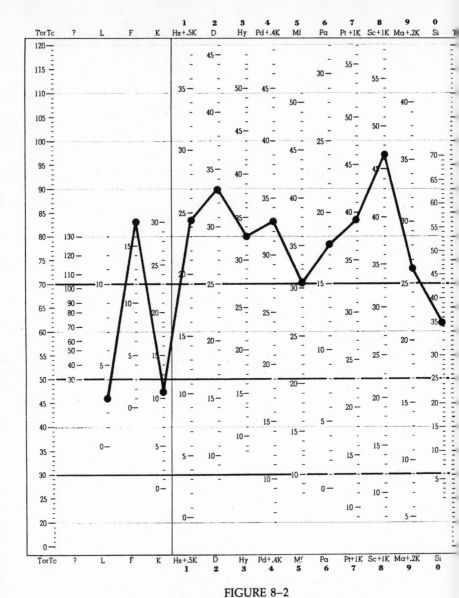

FIGURE 8–2

Mean MMPI Profile: Group 2—Lifelong Nightmare Group (N = 10)
NOTE: Copyright © 1948, renewed 1984 by the University of Minnesota. Reprinted by permission.

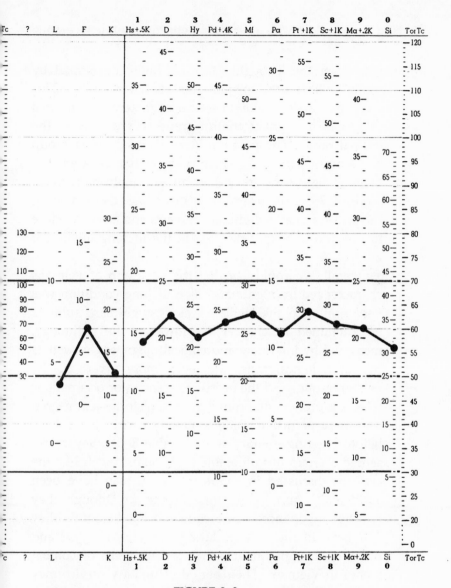

FIGURE 8–3

Mean MMPI Profile: Group 3—Combat Control Group (N = 11)

NOTE: Copyright © 1948, renewed 1984 by the University of Minnesota. Reprinted by permission.

scored on the Thought Disorder Index developed by Philip Holzman (Johnston and Holzman 1979). This score is usually quite low—close to zero—in normal subjects. The combat control group scored 0.53, in the normal range. The post-traumatic stress disorder group had a mean score of 7, which is somewhat elevated. The lifelong nightmare group had an extremely high mean score of 25. This, again, indicates some disturbance in the post-traumatic nightmare subjects and a severe, close to psychotic, thought disorder in the lifelong nightmare group.

Overall, we could say that the subgroup of veterans characterized by nightmares as a lifelong condition was very similar to the civilian lifelong nightmare subjects we examined in chapter 4. However, the pathology, measured by interview and clinical diagnoses as well as by psychological tests, was even more severe in the veteran group, and the artistic tendencies or occupations were less prominent. From their past histories it appeared that these particular soldiers already had had problems before entering military service (table 8–3); they represented a group of vulnerable individuals, much like the civilians discussed in chapter 4. They may have been additionally hurt by wartime experience, though they had not experienced acute combat-related trauma; they had been in the service during the Vietnam War and many of their nightmares included elements of combat scenes in Vietnam. Their period of military service may well have been a period of chronic stress for them which would have increased the frequency and severity of their nightmares.

The veterans with definite post-traumatic nightmares (Group 1) were different. They had been, as far as we could tell, in reasonably good mental health before they entered military service. These veterans' memories of trauma were separated or isolated from their waking lives; they emerged in the form of nightmares or occasionally waking flashbacks, both of which can be considered unusual states disconnected from wakefulness. All strong emotions now appeared dangerous to these veterans, who perhaps related them to the traumatic memory, and felt that emotion could "set off" or trigger a recall of the trauma. They had difficulty in becoming emotionally close to people, including their families. The interviewers and therapists described them as possessing some feelings of warmth, but also a good deal of sadness and guilt because of their difficulties in relationships. The ones I interviewed personally appeared heavily defended and wary, though not paranoid; they did not have the openness, vulnerability, and sensitivity of the lifelong nightmare sufferers.

Thus, we have answered at least one of our questions. Veterans with nightmares are not all alike; they are not all "vulnerable," with histories of lifelong sensitivity and boundary problems in the sense we spoke of previously. Those with clear post-traumatic nightmares differed greatly from the lifelong nightmare group. Another important question remains: Why did these veterans develop persistent post-traumatic nightmares while others who had been through equally severe stress did not? To investigate this question, we tried to find any possible difference between the post-traumatic stress disorder nightmare sufferers (Group 1) and the combat control group (Group 3), who had been in equally severe combat, but had not developed nightmares or other symptoms of post-traumatic stress disorder.

TABLE 8–4

Nightmares in Veterans: Military Experience—Post-Traumatic Stress
Disorder Group Compared with Combat Control Group

		Group 1[a] PTSD (N = 15)	Group 3[b] CC (N = 11)	p
Age first in Vietnam	Under 20	14	2	.0002
	20 or Over	1	9	
Emotional loss while in Vietnam: Family or girlfriend	none or slight	10	9	n.s.
	moderate or high	2	1	
Severity of combat exposure	slight or moderate	1	3	n.s.
	high	14	8	
Closeness of buddy network in Vietnam	slight or moderate	4	8	.026
	high	11	3	
Loss of person known to him in direct combat	moderate	0	4	.022
	high	15	7	
Lost close buddy in combat	no	1	7	.002
	yes	14	3	
Experienced wish for revenge after loss of buddy	none or slight	1	7	.003
	moderate or high	12	3	

[a] Group 1 (PTSD)—Frequent nightmares began during or after combat experience; diagnosed as suffering from post-traumatic stress disorder.
[b] Group 3 (CC)—No nightmares in past eight years; heavy combat experience.
n.s.—not significant
See legend, Table 8-1.

Several clear-cut findings emerged (table 8–4). Those who developed post-traumatic nightmares had been younger at the time of combat; strikingly, the mean age of the group at the time they had suffered the severe trauma that later recurred in their nightmares was just under eighteen. The men in the combat control group had a mean age of twenty-one at the time of combat.

Post-Traumatic Nightmares

The post-traumatic stress disorder subjects had had less education than the control group. And, perhaps most importantly, they had had an extremely close attachment to at least one buddy in Vietnam. Our impression is that these veterans were still living through the identity formation of adolescence and were involved in extremely close peer relationships with buddies. It was most often the death or injury of such a close buddy that provided the trauma that later entered the nightmare. By contrast, the veterans in the combat control group, older, more educated, stated that they had quickly learned not to get too close to anyone in Vietnam. Thus, even when serious combat stress occurred, including the death of someone fighting near them, it was *not* the case that a buddy to whom they were attached had died. Our veterans with post-traumatic stress disorder, but not the combat control veterans, could be considered late adolescents involved in narcissistic relationships, or narcissistic mergers with a group, at the time of their combat experience in Vietnam (van der Kolk et al. 1984). This agrees perfectly with the formulation of Richard Fox (1974). For these veterans, the trauma was so intense and their capacity to integrate it was so limited that it could not be dealt with as part of ordinary life.

Our findings of the onset of post-traumatic nightmares were consistent with one of Lidz's conclusions (Lidz 1946, p. 39): "With surprising frequency these patients had suffered a severe blow at the time of the onset of the neuroses [the nightmares] by the disruption of the single most important interpersonal relationship in their lives. The loss of a buddy, fiancée, or mother had left them feeling deserted and helpless." Lidz, as mentioned, noted that the severe chronic nightmares often did not start immediately after the combat trauma but later, with an additional trauma in the form of a loss or rejection. This was true in some of our group as well.

In any case, we have found at least two different sorts of nightmares and nightmare sufferers among these veterans. In about a third of the group, the nightmares were ordinary ones that, as we have seen, may incorporate stressful experiences and traumas into their content. These occurred in persons with a history of lifelong nightmares and apparently thin boundaries since childhood. A majority of the veterans were different; they had a different sort of nightmare—the true post-traumatic nightmare—and they had a diagnosis of post-traumatic stress disorder. They did not have the sensitive childhood and other characteristics of the lifelong nightmare subjects. They appeared to have had relatively normal childhoods, but at the time of combat had been late adolescents prone to very close merging relationships. And almost always the trauma initiating the nightmare involved the death or wounding of the buddy with whom they had had this close relationship.

In terms of our discussion of boundaries, the veterans with post-traumatic nightmares were not persons with lifelong thin boundaries. However, the traumatic event which formed the core of the nightmares involved a temporary merging, or confusion of boundaries. The relationship was so close that when the buddy died, a part of the soldier himself died as well; or the soldier became unsure as to whether it was a buddy or himself who had been killed.* And, in addition, the survivor

* Sometimes the merging relationship involves a group of three, four, or more buddies, rather than two; in this case, the death of any member of the group may produce these traumatic effects on the survivors.

often felt that he, not his buddy, should have died, a phenomenon known as survivor guilt. Thus, one veteran in our group had frequent nightmares that were elaborations of actual events in Vietnam: he went to a morgue in order to identify ten to twelve men from his unit. He went through the doors and saw two men who were taking care of the bodies.

> They tell us to wait. They are in the middle of doing their job on the guy. They cut down his clothes with a razor blade, hose him down with a garden hose, and poke into the wounds with a stick and count the holes. They write it down on a piece of paper and they tag the body and put the body into a clear plastic bag which is tagged and once again it is put into another green plastic bag which is tagged again. It is all very professional. They stack them up three deep and four high. You go in; they unzip the bag and they ask, "Do you know who this is?" and one after the other I recognize the guys. Then they had trucks outside. It was a very busy day. They were dairy trucks with the refrigeration units, with the same set-up as inside the morgue: the overflow. When we went out to the trucks, I identified a couple of guys and in my nightmare then—I identify myself! At that point I start to run and can't stop running until I wake up. Sometimes I wake up by myself or sometimes my wife will wake me up.

Or a dramatic nightmare suffered by a Vietnam veteran every night as reported by Harry Wilmer (1982):

> One day, we were in our camp when three men and a woman killed the guard at the gate and ran towards me and my sergeant. We were just waiting there with our rifles propped up. I hit the woman at about twenty yards. I remember the way her shirt jumped when the bullet tore out of her back. It was like a dream. Then we were under

attack for three weeks. I lost a buddy and took it real hard and I began shooting heroin. The dream is about the time my buddy was killed. In the dream I'm running away from my tent, which is tied down to a powder keg. I am crawling in a trench we dug and I am crying. I get the feeling I am going to get hit. The hair on the back of my neck stands up. When the shooting is over, I go to my tent. It is blown full of shrapnel holes. The powder keg has blown up. So far that's the way it really was. Then I stare into the tent. There is a body in my bunk with a big bloody gaping hole in his chest. I try to see who it is, but I always wake up before I can see his face. I wonder, "Is it me or my buddy?"

In these cases, even the nightmare itself depicts an unsureness of who was really killed and who survived.

Summary

WHEN DO POST-TRAUMATIC NIGHTMARES OCCUR?

In summarizing material on post-traumatic nightmares in general I shall consider primarily these questions: When—and to whom—do traumatic nightmares occur? And once they occur, how can we describe the process that leads in some cases to the chronic post-traumatic stress disorder? First, as we have seen, post-traumatic nightmares are common. They occur to some extent after any trauma—accident, violent crime, death—in children, adolescents, and adults. Their frequency diminishes somewhat with age. Children can be considered always vulnerable to some extent in that their ways of dealing with the world—and their boundaries in many senses— are still being formed. In an adult, post-traumatic nightmares require not only an external trauma, but an external trauma occurring in a situation of vulnerability so that, at least temporarily, his or her boundaries are thin or weak. This was so in young soldiers involved in intense late adolescent buddy relationships, as we have seen. And it can also happen if the nightmare situation replays or recalls a specific very disturbing earlier trauma.

> A veteran had a repetitive traumatic nightmare involving a human head lying on a road. This apparently referred to an actual scene after a battle in World War II. However, he eventually recalled that as a small child he had had a guinea pig which disappeared one day. A day or two later he recognized the head of the guinea pig in the family's spaghetti at dinner! (The family was poor and could not afford to buy meat.) (Greenberg 1981).

Thus, we could say that in persons who do not have the lifelong thin-boundary condition we have described, a trauma can produce long-lasting nightmares if it occurs at times of vulnerability or helplessness, especially when boundaries are temporarily confused or stretched thin. Perhaps there are times when we are all in this vulnerable situation. For instance, in childhood most of us have had nightmares, perhaps because our boundaries were still unformed. And in childhood, an external trauma that might not produce severe symptoms in an adult can result in traumatic nightmares (Stoddard 1982); a situation I feel to be extremely frequent. Again, being conscious but completely paralyzed—an awakening during an operation—may render one vulnerable enough or one's boundaries thin enough so that one has nightmares at least for a time. Other traumas which often result in post-traumatic nightmares in adults include torture, and longterm experiences in a concentration camp (Rasmussen and Lunde 1980, Hermann and Thygesen 1954). In these continuing conditions of trauma, being older is of little help; one cannot avoid being engulfed in the situation.

Under all of these conditions, one's basic stable assumptions about the world, one's basic foundations somehow collapse. One is absolutely stunned and asks not only, "What is going on here?" but also "Can this be happening to me?" "Is it really me?" And sometimes "Am I really alive while he/she is dead?" A corollary is that there are many times when apparently severe trauma—auto accidents, crimes, combat experiences—do *not* result in post-traumatic nightmares. This is so for adults who have solid boundaries and in whom trauma does not strike at any personal weak spots or points of vulnerability. As we saw, the veterans who had not developed nightmares after severe combat trauma were older and had protected themselves by not getting too close to others (buddies) so that they could not be hurt too much by their loss.

HOW DO POST-TRAUMATIC NIGHTMARES EVOLVE INTO POST-TRAUMATIC STRESS DISORDERS?

Once an acute post-traumatic nightmare has occurred, how can we understand its development into the sometimes debilitating condition of post-traumatic stress disorder? An acute trauma can be considered an extreme example of what happens every day—material arrives through the sensory channels; it must be handled by the central nervous system and integrated into the memory systems. The traumatic material enters in the same way but is more disturbing than other material, and is presumably more difficult to handle.

When traumatic material enters the system, there are two major paths it can follow. The first is the path of normal healing and resolution. Here, although the traumatic material stands out as distinct and disturbing for a few weeks or months, it is gradually thought about, fantasized about, and dreamt about; it is handled by the usual integrative process. The traumatic material is often dreamt about prominently for a while (acute post-traumatic nightmare) but it then fades into the background of other dream material and the dreams return to their normal mixture of dream content, assimilating new daytime material as usual. Dealing with the traumatic material in this way is part of the function of dreaming sleep; I consider it a special example of the more general functions that I and a number of other researchers have proposed for D-sleep (REM-sleep). Thus, I suggested (Hartmann 1973) that "D-sleep functions to make connections between daytime material and past material, past wishes and fears." It ties up loose ends or "wraps up the knitted sleeve of care," in Shakespeare's phrase, by making connections between new material and the basic memory structures of the mind. Most traumatic material can apparently be handled in that way, like other new material.

The second path is the more pathological one which I call encapsulation. The traumatic material does not merge with ordinary dream content and does not become integrated into the remainder of mental life. It is pushed away and avoided during normal waking, and thus is not thought about and fantasized about as most new material is. It remains separated from ordinary memory and consciousness. The nightmares may disappear for a time, and then suddenly may be reactivated by a later loss or rejection of some kind. The traumatic material has produced some kind of tear in the mental fabric; a part of the sleeve that cannot be "raveled up"; or to use a very different medical metaphor, it becomes a sort of encapsulated abscess, walled off, and painful to the touch. This path of development produces the longterm post-traumatic nightmare and along with other symptoms constitutes post-traumatic stress disorder, which can be considered a specific form of hyperarousal (Schoen, Kramer, and Kinney 1983).

Post-traumatic stress disorder is a complex biopsychological process only beginning to be understood. It involves an increased arousability or irritability so that a variety of stimuli—not always related to the stress—can set off an arousal reaction in the body. This can include post-traumatic nightmares at night and sometimes flashbacks (sudden intrusions of a traumatic memory) in the daytime. In fact, typical post-traumatic nightmares (as of the veterans in our Group 1) in which a fairly long scene is "replayed" sounds to a listener more like a terrifying memory (often with one "personal" addition) than like an ordinary dream.* The post-traumatic nightmare seems somehow burned or etched into the memory systems so

---

* Often the post-traumatic nightmare which is "played back" is not a precise memory of actual events but is altered in one detail: as we have seen, "It was me that was blown up; it was *my* dead body." This portrays the origin of the traumatic nightmare in a situation of helplessness and a situation in which there was a loss of self boundary as discussed above. Traumatic nightmares involve instances of intense identification with the victim—especially the dead buddy in wartime.

that it is separate but it can be "set off" by a number of disturbances. If anything touches on it or gets near it, the entire memory sequence (or rather the slightly-altered memory sequence) is triggered and runs in a completely repetitive sequence. This seems to happen especially easily at night, where it may be set off simply by the physiological shift from normal S-sleep to D-sleep (REM-sleep)—it can occur early in the night when there has not yet been a full D-period. It may even be set off occasionally by going to sleep—the hypnagogic period—or perhaps by any sudden awakening out of sleep. In other words, a variety of shifts in brain physiology can sometimes touch it off. (It is not always clear what sets off a flashback, which occurs in a state of wakefulness, but in some veterans an emotional memory—for instance, something that reminds them of their dead buddy—may set it off; in others, drugs such as marijuana have this effect.)

One cannot help thinking of the stored memories sometimes set off by electrical stimulation in the studies of Wilder Penfield and his colleagues (see, for instance, Penfield and Jasper, 1954). These studies showed that weak electrical stimulation of points in the temporal cortex sometimes produces a complete memory-sequence, which would be "run off" in an identical fashion each time the point was stimulated. In fact, Francis Forster (1978) described one case of a veteran who had experienced several epileptic seizures before going to Vietnam. He then went through severe combat experiences and afterward frequently experienced frightening post-traumatic nightmares reliving combat, from which he would wake up cold and clammy with clonic movements of his left arm. It was determined by electroencephalographic studies that he was having epileptic seizures and that the nightmare appeared to be set off as an "aura." (An aura occurs in epileptic patients just before their seizures when a feeling, a memory, or a sensory experience is activated, apparently by the spread of electrical discharge, just before the generalized motor activation of the seizure.) In this one case at least, the post-traumatic nightmare experience was apparently set off by an electrical discharge preceding a seizure. Although in other cases of post-traumatic nightmares no such clear seizures or abnormal EEG activity is found, it may still make sense to consider post-traumatic nightmares as being something akin to a subclinical epileptic discharge. If no other treatment helps (chapter 9), anti-epileptic medication may be worth trying.

We have now examined post-traumatic nightmares in a number of different situations. Perhaps we could extrapolate from what we have said about veterans and suggest that in every case after severe trauma there is some tendency for the trauma to be separated off and potentially become an encapsulated "abscess." We have examined the most severe cases of chronic post-traumatic nightmares where this actually happens—where a traumatic scene is isolated and then is activated nightly and runs off in an almost identical fashion for many years. In most cases, this does not happen. Usually, we assume that the traumatic event, if it is serious enough, begins this process of separation and walling off, and may produce a brief sequence of post-traumatic nightmares; but then connections are made between the trauma and the remainder of the person's mental life. This occurs in the daytime through recall, reliving, and, when available, psychotherapy, which helps the person to make connections, and helps him face the pain as he integrates the trauma with the remainder of his life. At night, the connections are made more or less automatically during D-sleep. We see in the less severe cases how a traumatic nightmare may be an exact replay of the trauma for a few days, but then begins to merge with more ordinary dream elements. Dreaming sleep may be performing at night the same function that reliving, connecting and psychotherapy perform in the daytime.

Thus, in the ideal case which resolves well, the post-traumatic nightmare is a transient phenomenon that is gradually integrated into the person's dream life as trauma is integrated into the person's mental life. In the most serious cases, the memory of the trauma with the additional personal identification—"It was me that got killed"—remains encapsulated. Presumably, there is a continuum between the two extremes so that in some persons, though the traumatic material is partially walled off, it is also partially being integrated; the nightmares then reflect a mixture of the pure post-traumatic memory and the more familiar long, frightening-dream kind of nightmare whose content is a mixture of various childhood events as well as aspects of the dreamer's everyday life.

The treatment of post-traumatic nightmares, as well as of ordinary nightmares and night terrors, will be taken up in the next chapter.

CHAPTER 9

Nightmares, Night Terrors, and Post-Traumatic Nightmares as Clinical Problems

MANY people who suffer from nightmares, night terrors, or post-traumatic nightmares seek professional help to find relief from these disturbing conditions. From the clinician's point of view, it is important to be sure of the diagnosis; to know what to expect over the course of time, what can make the condition better or worse, and what treatments may be useful. In this chapter we will look at the various treatments and consider which ones can be useful and under what conditions.

Nightmares (Frequent Nightmares, Not of the Traumatic Nightmare Variety)

Establishing the presence of nightmares—the diagnosis—does not present great problems if one remembers the distinction made between nightmares and night terrors. Nightmares (REM-nightmares) as such seldom require treatment. However, it is worthwhile for the clinician to examine the whole picture to determine whether the presence of nightmares indicates something else going on that might require further investigation and treatment. Children between the ages of three and six frequently have nightmares, which may simply indicate that the nervous system has matured to the point where a child can distinguish dreaming from waking activity and is now able to dream about fears and to relate the dreams to others. The themes involved are often primitive fears—loss of bodily integrity, loss of people close to him or her, castration, or mutilation—as well as fears of the child's own aggressive impulses. If the nightmares are of unusual frequency and severity, it may be worth looking for environmental situations or family dynamics that may make the child feel especially helpless or vulnerable.

Frequent nightmares (nontraumatic nightmares) continuing for long periods in older children, adolescents, and young adults suggest the sort of thin boundaries or vulnerability we have discussed in previous chapters. Treatment may sometimes be helpful. However, the decision would be made on the basis of the patient's overall psychological orientation including the way he or she handles interpersonal relationships, the way he or she functions at school and at home, etc. Treatment would not be aimed specifically at the nightmare but would be directed to providing structure and support in various ways. It could involve psychotherapy, perhaps including family or group therapy, and sometimes cognitive therapy for particular problem areas. It may be important to assist the child or adolescent to find ways to develop artistic talents if they are present.

The recent onset of nightmares in someone who has not previously had them suggests other possibilities. It is worthwhile for the clinician to obtain a careful history of drug use and use of any unusual substance, since sometimes these will be directly connected with the nightmares. In adults, nightmares often coincide with the beginning of medical treatment for hypertension, angina, or Parkinsonism. If the nightmares are very severe, they can be treated by reducing the dosage or changing the offending medication.

Nightmares that become more frequent over a period of weeks, accompanied by insomnia and daytime anxiety, may signal an impending psychotic condition that requires treatment. In such cases, antipsychotic medication reduces the incidence of nightmares, probably secondarily to reduction of the intensity of the underlying psychosis. As we shall see in chapter 10, these drugs (dopamine

receptor blockers) might be expected to reduce the incidences of such nightmares even if they were not related
to a psychosis, but this has not been tested directly. The
use of tranquilizers (such as the benzodiazepines) clinically appears also to reduce the incidences of nightmares.
In addition to medication, careful investigation of the
patient's situation is required to determine the need for
psychotherapy or other forms of treatment.

Occasionally, the nightmares themselves have been
the object of treatment. Behavioral treatments, such as
deconditioning, have been attempted and there are some
reports of success. Some clinicians have tried a method
involving teaching the patients to imagine fighting back
or resisting the danger or the attacker he or she encounters
in a nightmare and then trying to incorporate this
material into the dream, altering the nightmares, thereby
making the person feel better. I have doubts that this
sequence actually occurs. The sense I have obtained
clinically is that the reverse order is the more usual—
the person feels better, is more mature, learns to handle
problems better (with the help of therapy or without
any specific therapy) and then the nightmares reflect this
change by becoming less frequent or virulent (see
chapter 7). I believe behavioral treatments may be useful
principally in persons who have already improved, whose
lives are in good shape but who still have nightmares as
an annoying reminder of a time of disorganization or
illness.

CLINICAL EXAMPLES

Here are a few examples of patients, all of whom
suffered from nightmares, and some suggestions for
treatment:

Marie's mother comes to see me; she tells me Marie, aged five, has been waking frequently over the past year crying, complaining that something is chasing her. Marie's mother is becoming upset about this; she does not know whether she should allow Marie to come to bed with her and her husband when Marie is upset or make her sleep by herself. She is worried because Marie's crying and occasional screaming wakes her baby brother, who is sometimes a fitful sleeper himself. The mother also worries whether her occasional fights with her husband are having a bad effect on Marie. Marie has just started school; one of her friends has been diagnosed as hyperactive and is taking amphetamines. A teacher's assistant has mentioned to Marie's mother that perhaps Marie herself is a bit overactive and should be considered for medication as well.

What does one do here? Clearly, there is some cause for concern. If nothing else, the mother is becoming increasingly anxious, and her anxiety could make life difficult for the entire family. However, one gets the impression that Marie may well simply be going through a developmental phase. Marie should have a talk with her pediatrician. In this case, it turns out that Marie is a bright, charming girl with lots of friends in school. She adores her father, loves her mother but with some mixed feelings, and makes no bones about the fact that she does not especially care for her one-year-old brother. She enjoys the independence of going to school but, at the same time, is jealous of her little brother who gets to spend so much time at home with her parents. She invents a "baby school" and wishes the parents would immediately send her brother there.

Marie is a normal child experiencing some normal developmental problems. She appears to need no treatment of any kind, and she certainly needs no medication.

Nightmares as Clinical Problems

It is almost certain that her nightmares will become less frequent in the next year or two. Her mother may need some reassurance and perhaps even brief psychotherapy, if she is very anxious. She can be given information about the expected course of Marie's nightmares and be advised to spend more time with her. And she needs to be reassured that her child appears to be doing well in school and has no serious problems.

Leia, sixteen years old, does not come for help for her nightmares, but is brought to her doctor at the insistence of the police after she was mugged and almost raped while walking alone through a dangerous part of town two weeks before.

Leia has nightmares about twice a week now and in the last weeks they have involved the attack and attempted rape mixed with other content. She has had nightmares as long as she can remember, starting at perhaps age three: "The nightmares used to involve a white monster, kind of like a scarecrow with big teeth, coming after me." The nightmares never really stopped, but decreased somewhat at age seven or eight and have been increasing again in the past three years. The current nightmares involve wars, fights between gangs, tidal waves. She is usually a helpless victim, with one man, or with a whole group of people attacking her.

Leia is a poet who shows some talent. She writes her poetry only for herself, sometimes for one male teacher on whom she has a crush. Her parents seem to be decent and caring people. There are no overt problems in her home; nonetheless, Leia feels she had a very unhappy childhood: "I was always different; I was so easily hurt; everything seemed to get to me. My father was like that too. He and I were always the sensitive ones." She had a very disturbed reaction to the birth of her younger sister when she was three years old. She thinks this may be the time when she began to have nightmares, though she is not sure.

Leia has always done well in school, is considered intelligent and talented, but has not been popular and has had only one close friend. She herself attributes this to her being so easily hurt and turned off: "They don't even know they are hurting me. I think they probably mean well."

Although Leia has continued to do well in school, her grades have dropped somewhat in the past year. She spends a good deal of time daydreaming and in the evening spends hours crying by herself in her room. Her plans for herself alternate between seeing herself as a great writer and planning a dramatic suicide. She has recently experimented with alcohol and drugs in the hope that these would dampen her fears and sensitivity and perhaps make her more one of the group. However, she reports that alcohol simply makes her feel drugged and the one time when she drank heavily for a couple of days, she found she had more severe nightmares a day or two afterwards. She tried marijuana a few times. Although she enjoyed an initial relaxation, she reports that she quickly became scared of the people with her and felt that they were looking at her strangely. In her third experience with marijuana, she ran away from her friend's house screaming; she heard several men chasing her all the way home. She now realizes that there were no men chasing her and that this had been a hallucination. She has stayed away from marijuana since then and has not tried stronger street drugs.

Leia is obviously in trouble and needs help. Can we predict what is going to happen to her? Not exactly, but she fits into the lifelong nightmare group I have described in chapter 4. She is already having a difficult adolescence. It is possible that she may have psychotic episodes in the future and be diagnosed as schizophrenic. There is a danger that she will try to kill herself. She may continue to have nightmares and problems with relationships, lead a chaotic life for a time, but eventually settle into some more stable pattern at which time the night-mares will decrease in frequency and intensity. Finally, if Leia really has talent as a poet, she may be able to organize herself around her talent. She may through this part of herself fulfill wishes of becoming famous, or she may decide to teach writing to others. She may feel more comfortable among other writers and perhaps meet more compatible friends than she has so far. It is unlikely that Leia will ever become a typical, middle-class house-wife like her mother, nor indeed does she desire to be.

What sort of help does Leia need? Many forms of help might be useful to her. She needs a careful evaluation including psychological tests and a study of her family environment and problems. Certainly psychotherapy of some kind would be useful to her, perhaps therapy involving a long-lasting stable relationship with an older woman with whom she can identify. If she is very much involved in family struggles—and she may well be at sixteen—family therapy could help as well. If I were her therapist I would be honest with her and the family in the sense of letting her know that she is an unusual child, a sensitive child who may have artistic potential, but is probably also vulnerable to mental illness. Neither Leia nor her family should be encouraged to think she is just passing through a minor adolescent upset and that she will be perfectly all right in a couple of years.

Leia also needs some straightforward counseling in terms of safety (where she can safely walk, etc.), the seriousness of which may be difficult to impress upon her because, having thin boundaries, she is more trusting and less aware of danger. Her suicidal feelings can be a problem. Still, there is a part of her that wants to live

227

and to succeed, and an alliance needs to be made with that part of her. Group therapy might be useful to her, meeting with other sensitive adolescents like herself, because simply to know that she is not alone—the only one to have these terrible problems—can be a tremendous help.

The dangers of alcohol and street drugs should be carefully explained. The reaction she showed to alcohol and to marijuana are typical of many people like Leia. There is a rebound increase in nightmares and often anxiety and suicidal impulses in the period of withdrawal from alcohol, so it would certainly be best for Leia to avoid alcohol or use it very sparingly. Street drugs can be dangerous for her: even marijuana can precipitate a paranoid episode, and she has had one already. Leia may need medication should she encounter a stressful situation—initiated by a trauma or even by a bout with marijuana. Should the nightmares get a great deal worse, and should it appear as though she were headed for a psychotic episode, treatment with antipsychotic medication will be useful to her. One need not wait until one can make an unquestioned diagnosis. Of course it is possible that Leia may reject help at this time. However, if at all possible she and her parents should at least be made aware of the possibility of help along the lines discussed.

Let us take a minute to consider Carla:

Carla is twenty-six, a professional cellist, who had a history of lifelong nightmares. In adolescence Carla was much like Leia, except that Carla's interests were in music, not in poetry. She made a suicide attempt at age seventeen, followed by a brief hospitalization, and had psychotherapy for about two years. She has had several relationships with men and at one time had an affair with a woman for several months. She has been unsure about her sexual identity and unsure what to do with her life. However, in the last two years she has obtained a position with an excellent chamber music group and is now living with a man whom she hopes to marry soon. Their relationship seems to be going well. She still has nightmares about once every two weeks involving scary monsters and frightening men, but she now usually manages to escape in the dream, whereas previously she was always caught and helpless. She comes in now for advice about the future: Do the nightmares mean that she is mentally ill? Does she need psychotherapy? Should she take tranquilizers or other medication? Is there a danger her children will have nightmares or mental illness?

Carla does not need much help at this time. Her life is moving in a positive direction and the nightmares reflect this. Her childhood sensitivities, her artistic tendencies, her possible vulnerability to mental illness can be discussed with her. She can be reassured that nightmares and mental illness are not directly inherited, though there is a chance that "vulnerability" can be. She can be offered further psychotherapeutic help or counseling if needed, but the emphasis should be that she is getting better anyway and that she has been doing it herself. She has taken responsibility for her life and has been doing a good job of it, though she may sometimes need help with specific problems. She definitely does not need medication.

Margo is a fifty-year-old woman, who never had had nightmares until two months ago, but now she has been having them almost every night. Her dreams have become vivid and emotional, and sometimes terrifying: strange scenes of torture and single body parts—arms and legs without bodies. This frightens her considerably. There have been no recent traumatic or emotional upsets. She has been well physically; however, at her last physical examination she was found to have elevated blood pressure.

Margo's past is quite different from Leia's or Carla's. She had no particular sensitivities, had an uneventful childhood and a typical emotional but not really troubled adolescence; at present she has a happy marriage, two grown children with whom she is on good terms, and many friends. She expresses some slight anxiety about her younger daughter who is going out with a man Margo disapproves of, and she has some mild concerns about her high blood pressure—as well as the health of her husband, who had a heart attack three years ago. Aside from this her life has been happy and peaceful, and she can think of no reason for the sudden onset of her nightmares.

In this case, there appears to be no problem with boundaries and no traumatic events. On more detailed questioning, Margo reports that when her internist made a diagnosis of hypertension, he prescribed a small dose of the medication propranolol, and the nightmares began shortly thereafter. Clearly, the medication precipitated her nightmares (see chapter 10). Her nightmares will probably subside somewhat, even if she continues taking this beta-adrenergic blocking medication. She may benefit also from changing to alternate antihypertensive medication. There is a danger that Margo could become secondarily upset and anxious about the nightmares if she does not realize they are probably a simple result of medication. It is worth remembering that nightmares of sudden onset such as Margo's often have a straightforward cause such as medication or perhaps a recent traumatic event.

However, nightmares can sometimes be a sign of impending danger, as in the following case:

Nightmares as Clinical Problems

Jim, a twenty-one-year-old student, complained of night-mares during the past two weeks that were becoming increasingly severe. His student health physician gave him a physical exam, decided he was in good shape, and advised him to stop studying so hard. However, Jim's nightmares became more frightening and violent over the following weeks; he began to sleep less and less. He finally stopped eating because he felt his food was being poisoned, and he was admitted to a mental hospital with a clear-cut acute schizophrenic psychosis three weeks after he first saw his doctor with a complaint of nightmares.

In Jim's case, a careful history would have revealed that he had slowly become more frightened and more isolated at school over the past months, and would have alerted his doctor that the nightmares were to be taken seriously. It is quite possible that the prompt use of medication, combined with psychotherapy, and perhaps an environmental change such as giving up school for a time, could well have averted the hospitalization.

Night Terrors

Night terrors should be easy to recognize in most cases, even though the patient or the family may call them nightmares. Night terrors are most commonly reported in children at age three to eight. The parents often describe the child as screaming and then either returning to sleep or entering a sleepwalking episode with a glazed expression from which it is difficult to awaken him. Once awake, the child usually falls asleep again relatively quickly and has little memory of the event.

There is a tendency for night terrors to run in families, and some children may have a genetic susceptibility to them. Night terrors can be considered a minor abnormality in the brain's sleep-wake mechanisms producing unusual arousals. However, in a susceptible child, there is no question but that environmental or emotional factors play a part. Most often, no specific treatment is required. In cases beginning at the typical age in childhood, the condition is usually benign and the night terrors disappear spontaneously. Thus, reassurance to the parents is often the most important step. Otherwise, there is a chance that they will worry excessively, become anxious, and perhaps try inappropriate treatments. Most children who have transient night terrors between the ages of three and eight will have no further difficulties, though a minority will have recurrences of night terrors or sleepwalking in adolescence or early adulthood.

There are some additional measures worth keeping in mind. Since sleep deprivation and extreme tiredness aggravate night terrors, a regular sleep schedule allowing the child enough sleep is very important. Night terrors are also aggravated, and sometimes appear to be initiated by stress of many kinds. A child susceptible to night terrors may have a difficult period when a sibling is born, when the family moves, or when the parents' marriage is breaking up or under strain, etc. Thus, it is worth examining family relationships, school, and other aspects of the child's surroundings to determine possible sources of avoidable or treatable stress.

In a few cases, night terrors will begin in childhood

and will continue into early adulthood or throughout life. The reasons for this are not clear. These patients may simply have a greater degree of neurological susceptibility than others. I have seen cases in which there was no obvious medical or psychological abnormality; the persons functioned extremely well but continued to have occasional disturbing night terror episodes throughout life. It is possible that psychological predisposing factors are present in some instances. Some adults with night terrors have been noted to have phobic or obsessional personalities. There is sometimes a sense that these people are unable or unwilling to notice or express strong feelings in the daytime; in them, the night terror episodes may express a kind of outbreak of repressed emotion.

When night terrors do not begin in childhood but have their onset in adolescence or adulthood, they may be secondary to other factors. They are sometimes the first symptom of temporal lobe epilepsy. Occasionally, they follow various types of brain injury or brain pathology; for instance, I have seen one case in which severe night terrors lasting for years followed an episode of measles encephalitis. They sometimes appear to be caused by an overuse of alcohol or various drugs. These causes need to be kept in mind when the onset is at an unusual time, in adolescence or in adulthood, but of course these reasons occasionally may be responsible for the onset of night terror in children as well.

Night terrors are usually not a terribly serious or dangerous condition, but there have been exceptions when severe injuries, automobile accidents, and deaths took place during the episodes, especially when they were coupled with sleepwalking. Therefore, it is worth discussing treatment, even though in many cases, especially in children, the treatment will simply be reassurance that the condition will pass. When night terrors are serious and involve sleepwalking as well, the treatment first must include making the surroundings safe for the sleeper and for others. Glass windows, mirrors, and sharp objects should be removed from the vicinity of the sleeper, and he certainly should not sleep on a balcony or near the open window of an upper floor. A second element of treatment is the removal of exacerbating factors such as alcohol, street drugs, sleep deprivation, and stressful situations insofar as possible. Third, psychotherapy can sometimes be useful (see, for instance, Kales et al. 1982). I have had experience with several longterm night terror sufferers for whom shortterm psychotherapy did have a positive effect. In part, therapy may have reduced stress by helping the patient handle potentially stressful events in new ways. Therapy also gave patients an opportunity to examine their own dangerous emotions—anger and rage—in a safe daytime setting.

Finally, medication can be useful in the treatment of serious cases of night terrors. A small dose of benzodiazepines taken at bedtime reduces and sometimes eliminated the incidence of night terrors (Fisher et al. 1973a). The problem is that medication must be taken for a long time and the condition usually recurs when the medication is withdrawn.

Nightmares as Clinical Problems

CLINICAL EXAMPLES

Josh's parents are worried because for the past few years, since he was five, he has been "having these terrible nightmares from which we can't awaken him." What happens is that half an hour or an hour after going to sleep, Josh sits up in bed, often screams, and then wanders around in a daze looking terrified. His parents try to wake him up out of it, but often without success, for five or ten minutes. When he finally awakens, he does not seem to know where he is, but appears untroubled and usually falls back asleep and sleeps quietly for the rest of the night. Not so his parents: they have developed their own insomnia, sitting up wondering what in the world is the matter with Josh. They notice that these episodes happen most often on Saturday nights.

Josh has typical night terrors, and it is not unusual for them to start at age five and still be quite prominent at age seven or eight. His father had episodes of sleepwalking as a child, so there may be a familial connection, which is not unusual. What is special about Saturday nights is that Josh stays up late with his older brothers on Friday and Saturday nights so that he is usually very tired and worn out by the time he goes to bed, aggravating his night terror condition.

In a situation such as Josh's, it is certainly worth exploring what is going on in the family, since family stress or problems—a separation, perhaps, or a move— can initiate night terrors or make them worse. However, some children (boys rather than girls two-thirds of the time) appear to be predisposed to night terrors of this kind, and one may not be able to find any unusual stress, except perhaps something as simple as increased work at school or increased tiredness on some nights as was true in Josh's case.

235

The most important part of treatment would be simply reassuring Josh's parents about the nature of the condition, letting them know it will almost certainly become better with time and that factors such as stress and tiredness can make it worse. It may be worth exploring whether the parents are anxious only about Josh and his night terrors or have other reasons for their anxiety. It may also be useful to check on whether there are secondary problems. Possibly Josh's parents have made him so worried about his nighttime episodes that he is now becoming inhibited or afraid of doing anything that might set off an attack so that he may need some reassurance or supportive therapy as well. This is all that is likely to be necessary.

> Harold began to have strange episodes at age sixteen when he went away to school. About one hour after sleep onset, he would suddenly yell and scream and sometimes throw himself against the wall, at times producing injuries to his hands and head. Harold and his parents state that he had an entirely normal childhood with no night terrors, sleepwalking, enuresis, nightmares, or any particular psychological problem.

With Harold it was extremely important to obtain a careful history regarding all aspects of his life. Alcohol and drugs might have produced or aggravated his problem: however, he was not a user of alcohol or street drugs. He did not wear himself out and he was not sleep deprived. There was no particular recent stress in his life. No physical problem could be found to account for his night terrors. Their cause remained a mystery for some time. But in the year after the onset of the night terror episodes, Harold also began to have unusual daytime episodes during which he would appear confused or out of touch for several minutes at a time; he later would have no recollection of these episodes. This produced a strong suspicion that he might have a seizure disorder. Specialized EEG procedures demonstrated a probable temporal lobe focus. Harold was placed on anti-epileptic medication, which successfully brought to a stop both his night terror episodes and his daytime confusional episodes.

Acute Post-Traumatic Nightmares

Again, the diagnosis usually presents little problem; acute post-traumatic nightmares are frightening dreams replaying a traumatic experience that occur in the days and weeks immediately afterward. These include the post-operation dreams we have discussed, the dreams in children who have escaped from a fire or an automobile accident, and the dreams of soldiers just after a combat experience. Here, the nightmares can be considered one symptom—often the most important symptom—of an acute post-traumatic reaction. They follow two courses: Either—and this is the most common—the whole syndrome, including the nightmares, fades after a few weeks or months (as we have seen, when this occurs the nightmares become less like a straightforward memory of the trauma and become more dreamlike), or the post-traumatic nightmares remain and become incorporated

237

into a chronic post-traumatic stress disorder, which we will discuss later.

The acute post-traumatic nightmares do respond to treatment and it should be instituted as quickly as possible. Clinical improvement with immediate or rapid treatment have been documented in many different types of post-traumatic nightmare disorders (Grinker and Spiegel 1945, Blacher 1975, Terr 1981, Lidz 1946). Treatment is the type of psychotherapy sometimes called abreaction or ventilation whose main focus is to allow the trauma and its associations to become conscious and to be incorporated into the totality of the person's mental life. The patient is asked to retell the nightmare and the frightening event during waking in a variety of ways—recalling, reliving the emotions associated with the trauma and connecting them to times when similar emotions occurred, and so on. The therapist can try to understand insofar as possible what made the situation especially traumatic and provide understanding and support, as well as an opportunity to reexperience the emotions and make connections in a safe setting.

In the simplest cases, such as the post-operative dreams described by Blacher (1975), the explanation that the patient really had experienced something akin to his dreams has proven to be extremely useful. With the children who experienced trauma, it was very important to discuss the reality of the experience with them—how they had found themselves in that situation, how perhaps the events had been unavoidable—in an attempt to make a connection between the trauma and their usual lives. It is important to discuss and dispel unrealistic fears that the traumatic event will surely happen again, guilt that the child was responsible for the event, and hopeless feelings that things will never get any better. There are almost always some unrealistic elements that can be explored and discussed; these may involve dynamics such as survivor guilt, or rage at persons close to them who escaped injury or persons who were somehow held responsible. Treatment for such post-traumatic nightmares should be initiated quickly, but need not be long term. Prolonged psychotherapy or psychoanalysis is generally only helpful if there are other reasons for such treatment. Medication has not been found to be particularly useful in these cases. I believe there may be a danger to giving large doses of medication such as the typical tranquilizers. While medication may reduce anxiety and reduce the immediate intensity of the nightmares, it may make the connecting process more difficult, perhaps by reducing REM-sleep, thus making the traumatic nightmares more likely to become chronic.

It is worth emphasizing that acute post-traumatic nightmares represent one area where brief psychotherapy is definitely and almost uniformly useful. This is important to know since psychotherapy in this early period runs counter to the commonsense approach of "leave the poor girl alone," "let her recuperate," "don't bother her," etc. I feel quite certain that this sort of therapy is useful, even though there are no controlled studies to support this conclusion. In fact, I feel that often to deny therapeutic help can be detrimental to the patient and this needs to be kept in mind even when there appear to be more pressing physical problems to be dealt with. Thus, a soldier after a terrifying wartime experience or a child who has been in an accident or fire may often spend weeks having his physical wounds attended to while the mental wounds are neglected—no one pays attention to the onset of nightmares while the burns are still being treated. I believe this is a mistake and it may lead to the patient's suffering from chronic post-traumatic stress disorder with chronic nightmares, a condition much more difficult to treat.

CLINICAL EXAMPLE

Tad was an apparently normal eight-year-old boy doing well at school with nothing unusual in his past history. His house caught fire at night while the entire family was asleep. Tad escaped but had second degree burns over much of his face and shoulders necessitating a stay of several weeks in the hospital. One of his brothers had died in the fire. During the two weeks since the fire, Tad has had a nightmare every night. The nightmares always involve the fire, but they are not simple memories. They also incorporate accidents and war scenes that he has read about or seen on TV; in some of the dreams, it is he, rather than his brother, who is caught in the fire and killed.

At the hospital, he was given tranquilizers to reduce his anxiety. The hospital staff and his family tried to play games with him to turn his mind to happier things and they avoided discussing the accident.

Tad is, of course, having acute post-traumatic nightmares, which are to be expected in his situation. The condition will probably resolve itself in time. However, the trauma will be integrated better and he will probably be healthier afterwards if he is encouraged to talk repeatedly about the accident: his feelings about it and other scary things it reminds him of; his guilt that he escaped while his brother was killed; angry feelings he may have had towards his brother; and so on.

In cases like Tad's, I have a strong impression that the nightmares may actually play a helpful role in mental integration and the healing process. Tranquilizers, especially the benzodiazepines, greatly reduce dreaming-sleep time (REM-time) and usually reduce dream recall as well. I would recommend that Tad not be given anti-anxiety medication, or if medication is considered essential—for instance, to allow him to undergo necessary painful medical procedures—that he be given an anti-anxiety agent with a short half-life in the daytime so that it will have as little effect as possible at night.

Chronic Post-Traumatic Nightmares (Post-Traumatic Stress Disorder)

When an acute post-traumatic condition does not resolve itself and become integrated, perhaps in cases where it is too serious to be treatable, or where therapy was not available, then the condition of chronic post-traumatic nightmares develop, in which the frightening scenes, usually replays of the traumatic event, persist for many years. These are not typical REM-nightmares; they occur sometimes in stage 2 and sometimes in all stages of sleep and even at sleep onset; it is possible that the daytime flashbacks are a similar setting off of the traumatic material.

Aside from severity of trauma and lack of appropriate therapy, some factors that may lead to chronic post-traumatic nightmares have been discussed in chapter 8.

Those who developed the chronic post-traumatic night-mares in combat were unusually young—average age eighteen—at the time the wartime trauma occurred. These young men may have been in a particularly vulnerable state—they had formed very intense bonds of a narcissistic type with one or several buddies in their unit and it was when these buddies were killed or injured that the soldier felt damaged or betrayed and began to have nightmares. Occasionally it required an additional wound or trauma such as rejection by a girlfriend or the family to actually trigger the onset of a series of night-mares. In other words, among adults or adolescents, these serious nightmares occurred only when there was an unusually severe psychological wound. It occurred in young men who had had a part of themselves torn out, usually by the death of a close buddy, a wound sometimes deepened by an additional rejection occurring at close to the same time as the loss.

This trauma is encapsulated or "separated off." It is still there and emerges at night and occasionally in the daytime (flashbacks). The patients make an effort not to think about the trauma or anything connected with it and they try never to let themselves get into a vulnerable position in which they could get hurt in such a way again. This often means avoiding asking for help, avoiding close relationships, avoiding even love.

This situation is perhaps clearest in those veterans we discussed (chapter 8) who did not have a history of nightmares, and who suffered serious trauma and narcis-sistic injury at age seventeen or eighteen. However, the same mechanisms are probably involved at other ages and in the other situations. We saw that children often have post-traumatic nightmares. Their egos and their boundaries are less well formed; thus, it takes relatively less trauma to produce nightmares and they are usually less isolated and less long lasting. But with these children too there is a tendency to isolate their injuries and not to trust people, not to get involved in a situation in which they might be hurt again.

Once the condition has become chronic, treatment is very difficult. In some cases, the patients continue having nightmares for years or for their entire lives despite all attempts at treatment. However, there are cases of improvement, with and without treatment. It is much less clear that psychotherapy is useful in chronic, as opposed to acute, post-traumatic nightmares. In the cases that improve over time, with or without help from therapy, the nightmares gradually change from a direct memory to a more distorted, symbolic "dream-like" reference to the traumatic event, and the terrifying events merge with other more ordinary dream elements. Eventually, the person has normal dreams with only occasional reference to the trauma.

Many treatments have been tried for chronic post-traumatic nightmares (post-traumatic stress disorder), but there is no agreement at present as to what is the best treatment. Supportive individual psychotherapy, group psychotherapy, and family therapy are all sometimes used. Behavioral techniques such as deconditioning have been tried. All these have occasionally, but not routinely, been reported to be successful. In addition, a number of medications have been used and sometimes have been found to be helpful. These include the benzodiazepines, the antidepressants (especially monoamine oxydase inhibitors), the antipsychotics, and lithium (Hogben and Cornfield 1981, van der Kolk 1983). I would suggest two other possibilities that might be worth trying: L-tryptophan could help, since it has an anti-arousal and anti-irritability effect, probably related to increases in brain serotonin (Spinweber et al. 1983, Hartmann and Greenwald 1984); an anti-epileptic medication may be useful in cases that most resemble a seizure discharge even if there is no clear evidence of a seizure disorder. However, there is unfortunately no standard medication; the treating physician often has to try a number of medications, with little clear rationale, to find one that may help the patient.

CLINICAL EXAMPLE

Winston is a veteran, thirty years old. Several times every week for the past twelve years he has had a dream that is an almost exact replication of a scene he experienced. Winston and his best buddy are in a foxhole. It is nighttime. There is a lot of machine gun firing and shell bursts. A shell or grenade blows up right next to his buddy. He rushes out trying to get help. He finally finds someone to come, but when they get to the foxhole, it is too late and his buddy is dead. Winston sometimes screams and yells during the episode, waking his wife and children. He awakens bathed in sweat and is unable to get back to sleep. He sometimes has the same "dream" in the daytime as a flashback. The experience has greatly disrupted Winston's life. He is nervous and jumpy much of the time. He avoids emotion and avoids all sorts of closeness. He and his therapist have been working for a long time on his avoidance of closeness even with his wife.

Winston is one of many veterans with post-traumatic stress disorder (discussed in chapter 8). He is one of the unlucky ones who had unusually severe trauma, or was unusually vulnerable, or was not able to obtain or take advantage of abreaction and discussion in the weeks after the trauma, so that his traumatic nightmare did not become incorporated into the totality of his life but has remained "encapsulated" and walled off.

The prognosis is guarded, unfortunately. Winston's condition may improve in time, but one cannot be certain that it will. There are World War II veterans and survivors of the holocaust who have continued suffering post-traumatic nightmares since the 1940s. There is no agreement at present as to the best treatment for Winston and others like him, but the U.S. Veterans Administration and its counterparts in other countries are actively exploring a number of possibilities.

CHAPTER 10

The Biology of the
Nightmare

WRITERS on psychological topics, whether they are psychoanalysts, psychiatrists, or psychologists, often appear embarrassed by biology—by the fact that our thoughts, dreams, behavior are obviously influenced by our brains. Obligatory bows to biology such as "of course, organic factors must be considered as well" clearly contain the wish that biology would just go away and stop bothering us. On the contrary, I believe that biological studies may in fact present our greatest opportunity for advancing psychology. Psychology is a part of a larger whole—an upper story, perhaps, of a building whose lower stories are brain biology. Psychology can be considered to be a higher level biology of the intricate workings of our forebrains. Examining the effects of a chemical or neurological variable on nightmares is obviously important to a complete understanding of the nightmare and is not in principle different from examining the effects of trauma, or other external events.

Learning more of the biology of the nightmare has great potential importance: anything we learn of the specific biology of the nightmare may add to our understanding of the biology of dreaming, which has long been one of the chief interests of sleep researchers. And, since the nightmare is an unusually scary dream, and a series of nightmares sometimes heralds the onset of psychosis, understanding the biology of the nightmare may also help us with the biological link between dreaming and psychosis.

I shall follow two paths toward understanding the biology of the nightmare. First, since the nightmare as a psychological phenomenon is an intense dream, I shall discuss what we know of the biology of dreaming and some data suggesting that the biology of the nightmare involves an intense form of the biology of dreaming. Second, I shall examine data on specific neurological, physiological, and chemical situations or manipulations that can produce (or prevent) nightmares, looking for biological factors specific to nightmares, rather than dreams in general.

The Biology of Dreaming

In laboratory studies, nightmares always occur during D-sleep (REM-sleep) as we have discussed; and I have noted that spontaneously occurring nightmares in our laboratory took place in especially long D-periods late during the night: (arousals with nightmare reports came after twenty to thirty-five minutes of D-sleep.) Charles Fisher (1970) pointed out that nightmares arise from D-periods with relatively high levels of autonomic activity. Some reports suggest that these are D-periods with increased eye movements as well. It is known that the later and longer dreams of the night become increasingly intense and emotional and contain more experiences from early in the dreamer's life (Verdone 1965; Foulkes 1966). I have suggested that since a dream involves increasingly intense and emotional content as it continues, most dreams might contain "nightmare material"—fearful material from early childhood—if they continued long enough (Hartmann 1970a). All of this then suggests that the nightmare is an especially long, intense, and vivid dream arising out of a physiologically long and intense dream period. This is not particularly surprising and it leads us to the expectation that the biology of the nightmare may be an especially intense manifestation of the biology of dreaming.

Let us briefly examine our general knowledge of the biology of dreaming since this is obviously part of the biology of the nightmare. A huge amount of information is now available. I will emphasize here some general features that I think may be of special importance since they can be linked to chemical-pharmacological studies that we will discuss later.

It might be worthwhile to recapitulate the material covered in chapter 2 as it refers to dreaming sleep. First, and perhaps most important, there is now overwhelming evidence that most typical dreaming occurs during specifiable periods so different from the remainder of sleep that they are referred to as a separate biological state known as REM-sleep (rapid eye movement–sleep) or D-sleep (dreaming- or desynchronized-sleep). In humans, D-sleep or REM-sleep occurs four or five times every night. Similar periods are found among almost all mammals studied, though their spacing differs from species to species. D-sleep differs from the remainder of sleep called S-sleep (or non-REM sleep) on many different dimensions. In fact, in some ways D-sleep resembles active waking more than it resembles S-sleep. In physiological terms, D-sleep is characterized by arousal and variability in various autonomic measures such as pulse rate, respiratory rate, and blood pressure; also by penile erections in the male. Muscle tone is at its lowest during D-sleep so that in this sense it seems like a very deep sleep, although the EEG resembles that of light sleep. Arousal threshold is quite high: in almost all studies it is higher in D-sleep than its average level during S-sleep. D-sleep has been called paradoxical sleep because of these paradoxical features which make it appear light in some ways and deep in others.

D-sleep and S-sleep are found in all mammals (with one possible exception) and also to some extent in birds and reptiles. D-sleep always occupies a greater proportion of the night in newborn animals and this proportion gradually falls to the adult levels. D-sleep and S-sleep, as well as waking, are states that affect the entire brain and, in fact, the entire body. There is evidence that they are initiated and regulated by a number of centers in the brainstem. A broad, ill-defined region of the brainstem, known as the reticular activating system, contains a number of pathways that activate the cortex during waking. In the lower brainstem are several regions that play an important role in regulating the two sleep states, though the details are not yet certain.

There is considerable evidence that the raphé system, a small region in the brainstem containing large neurons that release serotonin as a neurotransmitter and have widespread terminations in the forebrain and elsewhere, plays a role in initiating or maintaining sleep (Jouvet and Renalt 1966, Koella, Feldstein, and Czicman 1968). There is evidence that these raphé neurons reduce their activity during the course of S-sleep and are almost totally inactive during D-sleep (Trulson and Jacobs 1981).

The locus coeruleus, containing norepinephrine neurons, also plays a part as evidenced in pharmacological studies of animals and humans (Hartmann 1970*b*, Hartmann, Bridwell, and Schildkraut 1971, Hartmann and Schildkraut 1973). I have suggested that the norepinephrine systems (originating in the locus coeruleus) are inactive and possibly are being repaired during D-sleep (Hartmann 1973); recent single-unit recordings confirm that most locus coeruleus neurons are inactive during D-sleep (Hobson, McCarley, and Wyzinski 1975, Foote, Aston-Jones, and Bloom 1980).

There is also evidence that the cholinergic neurons in the frontotegmental fields ("FTG" cells) are especially active during D-sleep or at the beginning of D-periods and that reciprocal interactions between the cholinergic FTG neurons, on the one hand, and locus coeruleus and raphé neurons, on the other, may regulate the onset and offset of D-periods (Hobson, McCarley, and Wyzinski 1975, McCarley and Hobson 1975).

The Biology of the Nightmare

So far, there is less evidence of the role of the equally prominent dopamine-containing neurons; the firing of those neurons does not change dramatically during sleep (Steinfels et al. 1983), though a great deal of indirect evidence suggests a role of dopamine in arousal or wakefulness (Malitz 1972, Sourkes 1972).

These brainstem regions—containing large neurons with widespread terminations in the forebrain—appear to be essential in turning the sleep and waking states on and off, but many other brain regions are involved in mammalian sleep, including the medial forebrain and the thalamus. And the cerebral cortex is involved in all types of sensory imagery and consciousness; thus, its activation is presumably necessary for dreaming as well as waking consciousness.

All of these features are part of the biology of dreaming. I have concentrated on the chemical transmitters in the pathways above because I consider these to be especially important and especially related to the psychological state we know of as dreaming. It is intriguing that we have available exactly the same brain and mind during waking as during the state of dreaming sleep, but it produces two very different types of consciousness: We are conscious during dreaming but in a quite different fashion from waking consciousness. I discuss the differences in these two types of consciousness in detail elsewhere (Hartmann 1976, 1982). We do not appear to turn off one part of the brain and turn on another during dreaming (though there has been some not very conclusive evidence of right cerebral dominance during sleep). Rather, the pattern of activation is different. Most probably the intriguing psychological differences have an underlying biology involving different patterns of activation of the forebrain by the brainstem, producing differences in the release of the biogenic amines or other transmitters in the forebrain. In other words, exactly the substances we have been talking about—norepinephrine, serotonin, acetylcholine—released in the forebrain by the neurons of the brainstem, are at least in part responsible for the differences between waking consciousness and dreaming consciousness. Since the nightmare is an especially intense dream, we might expect that intensifications or alterations of certain kinds in these systems may form at least part of the biology of the nightmare. Specifically, reduction of norepinephrine and serotonin influence, plus increased acetylcholine influence on the forebrain, probably constitutes part of the biology of the nightmare.

Biological Factors Specific to the Nightmare

Now let us approach the biology of the nightmare more specifically and ask what sorts of evidence exist. We have no adequate method of studying the brain biology of someone while the person is having a nightmare, though we can study the accompanying peripheral physiological changes. However, another approach is available: we can examine what biological manipulations or changes have an effect on nightmares, as opposed to dreams in general. We have spoken of the fact that frightening traumatic episodes, including surgical operations, fires, accidents, for example, can induce traumatic nightmares, but these are clearly nonspecific and the effect is probably related to the generalized stress and anxiety rather than any particular sort of body damage. One kind of evidence might involve neurological diseases. Does brain injury of one kind or another particularly generate nightmares or inhibit them? I have come across no reports of nightmares (ordinary REM-nightmares) being produced by a definite type of brain injury.* My impression is that nightmare and dream frequency in general are often reduced after brain injury, but no specific part of the brain can be singled out as being most important in this respect.

OXYGEN DEPRIVATION

However, there are many hints of biological factors in nightmares, most of them involving chemical factors. It may be worth discussing first several older chemical-biological hypotheses that are disproved or at least unsupported by recent data. A number of authors have suggested that nightmares can result from depriving the brain of oxygen (for instance, Radestock, 1879, Cubasch 1877). This view was based in part on the impression of being crushed, suffocated, or unable to breathe that sometimes occurs in nightmares.† This hypothesis was not tested experimentally since a test would have involved

---

* However, night terrors are sometimes symptoms of a temporal lobe epileptic condition, which can occasionally be a result of trauma, and I have mentioned a case in which measles encephalitis led to severe night terrors. Also, we have discussed one case in which post-traumatic nightmares appeared to be auras preceding an epileptic discharge (Forster 1978).

† Of course, for these nineteenth-century authors the term "nightmares" included night terrors.

either the unacceptable procedure of choking a subject or somehow reducing oxygenation, while carefully measuring it, to determine whether nightmares were produced, or the lengthy and only recently perfected procedure of measuring oxygen saturation every night until nightmares occurred and then comparing levels during nightmares with levels at other times during the night.

However, recent data concerning the illness known as sleep apnea demonstrate that a reduced supply of oxygen to the brain does *not* produce nightmares. Sleep apnea is a condition in which respiratory exchange ceases for periods of over ten seconds many times during the night either because of airway obstruction (obstructive sleep apnea) or failure in the neuromuscular signals necessary for respiration (central sleep apnea). Several thousand patients with sleep apnea have had their sleep apnea studied by means of all-night sleep recordings (polysomnography) usually including recordings of blood oxygen saturation. Many of these patients experience unusually low and even dangerously low O_2 saturation during episodes of apnea. This is an "experiment in nature" in which one can examine the effects of episodes of reduced O_2 supply to the brain. The immediate effects are usually brief arousals and awakenings during which breathing recommences. There are many longterm effects including morning headaches, daytime sleepiness, and eventual changes in the heart and lungs. However, nightmares are never or almost never reported by these apneic patients. Thus, demonstrated repeated reductions in O_2 supply (at least in this large group of patients) does not produce nightmares.

The Biology of the Nightmare

GASTROINTESTINAL DISTURBANCE

Another widely held view is the "pepperoni pizza" hypothesis—that eating spicy food produces nightmares. Presumably the mechanism would be that spicy foods induce increased intestinal movement or some other disturbance of gastrointestinal function, that the autonomic afferent nervous system senses these changes or "disturbances" and that these nerves at their central terminations produce unspecified changes that lead to nightmares. This widely held but untested hypothesis is consistent with the most common explanation of nightmares in the nineteenth century: that they were produced by some form of gastric or gastrointestinal disturbance. Ernest Jones (1931) reviews the conclusion of a large number of nineteenth-century physicians and scientists who supported this explanation.

Unfortunately there is no solid evidence for this view. There are no controlled studies, and case reports have not convinced me of the association. A number of people, knowing of my work on sleep and on nightmares, have indeed told me that they have nightmares after eating spicy food. However, the reports are usually something like "I had two nightmares this past month and I'm sure I had pizza on both of those evenings. Of course, I do eat pizza quite a lot." A convincing case report, or at least one worth following up, would be "I've kept a careful log and noted down every time I had a nightmare. I've had twenty the past year and they've all occurred on Wednesday nights. The past year's been a good year for me. There's been nothing disturbing or unusual happening. About the only thing unusual about Wednesdays is that I eat pizza—usually pepperoni pizza—with a group of friends and I never eat it on other days." However, I have never heard a report of this kind.

In examining this possible relationship, I questioned one hundred persons with frequent nightmares (the fifty in chapter 4 and fifty others) in detail about whether they had ever noticed that any foods they ate had any effect in producing or reducing nightmares. (I asked them these questions not only about food but about alcohol, other beverages, nicotine, street drugs, and so on.) In this group there was no association reported between spicy food and nightmares: only one person out of the one hundred said that foods made a difference, and she did not specify spicy foods but said that "eating unusual foods" of any kind sometimes seemed to bring on nightmares, and that not eating at all (skipping the evening meal) also sometimes had this effect.

Thus, in my opinion, there is little evidence for the "pepperoni pizza" hypothesis. However, it is not impossible that some relationship could exist. Since a nightmare involves an awakening from a long D-period (REM-period), it is possible that anything that either increases the incidence of long D-periods or the incidence of awakenings could increase nightmares. Eating spicy foods, or anything that irritates the gastrointestinal system, might well increase awakenings and thus have a slight effect. But this is not a specific enough effect to help us in our search for a biology of the nightmare.

There is one area in which we have additional useful data. There is considerable evidence that pharmacologic causes (medications) can produce an increase or decrease in nightmares; we will consider this correlation in more detail.

DRUG USE AND WITHDRAWAL

There are a number of reports that show various medications can induce nightmares. In a compilation of data pertaining to the side effects of drugs, there are reports that almost every drug known to man has occasionally produced nightmares as a side effect; but of course these data are not based on controlled studies. Hence, it is necessary to be somewhat selective. I will discuss here only what appear to be fairly solid and replicated findings.

First, it is well established that nightmares, bizarre dreams, and intense vivid dreams often occur during a period of withdrawal from depressant medication, including barbiturates, alcohol, and the benzodiazepine tranquilizers (Oswald and Priest 1965, Kales et al. 1969). Since this effect seems to occur with a number of different depressant medications whose mechanisms of action are not precisely known, we cannot attribute it as yet to a specific chemical change; however, it is likely that central nervous system depression by these drugs produces alterations in one or more groups of receptors during drug administration and that withdrawal of the medication produces changes in receptor number or sensitivity that manifest themselves as hyper-reactivity. This hyper-reactivity may have a direct effect on dream content, or may indirectly increase nightmares by producing long D-periods (REM-periods) with frequent awakenings. Indeed, sleep laboratory studies demonstrate that these depressant drugs produce a decrease in D-sleep during administration followed by a great increase during withdrawal (reviewed in Williams and Karacan 1976). Thus, the withdrawal period is characterized by increased D-time and long D-periods; and frequently this period is also characterized by more awakenings during the night. The combination of long D-periods with increased awakenings, as we have seen, is likely to result in long and more vivid dreams and probably nightmares. In any case, this sort of hyper-reactivity is one biological factor that appears to generate nightmares.

More directly relevant to a biology of the nightmare, there are medications that appear specifically to produce nightmares during administration rather than during withdrawal. The most consistent findings involve four groups of medications—reserpine and related drugs, the beta-adrenergic blockers, l-DOPA and related drugs, and centrally active cholinergic drugs. Let us examine these briefly and look for possible underlying mechanisms.

Reserpine, used widely as an antihypertensive, and used in the past as a tranquilizer, is frequently reported to induce intense, vivid dreams and nightmares (Azima 1958, Hartmann and Cravens 1973). Reserpine has been well studied and it apparently produces both its antihypertensive effects and its various mental effects by disturbing and preventing intraneuronal storage of the biogenic amines—dopamine, norepinephrine, and serotonin. The overall effect, by preventing their storage in vesicles, is to reduce the central nervous system levels of all three amines; therefore, the effects found may be due simply to reduced levels of amines in the brain.

The Biology of the Nightmare

However, some have suggested that reserpine effects may be due to sudden release of synthesized amines so that activation of receptors, rather than a reduction in levels of amines, might be involved. We cannot draw more specific conclusions. The data on reserpine and similar drugs tell us that the three biogenic amines are probably involved but do not tell us specifically what effect on which amine could be important. (I believe the effect of reserpine in producing nightmares and vivid dreams—an intensification of normal dreaming—is most likely related to its effects in reducing forebrain norepinephrine and/or serotonin levels; producing a state that can be considered an intensification of the normal reduced norepinephrine and serotonin activity during dreaming.)

A group of drugs increasingly used in recent years is the group of beta adrenergic blockers; the best known of these is propranolol. These drugs block certain effects of the sympathetic amines (norepinephrine and epinephrine) throughout the body including the central nervous system. They are used mainly for their cardiovascular effects. A number of studies have shown that these drugs—especially when first taken—produce an increase of vivid, detailed dreams and nightmares (Greenblatt and Shader 1972, Frishman et al. 1979, Waal-Manning 1979). Since as far as is known these drugs have little effect on serotonin or dopamine, the nightmare effect is most likely to be due to the blocking of norepinephrine, at least the blocking of certain norepinephrine receptors.* Together with the reserpine results, these findings provide some evidence that reductions in brain norepinephrine activity may be involved in producing nightmares.

* Although one cannot rule out the possibility that the effect is produced by some entirely different, as yet unrecognized, action of these drugs.

Perhaps most interesting are results following l-DOPA administration. L-DOPA is a direct precursor of brain dopamine. Administration of l-DOPA has been shown in animal studies to produce rapid increases in brain dopamine, but with little change in brain norepinephrine (Everett and Borcherding 1970). Patients with Parkinsonism have been shown to have deficits in brain dopamine, usually due to damage to certain brain dopamine-containing centers; to a certain extent, the neuromuscular symptoms of Parkinsonism can be reversed by administration of l-DOPA in large doses. These persons who are receiving large doses of l-DOPA, whose brain dopamine is increased not only in the areas (striatum) involved in Parkinsonism, but in the rest of the brain as well, often demonstrate marked psychological changes. Prominent among these are a report first of unusually vivid and detailed dreams followed often by a report of nightmares and then sometime later reports of frank psychotic episodes* (Klawans et al. 1978, Sharf et al. 1978, Moskovitz, Moses, and Klawans 1978). In almost all cases, the nightmares and the psychosis, if present, recede and disappear when l-DOPA administration is stopped. Here, the effect is most likely due to increased brain dopamine, although it is true that administration of l-DOPA also indirectly produces other effects such as reductions in brain serotonin that could be important.

Another group of relevant drugs is that known as cholinesterase inhibitors. Acetylcholine is one of the best studied neurotransmitters of the central and peripheral

---

* This is also intriguing because it lends support to the view we have mentioned several times that nightmares may represent something intermediate between ordinary dreaming and outright psychosis.

nervous systems. It cannot be administered directly, but the most powerful way to increase the activity of acetylcholine is by administering drugs that interfere with its usually very rapid destruction by acetylcholinesterase. These cholinesterase inhibitors have some medical uses—for instance in the treatment of a neuromuscular disease called myasthenia gravis—and they also have been studied as neurotoxins or poisons, and as antidotes for other poisons. These drugs have repeatedly been noted to produce intense, long, dreams and nightmares* (Grob et al. 1947, Holmes and Gaon 1956), which supports the view that increased activity of brain acetylcholine may play a role in the biology of the nightmare.

Thus far, aside from the fact that nightmares are produced when awakenings occur after long periods of D-sleep, we also have some hints as to a possible brain chemistry of the nightmare involving reduced activity of brain norepinephrine and serotonin systems and increased activity of dopamine and acetylcholine systems. To some extent, this parallels the chemistry of D-sleep (REM-sleep), which I have discussed above. Again, the nightmare may chemically simply turn out to be a more intense dream. However, there are differences: the finding of increased nightmares in patients receiving large doses of l-DOPA is especially intriguing in that it suggests that dopamine may be involved in intense dreams and nightmares, although dopamine has not been implicated in the physiological regulation of D-sleep. Its possible involvement is also interesting because there is a great

---

* There is also evidence that these cholinergic drugs cause D-periods to appear sooner (Sitaram et al. 1976) so that again the increase in nightmares could perhaps be related to increase in D-time or lengthening of D-periods.

deal of evidence implicating increased activity of brain dopamine in psychosis, especially in the psychosis of schizophrenia (for instance, the drugs that have anti-psychotic effects almost all turn out to be blockers of brain dopamine) (Carlsson and Linquist 1963, Snyder et al. 1974).

This body of evidence regarding the biological aspects of nightmares is suggestive but it should be studied under conditions of controlled laboratory experiments. This would involve trying to find out, for instance, whether experimentally increased brain dopamine or some of the other suggested changes would actually increase the incidence of nightmares. We have in fact recently performed such a study. Our hypothesis was that nightmares would be induced or their frequency increased by a small dose of l-DOPA and that they would be blocked by dopamine blockers. We used eleven of the people with frequent nightmares (previously discussed) who volunteered to be subjects for this study. Since it is well known that nightmares occur much more rarely in the sleep laboratory than at home, we chose as subjects persons who had reported as having at least one nightmare per week at home. We performed a study in which each subject slept in a sleep laboratory one night per week over a four-week period. Under double blind conditions, they received either two doses of l-DOPA or two doses of placebo each night. The two doses were very small (500 mg) compared to doses used clinically so that there would be minimal safety problems or problems of arousal produced by l-DOPA. L-DOPA was administered at a time such that the maximum effect would coincide with later REM-periods of the night

The Biology of the Nightmare

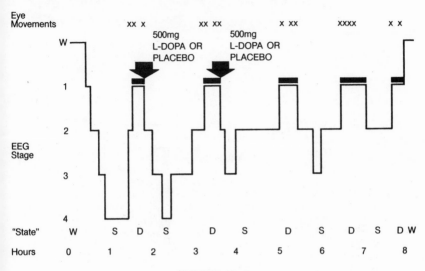

FIGURE 10-1
Times of DOPA Administration (see text)

(figure 10-1). Standard laboratory recordings were made of the sleep pattern and each subject, if he or she did not awaken spontaneously from the later REM-period and provide a report, was awakened when the technician judged a REM-period to be over, and was asked for a dream report (Hartmann et al. 1978). The subject was asked what had been going on when he was awakened, whether what he had experienced was a nightmare or similar to a nightmare and his or her report was recorded. Later, four judges, blind to sleep conditions, independently rated each dream definitely a nightmare, probably a nightmare, or definitely not a nightmare. The judges also rated each dream on a scale of "dreamlikeness," "vividness," "emotionality," and "detail" (Foulkes 1966).

Results are in figures 10-2 and 10-3. As expected, there were not many nightmares in the laboratory, even

263

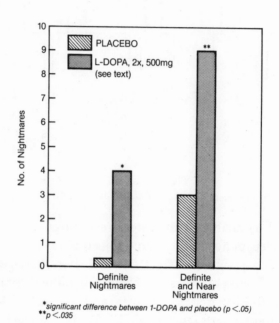

FIGURE 10-2
Nightmares after l-DOPA and after Placebo

among those subjects who were susceptible to them. There were four definite nightmares on which judges and subjects agreed, and eight "probable nightmares" in which there was some disagreement among judges but where the majority felt the dream was a nightmare. In breaking the code, it turned out that all four definite nightmares had occurred under the l-DOPA condition

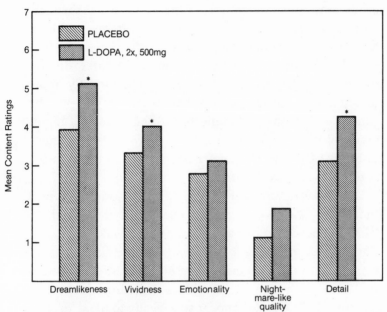

*significant difference between 1-DOPA and placebo (p < .05)

FIGURE 10–3
Characteristics of Dreams after l-DOPA and after Placebo

and that when nightmares as well as probable nightmares were combined, nine had occurred under l-DOPA and three under the placebo conditions.* The data support the notion that a small dose of l-DOPA tended to produce nightmares in these subjects; unfortunately, the numbers are small.

Although there were only a few nightmares, all subjects

* The results reach acceptable significance levels ($p < .05$, one-tailed) by Fisher's exact probability test.

reported many dreams so that data on the characteristics of dreams are considerably more solid since they are based on large numbers (a total of over one hundred fifty dreams). Figure 10–3 presents these results. It is clear that whether or not there were nightmares, dreams under the l-DOPA condition were significantly more dreamlike, vivid, and detailed than under the placebo condition. Four normal subjects with no history of nightmares went through the same study protocol with results, in terms of dream characteristics, similar to those in the nightmare subjects (Hartmann et al. 1980).

Detailed examination of the sleep recording showed that there was no significant change in the length of REM-periods, number of spontaneous awakenings, etc. Thus, we do not believe the results can be accounted for by some sort of nonspecific arousal or alertness produced by l-DOPA, though l-DOPA does sometimes have such an effect. L-DOPA did appear specifically to make dreams more vivid, detailed, and dreamlike as well as increasing the likelihood of having nightmares.

We had hoped also to do the opposite study and to test experimentally whether dopamine blockers would reduce the incidence of nightmares. However, in order to make this practicable, we would have had to study subjects with a high incidence of laboratory nightmares. Our results from the above study (under placebo conditions, twenty-two nights for eleven "frequent nightmare" subjects produced no definite nightmares and only three probable nightmares) alerted us to the difficulty or impossibility of the task.

There is much less information as to which drugs decrease the frequency of nightmares or make them less intense, at least as it applies to typical civilian (non-traumatic) nightmares. Our frequent nightmare sufferers had more severe nightmares when they were becoming psychotic or were under severe stress. In fact, we have noted that nightmares were frequent just before (or sometimes just after) a psychotic episode. Thus, it might be expected that dopamine blockers, which act as anti-psychotics, would decrease the incidence of nightmares. And such indeed was the case in our group of frequent nightmare sufferers, as mentioned; I do not have data from a controlled study, but I obtained many reports from these subjects and from patients indicating that dopamine blockers (antipsychotics) reduced the incidence of nightmares.*

On the other hand, dopamine blockers frequently have been tried in the treatment of post-traumatic stress disorder nightmares and usually without success. This is consistent with our view that those nightmares represent a different phenomenon than ordinary nightmares biologically as well as psychologically.

There may well be other drugs that reduce the frequency of nightmares, but this effect will often be missed, since only persons who have nightmares very frequently would make the connection. (Someone who experiences one nightmare per year can hardly be expected to notice a reduction to no nightmares). The subjects I studied with frequent nightmares did note a reduction in nightmares when using alcohol, followed by an increase when alcohol use was discontinued. One who had taken

* The effect of antipsychotics in reducing nightmares might of course be nonspecific; when psychotic anxiety is reduced, nightmares are reduced—this need not necessarily be related to an involvement of dopamine in the biology of nightmares.

barbiturates likewise reported a decrease in nightmares followed by a great increase upon withdrawal. And there is one study in which lithium was found to decrease nightmares as well as produce clinical improvement among certain adolescent mental patients with mixed diagnoses (Popper 1982). Lithium, generally used in the treatment of bipolar affective disorders (manic-depressive illness) has a number of actions on the brain (including interaction with the amine system we have discussed), but its true mechanism of action is not known. Overall, these data about nightmare-reducing drugs give us little specific information, with the possible exception of the effect of dopamine blockers.

Conclusions and Implications

What can we make of all this in approaching a biology of the nightmare? First, the nightmare is a long and intense dream and its biology is probably an intense form of the biology of dreaming, with perhaps additional factors producing the nightmarelike features. Thus, nightmares, like other dreams, have an underlying biology involving in part the activation of the forebrain by certain brainstem centers, and specifically an increased activity of acetylcholine in the forebrain with a decrease in activity of norepinephrine and serotonin. The addition of dopaminergic activity might be an additional specific factor that accounts for the difference between nightmares and other dreams: Nightmares may involve the same factors (perhaps to a greater degree) as those involved in dreams, but with the addition of dopaminergic activity at the forebrain. Persons who have frequent nightmares would be persons who have a tendency to greater or more rapid activation of these dopamine systems or who are more sensitive to such activation. It is possible that this same characteristic if present from birth might make these people more vulnerable to psychosis.

In other words, the biology producing a nightmare may involve an altered balance of the four neurotransmitters discussed such that a tendency towards nightmares is produced by relatively *increased* acetylcholine and dopamine or relatively *decreased* norepinephrine and serotonin released in and acting on the forebrain. This implies that a balance among these transmitters or modulators rather than the action of a single substance is involved.

From this model one could predict that the incidence of nightmares would be either high or low in certain patients with illnesses characterized by alterations in the same brain amine systems. (The predictions must be tentative since we do not know whether the postulated alterations in amine systems in these illnesses occur everywhere in the brain or only in certain regions and whether the latter would include the regions where effects on nightmares might be produced.) For instance, narcolepsy is thought to be produced by a brainstem abnormality involving either a decrease in norepinephrine activity or an increase in acetylcholine activity.* In either

* The decrease in norepinephrine activity is postulated because the drugs that specifically and dramatically improve narcolepsy are adrenergic (norepinephrine increasing) drugs. The acetylcholine postulate depends on actual findings of increased acetylcholine receptors in the brains of narcoleptic dogs (Dement 1983).

case—if either or both of these hypotheses are true—
our biological model would predict that narcoleptic patients would have a large number of vivid dreams and
nightmares; and such appears to be the case (Broughton
1982).

Severely depressed patients have an increased sensitivity to acetylcholine, according to recent studies (Gillin
et al. 1978). And the fact that antidepressant drugs
increase the availability of norepinephrine and/or serotonin suggests that some form of deficit of these two
substances may be involved in depression. From both of
these lines of evidence, our model predicts that severely
depressed patients should have an increase of nightmares.
And again, this appears to be the case on the basis of
many clinical reports.

Schizophrenic patients are believed to have an increased dopamine activity or sensitivity somewhere in
the brain and on this basis the model would predict an
increase of nightmares, which has been found to be true
(see chapter 5).

Finally, chronic Parkinsonian patients have a clear
decrease in dopamine activity, at least in some portions
of the brain, and thus one might expect that Parkinsonian
patients (as long as they are untreated) would have
unusually few nightmares. I know of no specific studies
on this point but when I asked neurologists who have
treated many such patients they often reported that
nightmares occurred upon treatment using l-DOPA or
similar drugs; they could not recall any nightmares in
chronic, untreated Parkinsonian patients.

This model predicts that any illness, any new drug, or
other condition that alters chemical balance by increasing

forebrain dopamine or acetylcholine, or decreasing forebrain norepinephrine or serotonin activity, would tend to produce nightmares, while a condition that produces the opposite effect would reduce them.

Further, the possibility exists that an altered pattern in the enzymes involved in the synthesis, release, and metabolism of these transmitters could represent a biological difference between those with a tendency to frequent nightmares and those who do not have this tendency and that it could therefore form part of the biology underlying frequent nightmares, sensitivity, and vulnerability to schizophrenia.

The biological findings discussed here are of course preliminary and theorizing must be tentative. However, our investigations of nightmares may indicate one way progress can be made in understanding various psychological phenomena. We began by identifying the psychological phenomenon of a nightmare. To do so we separated it from similar phenomena, then characterized it psychologically as precisely as possible. We then examined questions of when and in what persons it occurred—the personality of the nightmare sufferer—and I believe we have delineated a fairly specific personality type. This then led us to formulate psychological personality characteristics in terms of boundaries in the mind; we can now continue the exploration of the usefulness of this concept in many conditions aside from nightmares and seek a biology underlying this psychological construct.

The biology of nightmares and dreams may turn out to be our deepest level of knowledge, a level our expeditions are only beginning to approach and explore.

We can be most confident of the upper layers: we have solid data, reviewed in this volume, concerning the descriptive features of the nightmare, and the circumstances under which nightmares occur. And we have summarized a great deal of information about who has nightmares and when. We have delineated the possible relationship of frequent nightmares to creativity and to vulnerability to schizophrenia. This relationship contrasts with the very different situations we have explored in night terror sufferers and in persons with post-traumatic nightmares. This knowledge will help in the fuller understanding and treatment of all three groups. Finally, a consideration of biological factors involved in nightmares has brought us back once more to boundaries in the mind, a concept useful to us in succinctly defining the nightmare sufferer and a concept which may turn out to be important in exploring the biology underlying our mental functioning.

REFERENCES

Adler, G., and Buie, D. 1979. Aloneness and borderline psychopathology; the possible relevance of childhood development issues. *International Journal of Psychoanalysis* 60: 83–96.

Azima, J. 1958. The possible dream inducing capacity of the whole root of rauwolfia serpentina. *Canadian Psychiatric Association Journal* 3: 47–51.

Belicky, D., and Belicky, K. 1982. Nightmares in a university population. *Sleep Research* 11: 116.

Belicky, D., and Belicky, K. 1983. Personal communication to the author.

Benjamin, J. D. 1961. Some developmental observations relating to the theory of anxiety. *Journal of the American Psychoanalytic Association* 9: 652–668.

Bergman, P., and Escalona, S. 1949. Unusual sensitivities in very young children. *Psychoanalytic Study of the Child* 3/4: 333–352.

Beutler, L. E., Thornby, J. I., and Karacan, I. 1978. Psychological variables in the diagnosis of insomnia. In Williams, R. L., and Karacan, I., eds., *Sleep Disorders: Diagnosis and Treatment,* New York: John Wiley & Sons.

Bixler, E. O., Kales, A., and Soldatos, C. R. 1979b. Sleep disorders encountered in medical practice. *Behavioral Medicine* November: 1–6.

Bixler, E. O., Kales, A., Soldatos, C. R., Kales, J. D., and Healey, S. 1979a. Prevalence of sleep disorders in the Los Angeles metropolitan area. *American Journal of Psychiatry* 136: 1257–62.

Blacher, R. S. 1975. On awakening paralyzed during surgery: A syndrome of traumatic neurosis. *Journal of the American Medical Association* 234: 67–68.

Blatt, S., and Ritzler, B. 1974. Thought disorder and boundary disturbance in psychosis. *Journal of Consulting and Clinical Psychology* 42: 370–81.

Blatt, S. J., Brenneis, C. B., Schimek, J. G., and Glick, M. 1976. The normal developmental and psychopathological impairment of the concept of the object on the Rorschach. *Journal of Abnormal Psychology* 85: 304–73.

Bleuler, E. 1950. *Dementia Praecox or the Group of Schizophrenics.* New York: International Universities Press.

273

References

Blitz, R. 1983. Nightmares and the self. Unpublished doctoral dissertation, Boston University.

Boller, F., Wright, D. G., Cavalieri, R., and Mitsumoto, H. 1975. Paroxysmal nightmares: Sequel of a stroke responsive to diphenylhydantoin. *Neurology* (Minneap) 25: 1026–28.

Bowers, M. B., Jr. 1974. *Retreat from Sanity.* New York: Human Sciences Press.

Broughton, R. 1968. Sleep disorders: Disorders of arousal? *Science* 159: 1070–78.

Broughton, R. J. 1982. Neurology and dreaming. *Psychiatric Journal of the University of Ottawa* 7: 101–10.

Cameron, N., and Margaret, A. 1951. *Behavior Pathology.* Boston: Houghton Mifflin.

Carlsson, A., and Lindquist, M. 1963. Effect of chlorpromazine or haloperidol on formation of 3-methoxytyramine and normetanephrine in mouse brain. *Acta pharmacologica* (Kbh) 20: 140–44.

Chapman, L. J. 1961. A reinterpretation of some pathological disturbances in conceptual breadth. *Journal of Abnormal Social Psychology* 62: 514–19.

Cohn, J., Holzer, K. I. M., Koch, L., and Severin, B. 1980. Children and torture: An investigation of Chilean immigrant children in Denmark. *Danish Medical Bulletin* 27: 238.

Coleridge, S. (1803) 1912. The pains of sleep. In Coleridge, E., ed., *The Poems of Samuel Taylor Coleridge.* London: Oxford University Press.

Coursey, R. D. 1975. Personality measures and evoked responses in chronic insomniacs. *Journal of Abnormal Psychology* 84: 239–49.

Cox, G. W. 1870. *The Mythology of the Aryan Nations,* vol. 2, pp. 222, 253. London: Longmans and Green.

Cubasch, D. 1877. *Der Alp,* n.p., cited by Jones 1931.

Dahlstrom, W. G., Schlager, W. G., and Dahlstrom, L. E. 1960a. *An MMPI Handbook, Volume I: Clinical Interpretation.* Minneapolis: University of Minnesota Press.

Dahlstrom, W. G., Schlager, W. G., and Dahlstrom, L. E. 1960b. *An MMPI Handbook, Volume II: Research Applications.* Minneapolis: University of Minnesota Press.

Dement, W. 1983. Personal communication to the author. Based on as yet unpublished work by Mefford, I. N., Baker, T. L., Boehme, R., Barchas, J. D., Dement, W. C., and others.

Descarries, L., Watkins, K., and Lapierre Y. 1977. Noradrenergic axon terminals in the cerebral cortex of rat. III. Topometric ultrastructural analysis. *Brain Research* 133: 197–222.

Detre, T. P., and Jarecki, H. G. 1971. *Modern Psychiatric Treatment.* Philadelphia: J. B. Lippincott.

Diagnostic and Statistical Manual of Mental Disorders (Third Edition) 1980. Washington D.C.: The American Psychiatric Association.

References

Dreiser, T. 1983. *An Amateur Laborer.* Philadelphia: University of Pennsylvania Press.

Erlenmeyer-Kimling, L. 1975. "A prospective study of children at risk for schizophrenia: Methodological considerations and some preliminary findings." In Wirt, R. D., Winokur, G., and Roff, M., eds., *Life History Research in Psychopathology,* vol. 4, pp. 23–46. Minneapolis: The University of Minnesota Press.

Everett, G. M., and Borcherding, J. W. 1970. L-DOPA: Effect on concentrations of dopamine, norepinephrine and serotonin in brains of mice. *Science* 168: 849–50.

Fairbairn, W. R. D. 1952. The war neuroses: Their nature and significance. *Psychoanalytic Studies of the Personality,* pp. 256–80. Boston: Rutledge, Kegan, and Paul.

Federn, P. 1952*a*. The ego as subject and object in narcissism. In *Ego Psychology and the Psychoses,* pp. 283–322. New York: Basic Books.

Federn, P. 1952*b*. On the distinction between healthy and pathological narcissism. In *Ego Psychology and the Psychoses,* pp. 323–64. New York: Basic Books.

Feldman, M. J., and Hersen, M. 1967. Attitudes toward death in nightmare subjects. *Journal of Abnormal Psychology* 72: 421–25.

Fisher, C., Byrne, J. V., and Edwards, A. 1968. NREM and REM nightmares. *Psychophysiology* 5: 221–22.

Fisher, C., Byrne, J. V., Edwards, A., and Kahn, E. 1970. A psychophysiological study of nightmares. *Journal of the American Psychoanalytical Association* 18: 747–82.

Fisher, C., Kahn, E., Edwards, A., and Davis, D. M. 1973*a*. A psychophysiological study of nightmares and night terrors. The suppression of stage 4 night terrors with diazepam. *Archives of General Psychiatry* 28: 252–59.

Fisher, C., Kahn, E., Edwards, A., and Davis, D. M. 1973*b*. A psychophysiological study of nightmares and night terrors. I. Physiological aspects of the stage 4 night terror. *The Journal of Nervous and Mental Disease* 157: 75–97.

Fisher, C., Kahn, E., Edwards, A., Davis, D. M., and Fine, J. 1974. A psychophysiological study of nightmares and night terrors. III. Mental content and recall of stage 4 night terrors. *The Journal of Nervous and Mental Disease* 15: 174–89.

Fisher, S., and Cleveland, S. E. 1958. *Body Image and Personality.* Princeton, N.J.: Van Nostrand.

Foote, S. L., Aston-Jones, G., and Bloom, F. E.; 1980. Locus coeruleus neuronal impulse activity in awake rats and monkeys is a function of sensory stimulation and arousal. *Proceedings of the National Academy of Science USA,* 77: 3033–3037.

Forster, F. M. 1978. Comparison of auras and triggering factors in epilepsy. *Pavlovian Journal of Biological Science* 13: 206–10.

References

Foulkes, D. 1966. *The Psychology of Sleep*. New York: Scribner.

Fox, R. 1974. Narcissistic rage and the problem of combat aggression. *Archives of General Psychiatry* 31: 807–11.

French, T. M., and Fromm, E. 1964. *Dream Interpretation*. New York: Basic Books.

Freud, S. 1900. *Interpretation of Dreams*. Leipzig and Vienna: Franz Deutilie.

Freud, S. 1920. *Beyond the Pleasure Principle*. Leipzig, Vienna, and Zurich: Internationales psychoanalytischer Verlag.

Freud, S. 1939. *New Introductory Lectures to Psychoanalysis*. In *Standard Edition of the Complete Psychological Works of Sigmund Freud*, vol. 22, p. 80. London: Hogarth Press.

Freud, S. 1955. *Beyond the Pleasure Principle*. London: Hogarth Press and the Institute of Psycho-Analysis.

Frishman, W., Silverman, R., Strom, J., Elkayam, U., and Sonnenblick, E. 1979. Clinical pharmacology of the new beta-adrenergic blocking drugs. Part 4. Adverse effects. Choosing a beta-adreno-receptor blocker. *American Heart Journal* 98: 256–62.

Gastaut, H., and Broughton, R. 1964. A clinical and polygraphic study of episodic phenomena during sleep. *Recent Advances in Biological Psychiatry* 7: 197–221.

Geer, J. H. 1965. The development of a scale to measure fear. *Behavior Research Therapy* 3: 45–53.

Gide, A. 1948. In O'Brien, J., Trans., *Journals of André Gide*. December 20, 1924, p. 365. New York: Knopf.

Gillin, J. C., Wyatt, R. J., Fram, D., and Snyder, F. 1978. The relationship between changes in REM sleep and clinical improvement in depressed patients treated with amitriptyline. *Psychopharmacology* (Berlin) 59: 267–72.

Greenberg, R. 1981. Personal communication to the author.

Greenberg, R., Pearlman, C. A., and Gampel, D. 1972. War neuroses and the adaptive function of REM sleep. *British Journal of Medical Psychology* 45: 27.

Greenblatt, D. J., and Shader, R. I. 1972. On the psychopharmacology of beta adrenergic blockade. *Current Therapy Research* 14: 615–25.

Grimm, J. 1876. *Deutsche Mythologie*. Berlin: F. Dummler.

Grinker, R., and Spiegel, J. 1945. *War Neurosis*. New York: McGraw Hill.

Grob, D., Harvey, A., Langworthy, O., and Lilienthal, J. 1947. The administration of di-isopropyl fluorophosphate (DFP) to man. *Bulletin of Johns Hopkins Hospital* 81: 257–66.

Hammerton, J., ed. 1903. *Stevensonia*. London: Richards.

Hartmann, E. 1967. *The Biology of Dreaming*. Springfield, Ill.: Charles C Thomas.

Hartmann, E. 1970a. A note on the nightmare. In Hartmann, E., ed., *Sleep and Dreaming*. pp. 192–97. Boston: Little, Brown.

References

Hartmann, E. 1970b. The D-state and norepinephrine-dependent systems. In Hartmann, E., ed., *Sleep and Dreaming,* pp. 308–28. Boston: Little, Brown.

Hartmann, E. 1973. *The Functions of Sleep.* New Haven: Yale University Press.

Hartmann, E. 1976. The dream as a "royal road" to the biology of the mental apparatus (Discussion of: The changing use of dreams in psychoanalytic practice). *International Journal of Psychoanalysis,* 57: 331–34.

Hartmann, E. 1982. From the biology of dreaming to the biology of the mind. *The Psychoanalytic Study of the Child* 37: 303–35.

Hartmann, E., Baekeland, F., Zwilling, G., and Hoy, P. 1971. Sleep need: How much sleep and what kind? *American Journal of Psychiatry* 127: 1001–8.

Hartmann, E., Baekeland, F., and Zwilling, G. 1972. Psychological differences between long and short sleepers. *Archives of General Psychiatry* 26: 463–68.

Hartmann, E., Bridwell, T. J., and Schildkraut, J. J. 1971. Alpha-methylpara-tyrosine and sleep in the rat. *Psychopharmacologia* 21: 157–64.

Hartmann, E., and Cravens, J. 1973. The effects of long-term administration of psychotropic drugs on human sleep: II. The effects of reserpine. *Psychopharmacologia* 33: 169–84.

Hartmann, E., Falke, R., Russ, D., Oldfield, M., Sivan, I., and van der Kolk, B. 1981a. Who has nightmares? Persons with lifelong nightmares compared with vivid dreamers and non-vivid dreamers. *Sleep Research* 10: 171.

Hartmann, E., Greenwald, D., and Brune, P. 1982. Night terrors-sleep walking: Personality characteristics. *Sleep Research* 11: 121.

Hartmann, E., and Greenwald, D. 1984. Tryptophan and human sleep: An analysis of 43 studies. In Schlossberger, H. G., Kochen, W., Linden B., Steinhart, H., eds, *Progress in Tryptophan and Serotonin Research.* pp. 297–304. Berlin and N.Y.: Walter de Gruyter & Co.

Hartmann, E., Milofsky, E., Vaillant, G., Oldfield, M., Falke, R., and Ducey, C. 1984a. Vulnerability to schizophrenia: Prediction of adult schizophrenia using childhood information. *Archives of General Psychiatry,* in press.

Hartmann, E., Mitchell, W., Brune, P., and Greenwald, D. 1984b. Childhood nightmares but not childhood insomnia may predict adult psychopathology. Presented to the Sleep Research Society, Toronto, June 1984. *Sleep Research,* 13: 117.

Hartmann, E., Milofsky, E., Vaillant, G., Oldfield, M., Falke, R., Ducey, C., Brune, P., Greenwald, D., and Mitchell, W. 1984c. Childhood predictors of adult schizophrenia. Presented to the American Psychiatric Association (new research), May 1984.

Hartmann, E., and Russ, D. 1979. Frequent nightmares and the vulnerability to schizophrenia: The personality of the nightmare sufferer. *Psychopharmacology Bulletin* 15: 11–12.

Hartmann, E., Russ, D., Oldfield, M., Falke, R., and Skoff, B. 1980. Dream content: Effects of l-DOPA. *Sleep Research* 9: 153.

References

Hartmann, E., Russ, D., van der Kolk, B., Falke, R., and Oldfield, M. 1981b. A preliminary study of the personality of the nightmare sufferer: Relationship to schizophrenia and creativity? *American Journal of Psychiatry* 138: 794–97.

Hartmann, E., and Schildkraut, J. J. 1973. Desynchronized sleep and MHPG excretion: An inverse correlation. *Brain Research* 61: 412–16.

Hartmann, E., Sivan, I., Cooper, S., and Treger, F., 1984d. The personality of lifelong nightmare sufferers: Projective test results. *Sleep Research* 13: 118.

Hartmann, E., Skoff, B., Russ, D., and Oldfield, M. 1978. The biochemistry of the nightmare: Possible involvement of dopamine. *Sleep Research* 7: 186.

Hermann, K., and Thygesen, P. 1954. *K–Z Syndromet*. Copenhagen: n.p.

Hersen, M. 1972. Nightmare behavior: A review. *Psychological Bulletin* 78: 37–48.

Hertzman, J. 1948. High school mental hygiene survey. *American Journal of Orthopsychiatry* 18: 238–56.

Hobson, J. A., McCarley, R. W., and Wyzinski, P. W. 1975. Sleep cycle oscillation: Reciprocal discharge by two brainstem neuronal groups. *Science* 189: 55–58.

Hogben, G. L., and Cornfield, R. B. 1981. Treatment of traumatic war neurosis with phenelzine. *Archives of General Psychiatry* 38: 440–45.

Holmes, J. H., and Gaon, M. D. 1956. Observations on acute and multiple exposure to anticholinesterase agents. *Transactions of the American Clinical Climatological Association* 68: 86–101.

Holzman, P., Proctor, L. R., and Hughes, D. W. 1973. Eye tracking patterns in schizophrenia. *Science* 181: 179–81.

Holzman, P., Kringlen, E., Levy, D., Haberman, S., Proctor, L. R., and Yasillo, N. J. 1977. Abnormal pursuit eye movements in schizophrenia: Evidence for a genetic marker. *Archives of General Psychiatry* 34: 802–5.

Ježower, I. 1928. *Das Buch der Träume*. Berlin: Ernst Rowohlt Verlag.

Johnston, M. H., and Holzman, P. 1979. *Assessing Schizophrenic Thinking*. San Francisco: Jossey-Bass.

Jones, E. 1931. *On the Nightmare*. London: Hogarth Press.

Jortner, S. 1966. An investigation of certain cognitive aspects of schizophrenia. *Journal of Projective Techniques* 30: 554–68.

Jouvet, M., and Renalt, J. 1966. Insomnie persistante après lesions des noyaux du raphé chez le chat. *Comptes Rendues de la Societé de Biologie* 160: 1461–65.

Kales, A., Caldwell, A. B., Preston, T. A., Healey, S., and Kales, J. D. 1976. Personality patterns in insomnia. *Archives of General Psychiatry* 33: 1128–34.

Kales, A., and Jacobson, A. 1968. Clinical and electrophysiological studies of somnambulism. In Gastaut, H., Lugaresi, W., Berti-Ceroni, G., and Coccagna, G., eds., *The Abnormalities of Sleep in Man*. Bologna: Aulo Gaggi.

Kales, A., Malmstrom, E. J., Kee, H. K., Kales, J. D., Tan, T. L., Stadel, D., and Hoedemaker, F. S. 1969. Effects of hypnotics on sleep patterns,

References

dreaming and mood state: Laboratory and home studies. *Biological Psychiatry* 1: 235–41.

Kales, A., Soldatos, C. R., Caldwell, A. B., Charney, D. S., Kales, J. D., Markel, D., and Cadieux, R. 1980. Nightmares: Clinical characteristics and personality patterns. *American Journal of Psychiatry* 137: 1197–201.

Kales, J. D., Cadieux, R. J., Soldatos, C. R., and Kales, A. 1982. Psychotherapy with night-terror patients. *American Journal of Psychotherapy* 36: 399–407.

Kales, J. D., Kales, A., Soldatos, C. R., Caldwell, A. B., Charney, D. S., and Martin, E. D. 1980. Night terrors: Clinical characteristics and personality patterns. *Archives of General Psychiatry* 37: 1413.

Kardiner, A., and Spiegel, H. 1947. *War Stress and Neurotic Illness.* New York: Paul B. Hober.

Katan, M. 1962. A causerie on Henry James' "The Turn of the Screw." *Psychoanalytic Study of the Child* 17: 473–93.

Kestenbaum, C. 1982. Personal communication to the author.

Kety, S. S., Rosenthal, D., Wender, P. H., and Schulsinger, F. 1968. The types and prevalence of mental illness in the biological and adoptive families of adopted schizophrenics. In Rosenthal, D., and Kety, S. S., eds., *The Transmission of Schizophrenia.* Oxford: Pergamon Press.

Kety, S. S., Rosenthal, D., Wender, P. H., Schulsinger, F., and Jacobson, B. 1975. Mental illness in the biological and adoptive families of adopted individuals who have become schizophrenic: A preliminary report based on psychiatric interviews. In Fieve, R. R., Rosenthal, D., and Brill, H., eds., *Genetic Research in Psychiatry.* Baltimore: Johns Hopkins University Press.

Klawans, H. L., Moskovitz, C., Lupton, M., and Sharf, B. 1978. Induction of dreams by levodopa. *Harefuah* 45: 57–59.

Koella, W. P., Feldstein, A., and Czicman, J. 1968. The effect of parachlorphenylalamine on the sleep of cats. *Electroencephalography and Clinical Neurophysiology* 25: 481.

Koestler, A. 1964. *The Act of Creation.* New York: Dell.

Kohut, H. 1971. *The Analysis of the Self.* New York: International Universities Press.

Kohut, H. 1977. *The Restoration of the Self.* New York: International Universities Press.

Kris, E. 1952. *Psychoanalytic Explorations in Art.* New York: International Universities Press.

Landis, B. 1970. Ego boundaries. *Psychological Issues* 6 (Monograph 24): 1–177.

Lange-Eichbaum, W. 1928. *Genie, Irrsinn und Ruhm.* Munich: Ernst Reinhardt.

Lanyon, R. I. 1968. *A Handbook of MMPI Group Profiles.* Minneapolis: University of Minnesota Press.

Lavie, P. 1982. Personal communication to the author.

Lewin, K. 1936. *Principles of Topological Psychology.* New York: McGraw-Hill.

Lidz, T. 1946. Nightmares and the combat neuroses. *Psychiatry* 9: 37–49.

279

MacFarlane, J., Allen, L., and Honzik, M. 1954. A developmental study of the behavior problems of normal children between twenty-one months and fourteen years. Berkeley: University of California Press.

Mack, J. E. 1970. *Nightmares and Human Conflict.* Boston: Little, Brown.

Malitz, S., ed. 1972. *L-DOPA and Behavior.* New York: Raven Press.

McCarley, R., and Hobson, J. A. 1975. Neuronal excitability modulation over the sleep cycle: A structural and mathematical model. *Science* 189: 58.

Moses, R. 1978. Adult psychic trauma: The question of early predisposition and some detailed mechanisms. *International Journal of Psychoanalysis* 59: 353–63.

Moskovitz, C., Moses, H., and Klawans, H. 1978. Levodopa-induced psychosis: A kindling phenomenon. *American Journal of Psychiatry* 135: 669–75.

Myers, G. J., Colgan, M. T., and VanDyke, D. H. 1977. Lightning-strike disaster among children. *Journal of the American Medical Association* 238: 1045–46.

Oswald, L., and Priest, R. 1965. Five weeks to escape the sleeping pill habit. *British Medical Journal* 2: 1093.

Penfield, W., and Jasper, H. H. 1954. *Epilepsy and the Functional Anatomy of the Human Brain.* Boston: Little, Brown.

Perlmutter, E. 1979. Personal communication to the author, concerning poet Louise Bogan.

Petersen, A. C. 1981. A developmental study of adolescent mental health. NIMH grant, no. MH30252/38142. (Studies by Offer and Peterson 1975–82).

Pinches, T. G. 1906. *The Religion of Babylonia and Assyria,* p. 108. London: A. Constable & Co., Ltd.

Plath, S. 1971. *The Bell Jar.* New York: Harper & Row.

Popper, C. 1982. The use of lithium in children and adolescents. Syllabus and Scientific Proceedings, American Psychiatric Association, p. 153.

Radestock, P. 1879. *Schlaf und Traum,* pp. 126, 127. N.p., cited in Jones 1931.

Rasmussen, O. V., and Lunde, I. 1980. Evaluation of investigation of 200 torture victims. *Danish Medical Bulletin* 27: 241–43.

Reader, T. A., Ferron, A., Descarries, L., and Jasper, H. H. 1979. Modulatory role for biogenic amines in the cerebral cortex. Microiontophoretic studies. *Brain Research* 160: 217–29.

Reich, W. 1933. *Charakter Analyse.* Vienna: Sexpol Verlag.

Roskoff, G. 1869. *Geschichte des Teufels,* vol. 1, p. 146, n.p. Leipzig: Broch.

Rothenberg, A. 1971. The process of Janusian thinking in creativity. *Archives of General Psychiatry* 24: 195–205.

Rothenberg, A. 1981. Personal communication to the author.

Rotter, J. 1966. Generalized expectancies for internal vs. external control of reinforcement. *Psychological Monographs: General and Applied* 80: 1–28.

Sacks, O. W. 1974. *Awakenings.* Garden City, N.Y.: Doubleday.

Schoen, L. S., Kramer, M., and Kinney, L. 1983. Arousal patterns in NREM

References

dream-disturbed veterans. Presented to the Annual Meeting of the Sleep
Research Society, Bologna, July 1983.

Schlosberg, A., and Benjamin, M. 1978. Sleep patterns in three acute combat
fatigue cases. *Journal of Clinical Psychiatry* 39: 546–49.

Searles, H. F. 1960. *The Nonhuman Environment*. New York: International
Universities Press.

Shakow, D. 1963. Psychological deficit in schizophrenia. *Behavioral Science* 8:
275–305.

Sharf, B., Moskovitz, C., Lupton, M., and Klawans, H. 1978. Dream phenomena
induced by chronic levodopa therapy. *Journal of Neural Transmission* 43:
143–151.

Shelley, M. W. 1831. *Frankenstein* 1969. Ed. Joseph, M. K. Oxford: Oxford
University Press.

Sitaram, N., Wyatt, R. J., Dawson, S., and Gillin, J. C. 1976. REM sleep
induction by physostigmine infusion during sleep in normal volunteers.
Science 191: 1281–83.

Sivan, I. Boundary scoring system for the Rorschach test (unpublished).

Skelton, G. 1982. *Richard and Cosima Wagner: Biography of a Marriage*. Boston:
Houghton Mifflin.

Smitson, S. A., Walsh, J. K., and Kramer, M. 1981. MMPI Profiles: Lack of
discrimination among sleep pathologies. *Sleep Research* 10: 177.

Snyder, S. H., Banerjee, S. P., Yamamura, H. J., and Greenberg, D. 1974.
Drugs, neurotransmitters, and schizophrenia. *Science* 184: 1243–53.

Sourkes, T. L. 1972. Central actions of dopa and dopamine. *Revue Canadienne
Biologie*. 31: 153–68.

Spinweber, C., and Hartmann, E. 1977. Long and short sleepers: MHPG and
17-hydroxy-corticosteroid excretion. *Sleep Research* 6: 65.

Spinweber, C. L., Ursin, R., Hilbert, R. P., and Hilderbrand, R. L. 1983. L-
Tryptophan: Effects on daytime sleep latency and the waking EEG. *Electroencephalography and Clinical Neurophysiology* 55: 652–61.

Steinfels, G. F., Heym, J., Strecker, R. E., and Jacobs, B. L. 1983. Behavioral
correlates of dopaminergic unit activity in freely moving cats. *Brain Research*
258: 217–28.

Stoddard, F. 1982. Body image development in the burned child. *Journal of
American Academy of Child Psychiatry* 21: 502–7.

Stone, H. S. 1956. The TAT Aggressive Content Scale. *Journal of Projective
Techniques* 20: 445–52.

Stone, M. H. 1979. Dreams of fragmentation and of the death of the dreamer:
A manifestation of vulnerability to psychosis. *Psychopharmacology Bulletin*
15: 12–14.

Sullivan, H. S. 1962. *Schizophrenia as a Human Process*. New York: Norton.

Terr, L. C. 1981. Psychic trauma in children: Observations following the
Chowchilla schoolbus kidnapping. *American Journal of Psychiatry* 138: 14–
19.

References

Terr, L. C. 1983. Chowchilla revisited: The effects of psychic trauma four years after a schoolbus kidnapping. *American Journal of Psychiatry* 140: 1543–50.

Trulson, M. E., and Jacobs, B. L. 1981. Activity of serotonin-containing neurons in freely moving cats. In Jacobs, B. L. and Gelperin, A., eds., *Serotonin Neurotransmission and Behavior*, pp. 339–65. Cambridge, Mass.: MIT Press.

van der Kolk, B. A. 1983. Personal communication to the author.

van der Kolk, B. A., Adinolfi, S., Blitz, R., Hartmann, E., and Burr, W. A. 1981. Life long versus traumatic nightmares. *Sleep Research* 10: 178.

van der Kolk, B. A., Blitz, R., Burr, W., Sherry, S., and Hartmann, E. 1984. Clinical characteristics of traumatic and lifelong nightmare sufferers. *American Journal of Psychiatry* 141: 187–190.

van der Kolk, B. A., and Goldberg, H. L. 1983. Aftercare of schizophrenic patients: Psychopharmacology and consistency of therapists. *Hospital and Community Psychiatry* 4: 340–43.

van der Kolk, B. A., Hartmann, E., Burr, A., and Blitz, R. 1980. A survey of nightmare frequencies in a veterans outpatient clinic. *Sleep Research* 9: 229.

van der Kolk, B. A., Sherry, S., Blitz, R., Burr, W., and Hartmann, E. 1982. Rorschach responses in men with lifelong and traumatic nightmares. *Sleep Research* 11: 131.

Verdone, P. 1965. Temporal reference of manifest dream content. *Perceptual Motor Skills* 20: 1253–68.

Waal-Manning, H. J. 1979. Atenolol and three nonselective beta-blockers in hypertension. *Clinical Pharmacological Therapy* 25: 8–18.

Walker, J. I. 1981. Posttraumatic stress disorder after a car accident. *Posttrauma Stress* 69: 82, 84, 88.

Waller, J. 1816. *A Treatise on the Incubus, or Nightmare*, p. 7. N.p., cited in Jones 1931.

Webb, W. B., and Friel, J. 1971. Sleep stage and personality characteristics of "natural" long and short sleepers. *Science* 171: 587–88.

Weider, A., Wolff, H., Brodman, K., Mittelmann, B., and Wechsler, D. 1944. New York: The Cornell Index. Psychological Corporation.

Weight, F. F., and Swenberg, C. E. 1981. Serotonin and synaptic mechanisms in sympathetic neurons. In Jacobs, B. L., and Gelperin, A., eds., *Serotonin Neurotransmission and Behavior*, pp. 131–55. Cambridge, Mass.: MIT Press.

White, E. 1919. *The Song Of The Sirens*. New York: E. P. Dutton Co.

Williams, R. L., and Karacan, I., eds. 1976. *Pharmacology of Sleep*. New York: John Wiley & Sons.

Wilmer, H. A. 1982. Vietnam and madness: Dreams of schizophrenic veterans. *The Journal of the American Academy of Psychoanalysis.* 10: 47–65.

Wolf, L. 1972. *A Dream of Dracula*. Boston: Little, Brown.

Woodward, R. H., and Mangus, A. R. 1949. *Nervous traits among first grade children in Butler County schools.* Los Angeles: California Test Bureau.

Zucker, L. 1958. *Ego Structure in Paranoid Schizophrenia*. Springfield, Ill.: Charles C Thomas.

INDEX

INDEX

Childhood: adjustment of war veterans during, 200 (table 8-3), 201; fears, in interpretation of nightmares, 173–77, 182; fears in nightmares, 62; history of, in nightmare sufferers, 67, 70–71; mental development, boundaries of mind and, 136–37; nightmares beginning with, 112; sensitivity of, as characterization of nightmare sufferers, 70–71; traumatic, nightmare sufferers and, 105–7; "unusual," as characterized by nightmare sufferers, 70

Children: Ego of, nightmares and, 31; frequency of nightmares among, 28–32, 47, 221–22; night terrors of, 232–33; post-traumatic nightmares in, 188–90; 243; vulnerable to schizophrenia, as nightmare sufferers, 133–34

Cholinergic neurons, 250

Cholinesterase inhibitors, 260–61, 261n

Chronic post-traumatic nightmares (post-traumatic stress disorder), 241–46

Civilians, adults, post-traumatic nightmares in, 190–92; as nightmare sufferers, 116–18; MMPI test results, 116–17, 119

Clinical aspects of nightmares, 8–9

Clinical problems: acute post-traumatic nightmares, 237–41; alcohol and street drugs, 228; chronic post-traumatic nightmares (post-traumatic stress disorder), 241–46; nightmares, frequent, of nontraumatic variety, 221–31; nightmares, night terrors and post-traumatic nightmares as, 220–45; night terrors, 231–237; onset of psychosis, 222–23; psychotherapy, 227

Cleveland, Sidney, 92

Coeruleus, locus, 250

Cohn, J., 189

Coleridge, Samuel Taylor, 122

Colgan, M.J., 189

Conceptual boundaries, 137

Consciousness, during dreaming, 251–52

Cooper, Steven, 95

Cornell Index of nightmare sufferers, 55, 57, 96–97; of war veterans, 201–2

Cornfield, R. B., 244

Coursey, R. D., 81, 154

Cox, G. W., 39

Cravens, J., 258

Craziness of nightmares, 163

Creativity and madness, nightmares and, 128–30; "bissociation," 129; thin boundaries, 168–69

Cubasch, D., 253

Czicman, J., 250

Dahlstrom, W. G., 55

Das Buch der Träume (Ignaz Jeżower), 123

Dauthendey, Max, 124

Daydreams, 141

Daymare, 12 (table 2-1)

Death: thoughts about, nightmares and, 39; wish for, nightmares as, 183

Deconditioning of nightmares, 223

Defenselessness of nightmare sufferers, 103; as thin boundary, 162–63

Defense mechanisms, 150–51

Definition of nightmare, 10–24, 26n; night terror *vs.* nightmare, 10–13

Dehmel, Richard, 124

Déjà vu, nightmares and, 147

Delta waves, sleep and, 15

Dement, W., 269n

Depersonalization, 147

Depression, 117 (table 5-1); nightmares and, 28, 35; nightmare sufferers and, 67

Descarries, L., 170

Descartes, René, 124

Desynchronized sleep; *see* REM sleep

INDEX

Hypochondriasis, 117 (table 5–1)
Hysteria, 117 (table 5–1)

Id *vs.* Ego boundary, 149–50
Incubus attack; *see* Night terror
Insight, thin boundaries and, 168–69
Insomnia, 117; boundaries of the mind in, 154; nightmare sufferers and, 81, 83
Interpersonal boundaries, 141–43
Interpreting nightmares, 173–84; childhood fears and, 62, 173–77, 182; content, 173–74; hell, origin of, 177; holistic dreams, 179; mental structure and dynamics, changes in, 180–81; nightmares as dreams, 173–74; as person's "self," 179–80; state of body and, 182–83

Jacobs, B. L., 250
Jacobson, A., 20
Jamais vu, nightmares and, 147
James, Henry, 123
Jarecki, H. G., 35, 131
Ježower, Ignaz *(Das Buch der Träume)*, 123
Johnston, M. H., 115, 206
Jókai, Maurus, 124
Jones, Ernest, 35, 39, 44, 49, 160, 177, 183, 255; theory of clash of powerful wishes, 44
Jortner, S., 137
Jouvet, M., 250
Jullien, Madame, 124

Kales, Anthony, 20, 33, 39, 81, 116, 117, 117n, 118, 154, 234, 257
Kales, Joyce, 186
Karacan, I., 81, 154, 258
Kardiner, Abram, 194
K-complexes, 15
Keller, Gottfried, 124
Kerouac, Jack, 123

Kestenbaum, C., 133
Kety, S. S., 108
Kinney, L., 187, 216
Klawans, H., 260
Koella, W. P., 250
Koestler, Arthur, 129
Kohut, Heinz, 179, 194
Kramer, Milton, 22n, 83, 187, 216
Kris, E., 129
K scores, of nightmare sufferers, 83, 85

Landis, Bernard, 92, 137, 149n
Lange-Eichbaum, Wilhelm, 128
Lanyon, R. I., 83, 156
Lapierre, Y., 170
"Last Judgement, The" (Bosch), 178 (figure 7–1)
Lautréamont (Isidore L. Ducasse), 123
Lavie, Peretz, 22n, 188
L-DOPA, nightmares and, 36, 260, 262–66, 270
Lewin, Kurt, 137, 142
Lidz, Theodore, 183, 193, 194, 209, 238
Lifelong nightmares, of war veterans, 112–15
Linquist, M., 262
Lithium: decrease of nightmares from, 268; for post-traumatic nightmares, 244
Locus coeruleus, 250
LSD, nightmares and, 164
L-Tryptophan, for post-traumatic nightmares, 244

McCarley, R. W., 250
MacFarlane, J., 29n
Mack, J. E., 31, 35, 42, 45, 46, 49
Madness; *see* creativity and madness
Male/female distinctions: sexual identity and, 143–44; in testing of nightmare sufferers, 99–102
Males, adult, reluctance in admitting nightmares, 125
Malitz, S., 251

Nightmare sufferers *(continued)*
Locus of Control test, 97; schizophrenia and, 107–8; sensitivity of,
103–4; sleep patterns of, 64–65;
Thematic Apperception Test (TAT),
94–96; two studies described, 52–58;
vs. vivid and ordinary dreams, 102;
see also Artists; Civilians; Schizophrenic Patients; Students; War Veterans
Night terror(s), 4, 5, 12 (table 2–1),
117; in adults and adolescence, 233;
brain injury and, 233, 253n; of children, 232–33; clinical problems of,
231–37; genetic acceptability to, 232;
medication for, 234; oxygen deficiency and, 41; as post-traumatic
nightmares, 186–87; psychotherapy
for, 234; sleepwalking and, 234; sufferers, thin boundaries and, 155–56
Night terror *vs.* nightmare, 10–11, 16,
19 (figure 2–2), 19–21, 25n, 46, 47;
as arousal from sleep, 18; "hypnagogic" episode, 22, 23; "hypnagogic"
imagery, 22; personality characteristics and, 23–24; post-traumatic
nightmares, in soldiers, 22; schizophrenic and borderline features, 24n;
"stage 2 nightmare," 21–22; *see also*
Clinical problems
Nocturnal myoclonus, 154
Nonnightmare features of nightmares,
61
NREM–sleep (nonrapid eye movement
sleep), 12, 17 (table 2–1); S–sleep
depth, 17–18
Nonrepetitive nature of nightmares, 61
Norepinephrine, 170, 252, 269, 270,
271; systems, 250

Occupations, of nightmare sufferers, 65
Occurrence of nightmares, 34–38
"Openness" of nightmares, as thin
boundary, 162
"ordinary dreamer," 63; DSM–III diagnosis and, 72; MMPI test, 77; Rorschach test of, 91; *vs.* nightmare
sufferer, 102
Ordinary sensory *vs.* extrasensory experience, 151–52
Oswald, I., 257
Oxygen: deficiency, as theory of nightmare, 40–41; deprivation, nightmares
and, 253–54

Paranoia, 117 (table 5–1); tendencies,
thin boundaries and, 159
Parkinsonism, nightmares and, 35, 260
Pathology: brain injury, night terrors
and, 233; of nightmare sufferers, 102–
3
Patients: disadvantages of gathering
information from, 50; of physicians,
frequency of nightmares in, 27
Pearlman, C. A., 187
Pendulum Tracking Test, 58; nightmare
sufferers and, 98
Penfield, Wilder, 217
Penile erections, sleep and, 16
"Pepperoni pizza" hypothesis of night-
mares, 255–56
Peretz, Lavie, 22n
Perlmutter, Elizabeth, 123
Personality: adult adjustment and, of
nightmare sufferers, 65–67; night
terrors *vs.* nightmares and, 23–24
Peterson, Anne, 30
Pharmacology of nightmares; *see*
Chemistry of nightmares
Phobics, nightmare sufferers as, 160
Physical dimensions, as boundary, 148
Physical education majors in college,
nightmares and, 118, 119 (table 5–
2), 120
Physical illness: frequency of night-
mares and, 34–35; of relatives of
nightmare sufferers, 74
Pinches, T. G., 39
Plath, Sylvia *(The Bell Jar)*, 179
Plato, 128
Play *vs.* reality, 141
Poe, Edgar Allan, 123